Advance Praise for *The Leading Brain*

"*The Leading Brain* is the best integration of neuroscience and leadership that I have ever seen."
—Dr. Jonathan Schooler, neuroscientist and professor, University of California, Santa Barbara

"Breathtaking. It's both a lecture on modern sciences and kind of a thriller. I've never read a book on management so fast."
—Peter Gerber, CEO, Lufthansa Cargo

"Real leadership begins and ends in the brain. Science has changed the world throughout the ages and thanks to this book, it can now finally also change leadership for the good of mankind."
—Liam Condon, member of the board of management, Bayer AG, and CEO, Bayer CropScience

"What an interesting and helpful book. Fabritius and Hagemann have introduced the most important findings of modern neuroscience to the business community—offering us a host of new skills to excel at work, and even with friends and family. It's highly original, remarkably informative and insightful, even humorous in many spots. I am so happy to have read it! You will be too."
—Helen Fisher, PhD, senior research fellow, The Kinsey Institute, and bestselling author of *Anatomy of Love*

"Enjoyable and informative. Covers much of what I teach my students, that they must take command of their own psychological machinery to be successful in any endeavor."
—Ken Singer, managing director, Sutardja Center for Entrepreneurship and Technology, University of California, Berkeley

THE
LEADING
BRAIN

*POWERFUL SCIENCE-BASED
STRATEGIES for ACHIEVING
PEAK PERFORMANCE*

FRIEDERIKE FABRITIUS, MS,
AND HANS W. HAGEMANN, PhD

A TarcherPerigee Book

tarcherperigee

An imprint of Penguin Random House LLC
375 Hudson Street
New York, New York 10014

Most TarcherPerigee books are available at special quantity discounts for bulk purchase for sales promotions, premiums, fund-raising, and educational needs. Special books or book excerpts also can be created to fit specific needs. For details, write: SpecialMarkets@penguinrandomhouse.com.

LIBRARY OF CONGRESS CATALOGING-IN-PUBLICATION DATA
Names: Fabritius, Friederike, author. | Hagemann, Hans Werner, 1959– author.
Title: The leading brain : powerful science-based strategies for achieving peak performance / Friederike Fabritius, MS, and Hans W. Hagemann, PhD.
Description: New York : TarcherPerigee, 2017. | Includes bibliographical references and index.
Identifiers: LCCN 2016038838 (print) | LCCN 2016051763 (ebook) | ISBN 9780143129356 (hardcover) | ISBN 9781101993200 (ebook)
Subjects: LCSH: Leadership—Psychological aspects. | Performance—Psychological aspects.
Classification: LCC BF637.L4 F33 2017 (print) | LCC BF637.L4 (ebook) | DDC 158/.4—dc23 LC record available at https://lccn.loc.gov/2016038838

Printed in the United States of America
1   3   5   7   9   10   8   6   4   2

Book design by Spring Hoteling

Friederike:
To my husband, Jochen, and our children, Benita, Wolf, and Heinrich. You fill my life with love and joy.

Hans:
To my wife, Heinke, and our children, Oskar, Anton, and Tom. It is wonderful to share my life with you.

CONTENTS

CONTENTS

INTRODUCTION:
THE SCIENCE OF LEADERSHIP

LEADERSHIP has long been treated as an art, a fuzzy philosophy based more on fads than on facts. That accounts for the endless stream of "game-changing" management books that seem to come and go almost as rapidly as Paris fashions. It also explains why today's leadership guru, so much in demand, is often tomorrow's forgotten footnote.

But effective leadership isn't an art. It's a science. It shouldn't be dependent on buzzwords or slogans. It should be based on a bedrock foundation of our understanding of the brain. The ways we act, react, and interact are all products of distinct cognitive processes. What motivates us, what bores us, how we respond to threats and rewards, both as individuals and as groups, are dependent on the elaborate and seemingly miraculous neuronal networks that operate just behind our foreheads and above our ears.

Until recently, the brain was sort of a black box. Much of what goes on inside it was a mystery. But thanks to breakthroughs in neuroscience, such as functional magnetic resonance imaging, or fMRI, we no longer have to merely speculate on the behavior of our brains. We can actually watch them in action. What we've learned from rigorous scientific studies has the potential to radically change the way we lead and succeed.

Suddenly, news about neuroscience is booming. What's been known and discussed at the laboratory level for years is finally making its way into best-selling books. Nearly everyone, it seems, is curious to learn more about how our brains work and what that knowledge can do to improve life both at home and at work.

It hasn't always been that way. Just a few years ago, when one of us was working at a big traditional management consultancy, nobody there seemed the least bit interested to hear about neuroscience. This lack of enthusiasm worked both ways. When we asked some leading brain researchers to look for business applications for their findings, most of them seemed either unwilling or unable to search for any links.

As a result, when we first started to integrate these exciting discoveries into business seminars and coaching sessions, we were among just a handful of consultants who were making this crucial connection. After presenting our brain-based business approach to companies all over the world, we received a response from senior executives that was almost uniformly enthusiastic.

Given the audience, this was surprising and extremely rewarding. After all, senior executives can be a pretty tough crowd. They are often understandably skeptical about coaching and leadership development because they perceive these fields as too "soft." Our science-based approach really filled a gap. It has been amazing and highly gratifying to witness the positive transformation of individuals and organizations since we started applying the knowledge from cutting-edge research and establishing what in retrospect seems like a natural bridge between neuroscience and business. Clients who have attended our seminars have described them as "highly applicable" and even "life changing."

One question we were asked over and over again at the end of our seminars was whether we could recommend a business-world-compatible book that elaborated on the neuroscience topics we discussed in our presentations. At the time we were unable to recommend such a book. But now we can.

In its nine chapters, *The Leading Brain* takes you on a journey that starts with using brain science to consistently achieve individual peak performance and concludes by helping you apply these findings to create high-performing teams.

Part 1, "Reaching Your Peak," explains not only how to achieve optimal performance but also how to sustain it. Chapter 1, "Find Your Sweet Spot," provides the ingredients for the neurochemical cocktail that produces peak performance and explains why that recipe will often be different from one executive to the next. Chapter 2, "Regulate Your Emotions," explores the X factor that can make or break that performance, depending on how you use it. Chapter 3, "Sharpen Your Focus," offers a brain-based solution for a growing problem, effectively maintaining and sustaining your attention in a world awash in information.

Part 2, "Changing Your Brain," explodes the myth that our mental processes are largely locked in and hardwired. Chapter 4, "Manage Habits," tells you how to do just that. By learning the neuroscience of how habits operate, you'll gain an upper hand on adopting good routines and eliminating bad ones. Chapter 5, "Unleash Your Unconscious," takes things a tantalizing step further, by showing you how to tap into the impressive strength and efficiency of a part of your brain that, by definition, you are unaware of. Chapter 6, "Foster Learning," introduces the exciting concept of neuroplasticity, which shows how you can keep rewiring your brain and improving your abilities throughout your entire life.

Part 3, "Building Dream Teams," combines and expands the brain-based insights from the previous chapters into a group context. Chapter 7, "Thrive on Diversity," redefines the concept of diversity, maps out the brain chemicals that make people different, and offers ways to assemble the best combinations of coworkers. Chapter 8, "Cultivate Trust," focuses on one of the most important and yet largely underappreciated aspects of effective teams and outlines the crucial levers that can either draw people together or drive them apart. Finally, in chapter 9, "Develop the Team of the Future," we show you how to do just that. We explore the science behind finding and training top talent and describe the factors that can enable teams to achieve a remarkable level of energy, productivity, and satisfaction.

During the time that we've spent researching and writing this book as well as the hours and hours of training that we've done with senior executives throughout the world, we have grown even stronger in our original conviction that brain science can have a dramatic effect on the way in which we do business. We firmly believe that neuroscientific research results will change the way we lead, communicate, and interact in companies. The insights in this book aren't simply based on science but have been successfully applied in a remarkable variety of business environments and have led to increased satisfaction and performance. We can see a new era of leadership emerging that will fundamentally transform the ways we deal with each other, taking communication in companies to an exciting new level.

Munich, February 2017
FRIEDERIKE FABRITIUS AND HANS W. HAGEMANN

PART 1
REACHING YOUR PEAK

CHAPTER 1
FIND YOUR SWEET SPOT

How Do You Gain the Right Mix of Neurochemicals to
Perform at Your Very Best When You Need To?

ON May 15, shortly before dawn, Leroy Gordon Cooper Jr.,
wearing a new suit and carrying a metal box about the size of
a large briefcase, took an elevator up ten stories,[1] got off, and
was promptly strapped into a padded chair by waiting atten-
dants who were dressed in white coats. The area around him
was extremely cramped, similar to what you'd find in a typical
commercial airline restroom. But Cooper, known as Gordo
by his friends, wasn't sitting in an airline bathroom. He was
sealed inside a cone-shaped aluminum space capsule that was
perched atop 200,000 pounds of extremely flammable liquid
oxygen and was about to embark on a journey of 546,167
miles.[2]

The year was 1963, and astronaut Gordo Cooper was
scheduled to be just the sixth American to venture into outer
space. This was no joy ride. Several of the previous flights had
encountered problems. Serious problems. A little more than a
year earlier, Cooper's colleague John Glenn narrowly missed

being incinerated in the Earth's atmosphere after his space-craft's heat shield had come loose.[3] Despite the fact that the astronauts were all experienced pilots who had been chosen for their mental toughness, Cooper's mission was bound to place even the hardiest fighter pilot under significant stress.

A series of holds in the mission's countdown were agonizing even for the control room's seasoned technicians. As Cooper was forced to endure yet another delay, doctors on the ground were closely monitoring his biomedical telemetry. What they saw from their readouts shocked them to the point of disbelief. Although it seemed almost inconceivable, astronaut Gordo Cooper was actually taking a nap![4]

OUTSIDE a modest laboratory in Lille, France, hours after the workday had officially ended and more than a century before Gordo Cooper traveled into space, a solitary bearded man, dressed in a dark vest and jacket, could be seen pacing up and down a long corridor, deep in thought, betraying a noticeable limp, and occasionally jingling the keys in his pocket to provide a kind of rhythm to his ruminations.[5]

The man was Louis Pasteur, and his steadfast dedication to science and study revolutionized practices in both medicine and industry. Working with extreme caution, he never left anything to chance.[6] For Pasteur, hitting his performance sweet spot required incredible patience and sustained concentration. A thoughtful, reflective man, he was well aware of the secret of his success: "My strength," he explained, "lies solely in my tenacity."[7]

THE PURSUIT OF PEAK PERFORMANCE

No one would have confused cocky, clean-shaven Gordo Cooper with bearded, contemplative Louis Pasteur; nor could they have ever swapped jobs. Yet both were masters at reaching a level of excellence that we commonly refer to as peak performance. Pasteur's peak performance led to groundbreaking discoveries in science and medicine. Cooper's peak performance didn't come while he was sleeping. The fact that he could sleep through the preparations for a dangerous journey underscored the wide range of differences in the conditions for when people perform at their best. Whereas Gordo had the temperament of a sprinter, Pasteur had the mind-set of a marathoner. Although Cooper slept peacefully inside the cramped confines of his capsule, which he'd named *Faith 7*, before his *Atlas 9* rocket left the launchpad, his challenge and his crucial moment of peak performance were still to come.

THE U THAT MOTIVATES YOU

Anyone who has ever held a tennis racket, wielded a baseball bat, or swung a golf club knows about the sweet spot, the place where the ball responds in the best possible way. All of us strive to find our sweet spot of performance, that zone where we're at our most productive and our most effective. What's more, most of us know it when we get there. But *how* do we get there? What does it take? Without knowledge about the brain and the ability to use this knowledge, opportunities to perform at our best are squandered and the potential for great achievements remains unfulfilled. The good news: The skills it takes to improve one's mental game in business and in life can be learned, trained, and improved.

In 1908, two psychologists, Robert Yerkes and John Dillingham Dodson, found that subjecting rats to mild electric shocks actually improved the animals' performance in navigating a maze. But if the shocks were increased beyond a certain point, the rats' ability to travel through the maze degraded rapidly. Instead of being focused and alert, the rodents would grow increasingly panicked and attempt to escape. Yerkes and Dodson referred to the electric shocks as "arousal." We commonly call this "stress."

The two psychologists were able to illustrate the relationship between arousal and performance on a remarkably simple graph that has come to be known as the Inverted U (see fig. 1). Peak performance comes at the top of the graph, the spot where the level of arousal is sufficient to provide optimal focus and attention. Without adequate arousal, we're likely to feel bored or apathetic. And when arousal's too high? Those are the instances in which our focus deteriorates into a situa-

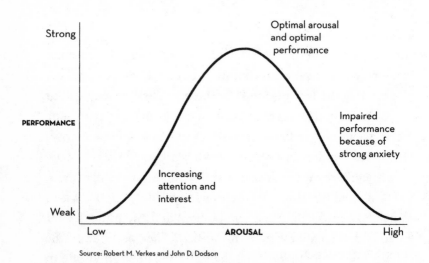

Source: Robert M. Yerkes and John D. Dodson

Figure 1. Peak performance curve

tion of stress—or even worse, panic. Our pursuit of peak performance is a little like Goldilocks's tasting of the Three Bears' porridge. Our goal is to find a level that is neither too cold nor too hot but just right.

Although it's useful to be able to have a way of visualizing peak performance, that's obviously not the same as achieving it. To gain a better grasp of just what it takes to find and reach your sweet spot, it helps to understand how the brain is operating when you're performing at your best—and at your worst.

THE ANATOMY OF AROUSAL

The wiring in your brain isn't really wiring at all but a series of signals that hop from one cell to another. Working together, these microscopic messengers are responsible for every action, reaction, and emotion that you experience, including the condition that Yerkes and Dodson called arousal.

NEUROTRANSMITTERS

There are approximately 1 trillion nerve cells in your brain, each of which measures about one-hundredth of a millimeter.[8] Physically, each nerve cell, known as a neuron, looks a bit like a splatter on your kitchen counter. There's a blob in the middle with tiny tentacles of neuronal matter radiating from the center. Different neurons may have slightly different shapes and functions, but the basic kitchen splatter design is the same from one neuron to the next. Although these billions of neurons are tightly crowded inside your brain, their tentacles don't physically connect. They maintain microscopic gaps called synapses and employ chemical messengers called neurotransmitters to cross the remaining distance. Like tiny cell phones, neurons are capable of both sending and receiving signals.

Where the Axon Is

The senders are known as axons, and each neuron comes with only one. Yet it has plenty of dendrites, which, although they sound like members of an obscure religious sect, are actually neuronal receivers. The fact that the nerves don't physically connect is a plus. This gives them a remarkable ability to create brand-new circuitry known as neuronal pathways without the need to get out a soldering iron or call an electrician. And like the path you make when you leave the sidewalk and cut the corner by crossing through a neighbor's lawn, these neuronal pathways, although they don't kill any grass, become increasingly well defined the more they are used.

This aspect of nerves isn't limited to performance. It also explains how we learn and how habits, good ones and bad ones alike, ultimately become actions we engage in without even thinking. The path becomes so well defined over time that the neurotransmitters can almost make the journey with their eyes closed. Or, as the saying goes among cognitive scientists: Neurons that fire together wire together. And, once again, this wiring isn't permanent, just as a path isn't permanent. But if you keep using it, it becomes as passable as a paved road. By the same token, if you stop going that way, the route gradually becomes fainter over time. That explains in part why you can recall your own phone number with relative ease but can't remember any of your high school French.

Although more than one hundred neurotransmitters have been identified, from the standpoint of peak performance, only three are truly important: *d*opamine, *n*oradrenaline, and *a*cetylcholine. We call them the "DNA of Peak Performance."

DOPAMINE

Dopamine, as one journalist suggests, has become "the Kim Kardashian of neurotransmitters" for the way in which it has spiced up the science pages with tales of pleasure, addiction, and reward.[9] It seems to have captured the public's interest and imagination, probably because of its association with excitement, novelty, and risk.

Dopamine is involved in your ability to update information in memory and also affects your ability to focus on the task at hand.[10] It provides a druglike reward that makes you want more. And, as with many drugs, the high wears off and you often need more the next time to get the same effect. That's why dopamine is known as a novelty neurotransmitter. Its effects are strongest when the stimulus that generates it is new. This explains in part the enthusiasm you may feel when you start a new project and why the thrill isn't usually as strong after you've been working on it for a while.

Dopamine plays a number of roles in the body, including aiding motor control. But in the context of the brain and peak performance, it's the fun chemical. To truly be performing at peak level, you should be having fun. The experience should feel rewarding. If you aren't feeling this way, you may still be performing better than usual, but you probably haven't reached your peak.

WHAT'S ALL THE RUSH? NORADRENALINE!

Almost everyone is familiar with noradrenaline (also known as norepinephrine), or at least thinks they are. It's the rush we get both when we bungee jump and when we react in surprise to the sudden lunge of a neighbor's "friendly" dog. Noradrenaline's primary purpose is to ensure your survival. It was evolutionarily designed to help you respond quickly to any threat, real or perceived. It does so by regulating your attention and alertness. Studies indicate that higher levels of noradrenaline lead to greater accuracy when detecting errors in a visual error-detecting task when we are awake, alert, and up to the task.

Noradrenaline is at an optimal level when you feel slightly overchallenged; it leads to a "this is tricky but I think I can handle it" feeling. It is also released when you push yourself to perform a difficult task better, faster, or with fewer resources.

FROM SPOTLIGHT TO LASER: ACETYLCHOLINE

The third of the three neurochemicals that make up the DNA of Peak Performance is acetylcholine, which is found in abundance in a surprising segment of the population. In fact, there's a very special group of human beings that can probably teach you a great deal about peak performance. Look around and you'll find that they seem to be practically everywhere. Are they dedicated research chemists? World-class professional athletes? Risk-taking entrepreneurs? Chess grandmasters? Award-winning sales reps? Politicians? Not even close. And yet, you might even have one of them living under your very roof. And no, it isn't your mother-in-law. Or that sullen twentysomething who still lives at home and has mistaken your house for a combination all-you-can-eat restaurant and Laundromat. It's an infant. That's right: babies!

If you've ever spent any amount of time with babies, then you probably recognize that they're some of the most alert and observant little people on the planet. Although they may be excreting a lot of unpleasant stuff, they're simultaneously soaking up sights, sounds, tastes, and smells like high-powered, turbocharged, diaper-wearing cognitive vacuum cleaners. The same mechanism you use to achieve peak performance every now and then, a baby is operating practically nonstop for the first few years of her life. And the chemical behind this extraordinary performance is acetylcholine.

Acetylcholine comes from a part of the brain called the nucleus basalis. Babies release acetylcholine without even trying. Neuroscientists refer to this as the "critical period of neuroplasticity," a time when brand-new brains are extremely receptive to new information and are constantly establishing neuronal pathways. As neuroscientist Michael Merzenich explains it, during critical plasticity "the learning machinery is continuously on."[11] As adults we're not so lucky. The automatic mechanism for extraordinary focus shuts down when we're still quite young and must be operated manually from then on.

So how do we as adults flip the switch that turns on acetylcholine? Once this critical period is over, there are only a handful of ways we can do it: when we make a conscious effort to pay attention, when we get physical exercise, or when we are exposed to something important, surprising, or novel—in other words, when our brain releases dopamine.

Another way to look at the DNA of Peak Performance is to think of it as a prizewinning photograph. Noradrenaline prompts you to point your camera in just the right direction, dopamine helps you to zoom in until you have a pleasing composition, and finally there's acetylcholine, which enables you to sharpen your focus until it's picture-perfect. Get only one or two of these elements just right and what you have is a snapshot. Add the third and suddenly it's a work of art.

ONE SIZE DOESN'T FIT ALL

The depiction of the performance curve as a simple inverted U provides a clear and concise explanation for how performance works. But as you may have already noticed, the graph doesn't have any units. How do you measure arousal? In inches? In ergs? In Scoville units?* In other words, exactly how much arousal is required to reach peak performance? The short answer is that we can't really say.

There's no universal standard for optimum arousal.

The longer answer is that it can vary dramatically from person to person and from one task or situation to another. There's no universal standard for optimum arousal. In that respect, arousal has a lot in common with spicy food.

SPICY, BUT NOT AS SPICY AS HERS

Put yourself for a moment in the role of a server at a Thai restaurant in California. A well-dressed couple stroll in and sit down in a booth just below the framed pictures of the king and queen. When you come over to take their order, she orders "Thai basil with pork, very spicy," while he asks for the same dish, but with chicken, adding, almost as an afterthought, "but not as spicy as hers." What are you going to tell the chef? You have a hunch that if he makes the dishes "very spicy" according to the standards of the small village outside

---

* Scoville units are used to measure the spicy heat of chili peppers. Whereas a perky jalapeño pepper has a Scoville range of 3,500–10,000 units, the red-hot habanero can be anywhere from 10 to 100 times as hot, with a range of 100,000–350,000 Scoville units.

Bangkok where he grew up, your customers may single-handedly worsen one of the state's periodic droughts by constantly asking to have their water glasses refilled. Who knows? They may even sue.

The definition of spicy in a Thai restaurant is a bit like the definition of arousal in a Yerkes-Dodson graph. One person's standards for what constitutes arousal can vary widely from another's. Some of us are "right-side performers" like Gordo Cooper. Others are "left-side performers" like Louis Pasteur. Still others lie somewhere in between. Luckily, we have a kind of spiciness test that we administer to our seminar attendees to gauge each one's optimum level of arousal.

THE LAST-MINUTE ASSIGNMENT

Imagine yourself in the following predicament. You and your colleagues have been attending one of our peak performance seminars. So far you've been having a great time. You've found the sessions to be intriguing, informative, entertaining, and useful. But not long after we've divided you into groups, the announcement comes: Your boss will be making a surprise appearance at the seminar, and each group will have a little more than an hour to prepare a presentation to deliver in the evening while he's here.

How would you feel? Well, when we delivered this news, some of the groups were positively terrified by the prospect, while others seemed completely energized and actually appeared to be looking forward to the evening's events.

We could've predicted those reactions.

That's because, unbeknownst to the participants, we had divided up the seminar attendees according to how they scored on the State Trait Anxiety Index, a test that assessed their requirements for arousal to achieve peak performance.

We put the right-side performers in one group and the left-side performers in another, and grouped others who landed in similar spots along the performance continuum.

Not surprisingly, the group on the left side felt under considerable pressure and didn't believe they had enough time to have the presentation ready. The group on the right seemed to relish the challenge. They weren't bothered at all by the short turnaround.

Then we let the other shoe drop.

Our announcement of their boss's impending appearance had been a hoax. The boss wasn't coming, and there was no need to prepare a presentation.

You could hear a huge sigh of relief emanating from one part of the room and sense some genuine disappointment coming from the other. And yes, there was some grumbling. But, luckily for us, no group grabbed torches and pitchforks and attempted to run us out of town.

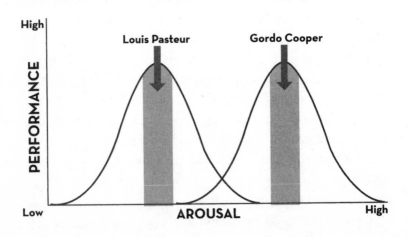

Figure 2. *Both Louis Pasteur and Gordo Cooper achieved optimal performance but with markedly different levels of arousal.*

We all survived the exercise, and an important point was made: Peak performance isn't the same for everyone. There are great individual differences in the degree of emotional arousal leading to peak performance (see fig. 2).

PEOPLE ON THE RIGHT

The further to the right on the curve you are, the easier it is for you to access a state of peak performance under pressure. You may be bored on a normal day at the office, but whenever there is a crisis, you are the person to call. (Gordo Cooper provides a classic example.)

In many companies, people who fall on the right side of the arousal scale are treated as corporate heroes. Their exploits in and out of the office are viewed with a hushed reverence. When one of the firm's partners casually confesses, "I need to spend my Sundays paragliding in order to relax," awed junior executives take careful note. When you work in an atmosphere where sayings like "Only under high pressure can diamonds develop" are unofficial policy, it's no surprise that everyone—whether consciously or not—seeks to emulate that ideal.

How do these sensation-seeking right-siders survive in a sometimes-stifling office environment? The truth is, many don't. The leaders who have managed to last in these settings have devised their own secret weapons over time. To remain fully engaged at work, they sometimes manufacture emergencies to provide the chemical cocktail they crave for optimal performance. They start work on a crucial presentation just a few hours before they have to step onstage to deliver it. They leave for an international flight at the last possible minute. A sensation-seeking news editor we knew would frequently redesign the front page just minutes before the paper had to go to press. Many of his colleagues were convinced that he was some sort of sadist, when in truth he was probably just artificially raising the stakes in order to perform at his best. The amount of stress that would induce heart palpitations in others makes these right-siders feel more focused and creative. They find routine tasks and long, unproductive meetings far more stressful than skydiving and they frequently check their smartphones for incoming email and text messages to distract themselves from what they perceive to be almost unbearable boredom.

Not surprisingly, people who fall on the right side of the performance curve tend to take a dim view of those who lean more toward the left. When we asked a group of right-side executives what kind of people they thought would perform best on the far left side of the curve, they had some quick answers. "Primary school teachers," someone ventured. "Bureaucrats," someone else chimed in. Overall, there did not seem to be a whole lot of respect for individuals who needed predictability and certainty, loved rules and systems, and abhorred tight deadlines, emergencies, and all sorts of stress. They were quick to judge those who performed on the far left of the curve as underachievers.

PEOPLE ON THE LEFT

The knee-jerk tendency to ridicule or dismiss left-side peak performers began to diminish once our group of right-side executives had a little more time to think things through. "What about Nobel Prize winners?" someone asked. "Aren't they extremely meticulous and detail driven and sometimes working for decades on the same molecule?" "And authors who rewrite their novels seventeen times?" wondered another. Clearly, there are high-performing individuals who don't require a lot of external stimulation. Although no one mentioned Louis Pasteur, he would've provided an excellent example. It ultimately became clear that the people on the left are just as important for organizations and society at large as the dopamine-dominant thrill seekers on the right.

FINDING YOUR HOME ON THE RANGE

At first blush it might seem that right-siders and left-siders come from totally different planets, much like the popular notion that men are from Mars and women are from Venus. Once a Martian, always a Martian? Are you destined to dwell on one side of the scale or another? Definitely not. Gender, genetics, age, environment, and experience all play a role in determining the position of your personal peak performance curve.

Gender. The Mars/Venus dichotomy may be an oversimplification, but it turns out that there's some scientific basis behind this divide. Countless tests have arrived at the same conclusion: Men are statistically more likely to be sensation seekers than are women. As we'll see in chapter 7, one of the key elements that determines where you are situated on the performance scale is testosterone. Although testosterone is best known as a male hormone, both men and women have it in differing degrees. But because men, on average, have more of it, that usually pushes them further to the right.

Genetics. In addition to gender, some other genetic factors can influence your position on the performance scale. For example, the dopamine receptor gene DRD4 is associated with novelty seeking, a key factor that can also push your curve significantly to the right. Again, as we'll see in chapter 7, high-ranking executives often have an unusually active dopamine system.[12]

Another set of genes appears to influence your overall response to stress. A recent study conducted by researchers at the Medical University of Vienna found that a trio of genetic variants can interfere with your ability to bounce back from stressful situations. If you have one or more of these variants, you may find it more difficult to recover from a challenging life event and may be more sensitive to other stressful situations. On the other hand, if you lack these at-risk genetic variants, each stressful situation can actually make you stronger.[13]

Does this mean the die is cast? No. At least, not always. The mere presence of certain genes doesn't automatically determine your destiny. Personality traits remain a combination of both nature and nurture. Estimates suggest that genes can influence your personality anywhere from 20 to 60 percent.[14] For a gene to have an effect, it must be switched on, or, as geneticists put it, "expressed." As a result, certain genetic dispositions can remain dormant throughout your life. As University of Wisconsin psychologist Richard Davidson suggests, the genes in your DNA are like the albums in your music collection: "Just because you have a CD doesn't mean that you will play it . . ."[15]

Age. The tendency to be irresponsible in adolescence and gradually grow more cautious and conservative with age is common but by no means universal. A key factor in what some consider budding wisdom and others view as steady steps toward stodginess is a decrease in levels of testosterone. Researchers in Australia have theorized that rather than being caused by aging, testosterone drops are associated with obesity and depression, two characteristics more common in older men.[16] Regardless of the cause, the outcome is the same. Men (and women) experience a decrease in testosterone levels as they grow older. And a drop in testosterone will almost always move you further left on the performance scale. (Interestingly, new fathers—and new mothers—often experience a drop in testosterone too.[17])

Environment. Of all the factors that influence your position on the performance scale, environment is the one over which you have the most control. Many consultants who initially seem to thrive in the high-pressure world of international business, with its constant travel and unforgiving deadlines, find that after a few years they prefer to move to an atmosphere that is not quite as relentless. Companies are now taking these preferences into account by creating separate tracks for "generalists" and "experts." Although the expert track may not be as fast-paced, it still attracts and requires top-notch talent. Experts are neither better nor worse than generalists. They just prefer a different way of working. The two options make it possible for both to find an environment where they can thrive.

Experience. Of course, not everyone automatically feels the need to shift from the generalist to expert track after a few years in the field. Some consultants can crisscross the globe their entire careers without getting burned out. In fact, many find the demands to be less and less of a burden as time goes on and actually crave steadily increasing challenges in order to avoid feeling bored. This hints at another factor that can influence your performance: experience. Often, the more practiced and experienced you are, the more tasks you can handle automatically by relying on your unconscious brain (see chapter 5). This not only makes your job easier, but it also makes it easier to handle stressful situations as they arise.

GOING UP, GOING DOWN

When it comes to peak performance, self-awareness is essential. Pinpointing your position on the curve from time to time and from task to task can be critical to your success. "When looking at all the individual differences regarding stress resistance and reactions to different environments," says eminent neuroscientist Wolf Singer, "it is perhaps the most important task in life to find out early what the individual strengths and weaknesses are and to work with the strengths."[18] Once you're aware of the situations when you're at your best, you can adjust to your environment to play to your strengths and then fine-tune conditions so you can reach your peak when you need to.

TAKE YOUR TEMPERATURE

Of course, none of us consistently maintains a steady level of arousal. To do so would be unsustainable. Or dull. Our arousal levels rise and fall throughout the day, driven by various factors in our environment as well as by elements of our individual temperament. Do weekly staff meetings drive you crazy with boredom or stress, while one-on-one meetings leave you feeling alert and extra energized? Do you relish big-picture discussions and animated give-and-take but dread poring over documents and slogging through details? As we've seen, when it comes to reactions to day-to-day tasks, one size definitely doesn't fit all. The parts of the day when you're at your best may be the same ones when your colleague in the next office is feeling overwhelmed.

What things get you hot under the collar? What things cool you down? To gain a clearer picture of your personal peak performance profile, start by making a list of your tasks and activities throughout your typical workweek. Then rate each according to how it makes you feel: overaroused, underaroused, or at the top of your game.

If drawing up a detailed list doesn't seem like your style, you can try the approach that psychologists often use. Start by setting an alert on your smartphone at ninety-minute intervals throughout the day. Each time the alarm goes off, do a quick inventory of your current performance level. Are you feeling bored, uninspired, or apathetic? If so, add an *L* for "low" (the low end of the performance curve) to your calendar for that time period. If, on the other hand, you're feeling overstressed or under the gun, add an *H* to your calendar for "high." And, of course, if you were performing at your peak when the alert went off (we apologize in advance for taking you out of the zone!), put a *P* for "peak performance" in your calendar.

Regardless of the approach you take, you should find that a pattern emerges, giving you a clearer sense of the factors that influence your performance. The more you learn about the rises and falls in your typical week, the greater control you will gain in hitting your performance sweet spot precisely when you need it most—and the better sense you'll have of whether you're a good fit in your current job.

LOCATION, LOCATION, LOCATION

As the old adage suggests, the three most important considerations in purchasing real estate are 1) location, 2) location, and 3) location. The same wisdom applies to finding your performance sweet spot. Nothing is more important. And when we say "location," we don't necessarily mean whether you work in a high-rise, at your kitchen table, or on the deck of a yacht. We're talking about the overall atmosphere of your workplace environment. It doesn't take a trained neuroscientist to realize that Louis Pasteur would've been a disaster as an astronaut and that Gordo Cooper would've been a liability in a laboratory. Above all, your success depends on finding an environment that matches your performance profile. If you find yourself constantly over- or underaroused, then you need to either alter the environment or make a serious change to the kind of tasks you handle or the way you are working. If you are the Pasteur type, don't go to work for an investment bank, and if you are a sensation seeker like Gordo Cooper, working in a highly controlled environment like Pasteur's laboratory will probably leave you feeling bored or frustrated or both.

> **Your success depends on finding an environment that matches your performance profile.**

In many cases the solution doesn't have to be as drastic as switching jobs. Try to find out exactly what is putting you into over- or underarousal and work to change these situations. Altering your hours, changing your work environment, or reallocating responsibilities with coworkers can all help. Talk about your needs with your supervisor and colleagues. The simplicity of the performance curve makes it relatively easy to discuss with friends and colleagues. As we'll see in chapter 4, sometimes seemingly small changes can make a very big difference.

TOO MUCH OF A GOOD THING

Although achieving peak performance should be your goal, staying at the top of the curve for an extended period is neither desirable nor beneficial. You should rise to the occasion when it's needed most. Attempting to maintain the optimum mix of dopamine, noradrenaline, and acetylcholine for a prolonged period would likely overtax the system and deplete the neurotransmitters, resulting in burnout and exhaustion. Think of cello virtuoso Yo-Yo Ma or top-ranked snowboarder Shaun White. It would seem absurd to ask either of them to perform at world-class level 24-7. Instead, they practice, rest, perform, and recover according to specific plans in order to be in an optimal state exactly when it counts.

Finding a daily, weekly, and monthly rhythm that leads to optimal energy management is equally important in the corporate world, where the demands on executives often rival the challenges faced by professional athletes in terms of difficulty and intensity. "Being in a high-performance state all the time is detrimental; being in a high-performance state when it counts is a winning strategy," says Axel Kowalski, a psychologist and neurofeedback expert who uses computer technology to help business leaders achieve peak performance. "The key is flexibility," he says.[19] Only leaders who can switch to the optimal states of arousal for the task at hand are really managing their neurological resources well.

PERFECT YOUR PERFORMANCE

Once you have made sure that you are in the right environment, you can use powerful techniques to fine-tune your position on the performance curve depending on the demands of a particular task or situation. But before you engage in that, make sure you are in the right spot! Keep in mind that these are minor tweaks intended for performance adjustments, not total game changers designed to transform a bad job into a good one. The more you are in balance and are selecting environments that are in line with your strengths, the less you will need these arousal-adjusting tricks.

Raising Arousal

Over time, most people gain an intuitive sense of when their arousal level is too low, too high, or just right. Those who find it difficult to assess their own stress level can measure it more scientifically by using the Perceived Stress Scale (PSS), a fourteen-item instrument devised by psychologists from Carnegie Mellon and the University of Oregon.[20] If you use the PSS or simply do a mental diagnosis and find that your arousal level is lower than you need it in order to be effective, there are a number of ways to artificially raise it.

Imagining a mild fear, even if it isn't related to the work at hand, can sometimes increase your level of noradrenaline and move you further to the right. When he needs an extra boost of noradrenaline, one colleague we know likes to envision the specter of a rapidly approaching deadline and the faces of unhappy stakeholders if he somehow fails to meet it.

If you're feeling bored, unengaged, or unmotivated, or if work simply doesn't seem fun, what you may lack is dopamine. To increase your level of dopamine, humor, positive thinking, and changing your location or approach can all help. In addition, aerobic exercise not only sweeps away the midafternoon blahs but can also add a welcome burst of dopamine to a humdrum day.

Lowering Arousal

If you're getting ready to push the panic button, you can employ a few effective strategies to dampen the threat response and move further to the left on the performance curve. It's important to remember that stressful experiences often result from the killer combination of high demands and low control. To temporarily take your foot off the gas, try engaging in some of the daily activities that you can do on "automatic pilot," like straightening your desk or deleting some e-mails. If you're feeling a loss of control, focus on those aspects of the process you can control, such as the general strategic direction of the solutions for the client rather than the developments in the stock market. And finally there's exercise, a versatile solution that can both increase your energy and reduce your stress. A lunchtime run or even a quick trip up and down the stairs can lower the level of damaging cortisol in your bloodstream. If these options aren't available, then follow the example of Louis Pasteur and take a walk through your office hallway.

ALL the nervous pacing that Louis Pasteur did outside his laboratory in Lille eventually paid off. Driven by a deep desire for the betterment of health and humanity, he set a secret goal to find a cure for contagious diseases.[21]

A series of escalating scientific breakthroughs paved the way to his dream. Solving the mystery of fermentation unlocked a door to the discovery of the role of microbes, which in turn led to his efforts to contain and eradicate infectious diseases. This ultimately led to the development of a number of lifesaving vaccines against deadly illnesses. Perhaps most important, his careful study of microorganisms revolutionized the procedures that surgeons use when operating on patients. The sterile conditions that characterize a modern hospital operating room can be traced back directly to the tenacious and dedicated work of Louis Pasteur.

TROUBLE started for astronaut Gordo Cooper during the nineteenth of twenty-two unprecedented Earth orbits when his capsule's electrical system started shorting out. An orbit later, it lost all altitude readings. Then, with just one trip around the Earth left to go, the automatic control system promptly went AWOL.[22] Suddenly, Cooper inadvertently got what he and his fellow astronauts had been demanding since the beginning: complete control over the spacecraft. In a case of "be careful what you wish for," he was abruptly transformed from passenger to pilot.

It was white-knuckle time for the chain-smoking engineers down on the ground, but Leroy Gordon Cooper Jr., a right-side peak performer if ever there was one, was calm, alert, and completely in his element. As author Tom Wolfe explained in *The Right Stuff*, Gordo was handling the whole crisis with the nonchalance of a commercial airline pilot. Although you certainly couldn't call it uneventful, Cooper's completely manual landing proved to be almost picture-perfect: one of the most precise that the space program had ever seen—and a triumph of optimal performance.[23]

WHEN you remember the DNA of Peak Performance—dopamine, noradrenaline, and acetylcholine—finding your sweet spot where and when you need it can seem remarkably straightforward and even simple. But experience tells us otherwise. To reliably achieve peak performance, two key obstacles must be overcome: 1) the highs and lows in our moods that can sometimes wreak havoc on our ability to think clearly, and 2) our strong and instinctive tendency to have our attention diverted by distractions, both in our minds and in our environment.

Ultimately, achieving peak performance requires learning how to regulate your emotions and to focus your attention. Not coincidentally, these are precisely the skills we'll look at in the next two chapters.

CHAPTER 1 IN A NUTSHELL

KEY POINTS FROM "FIND YOUR SWEET SPOT"

It all depends on arousal. You need an optimal level of emotional arousal (commonly called stress) to achieve peak performance.

Have fun. When you have fun, your brain releases dopamine. Without fun, peak performance is practically impossible.

Challenge yourself. The highest performance comes not when you're bored or in a state of utter panic but when you're feeling slightly overchallenged. That's when the brain releases just the right amount of noradrenaline to keep you at your best.

Zero in on what's important. Peak performance never comes when you're doing more than one thing at a time. Only when you are in a state of focused attention, working single-mindedly without constant interruptions, is it possible to perform optimally.

One man's meat is another man's poison. When it comes to achieving peak performance, the same stimulation that invigorates one person may be overwhelming for another.

One type of peak performer isn't better or worse than others; they're just different. There is no appreciable difference in intelligence and overall performance between people to the left and those to the right on the peak performance graph. They just require different conditions to reach their peak.

Both gender and age can affect your performance profile. Women in general tend to be more to the left on the peak performance curve, whereas men on average are more to the right. With age we all tend to move further to the left.

Match your environment to your personal performance profile. If you are constantly over- or under-aroused at work, the single most important thing you should do is to check whether your natural predisposition is in line with your environment.

Cultivate an optimal environment for your employees too. If you're a leader, try to adapt the workplace environment to allow people to operate more in line with their individual performance profiles. Aim for enough flexibility in working conditions so that everyone can more readily reach his or her peak.

Use mental training techniques for fine-tuning, not life-changing. Only after you've found the right environment can you use mental training techniques to adjust your level of arousal so that you're at your very best just when you need it.

CHAPTER 2
REGULATE YOUR EMOTIONS

Learn How to Gain Greater Control
of Your Emotional Temperature

ZINEDINE Yazid Zidane, known to millions of fans as "Zizou," is perhaps the greatest soccer player that France has ever known. Yet, for much of his international audience, the first thing that comes to mind when they think of Zizou is a single ugly incident in 2006 that took just a few seconds to transpire.

In the 2006 World Cup Final between France and Italy, it was Zizou who put France on the scoreboard with a penalty kick that ricocheted off the crossbar and landed behind the goal line. Twelve minutes later, Italy's feisty center fullback, Marco Materazzi, evened the score at 1-1 by deftly heading in a deflection off a corner kick.

After ninety minutes of fierce play from both sides, Zidane and Materazzi still accounted for the only goals. What happened next was both controversial and devastating. Two-thirds of the way through extra time, as the two men jogged by each other, they both stopped briefly and Materazzi tugged at Zizou's jersey. Although Zidane seemed at first to be walking away from the confrontation, he suddenly turned to face Materazzi and threw himself at him with full force, knocking him to the ground with a violent head butt to his chest.

Fans all over the world watched in utter disbelief. It's not clear whether any of the referees personally witnessed the incident, but the act was so brazen and breathtakingly unsportsmanlike that officials felt they had no choice. Zinedine Zidane was issued a red card and ousted from the match.

Deprived of its leader as well as one of its most skillful penalty kickers, France lost in the shootout round, and Italy emerged as the 2006 World Cup champion. Although soccer is a game of great complexity and a certain amount of luck, it could be reasonably argued that a few-second lapse in one man's emotional regulation cost his country a world championship.

OUR PRIMITIVE NETWORKS

It may not have had the violence or the international profile of Zidane's infamous head butt, but perhaps you've witnessed an emotional outburst at work that was nearly as devastating. Who knows? You may even have been the instigator. If you were, you almost certainly felt regret once you calmed down. Many people who experience lapses in emotional regulation ask themselves the same question: "What was I thinking?!"

Granted, that question is meant to be rhetorical, but it still has a neuroscientific answer: You weren't actually *thinking*. You were *reacting*. Emotional outbursts occur when the more civilized, conscious region of your brain is hijacked by a more powerful, primitive, and largely unconscious part. It's just one skirmish in a constant battle between your prefrontal cortex and your limbic system, which is the source of your two most fundamental responses. As humans, we are capable of displaying a remarkable array of emotions. Yet most of them grow out of just two very basic and very primitive networks in our brains: the threat circuit and the reward circuit.

THE THREAT CIRCUIT: STAYIN' ALIVE

Although the brain exhibits an impressive number of skills and abilities (everything from sinking a putt to deciphering an income tax form), make no mistake: Its primary business is to keep you alive. So you'll have to forgive it for being a little oversensitive whenever it gets even an inkling of something that might put you in jeopardy. Like a bodyguard with an itchy trigger finger, it shoots first and asks questions later.

Many of the threats that primitive humans faced are no longer a factor, but the software that was designed to respond to them is still up and running. Instead of replacing our outmoded survival instincts with newer ones, our modern brain was actually built on top of our caveman-era thinking system. And because our older brain systems are more entrenched and more powerful, they are usually the first to react to any stimulus we encounter. What this means is that the suave, well-dressed, college-educated employee in your company meeting room is apt to react like an angry, bearskin-wearing, club-wielding savage if you happen to push the wrong buttons.

Now that saber-toothed tigers are extinct, we may mistakenly feel as though we live in a safer world, when in fact the situations that can trigger a stress response have increased dramatically: the unexpected message from your superior, who needs the concept within the next hour; the client who calls and is "totally dissatisfied with the proposal"; the colleague who "helpfully" informs you that he's getting promoted next month and that you aren't; the calendar alarm that tells you there are now only two days left until the client visit takes place. And then, just when you think nothing else could possibly go wrong, you get a call from the school, notifying you that your ten-year-old is sick and needs to be sent home.

When we see something that we perceive as putting our survival in danger, we react, quickly and often unconsciously. The car that suddenly darts out into our lane and the co-worker who questions our competence are both treated in remarkably similar fashion by our brains. They have both been perceived as challenges to our current existence. In the case of the car, we should be grateful that we're equipped with such a hair-trigger alarm system. We hit the brakes or swerve suddenly to avoid an accident, and we usually do it so quickly that our conscious mind doesn't catch on to what we're up to until our unconscious reaction has already occurred. Our heart beats faster, our senses become more alert, our long-term cognition is momentarily shut down, and our focus is suddenly laserlike. We avert disaster and only realize it after the fact by the pounding in our chest or the sweatiness of our palms.

The ability to instantly avoid an oncoming car can literally save our lives. In contrast, our response to a social snub is rarely lifesaving these days. That's not because it isn't as quick as our reaction to a car. It's just that our lives were probably never in jeopardy when a colleague asked pointed questions about a discrepancy in our monthly report. Our executive brain almost certainly realizes this, but by the time it does, our threat circuit has already kicked in, responding to the co-worker almost exactly the same way it would if she were an oncoming car.

The net result is remarkably similar: pounding heart, sweaty palms, increased alertness, and a momentary lapse in our more reasonable faculties. For humans in a reportedly civilized society, this is a decidedly precarious moment. Keep in mind that the colloquial name for our brain's threat circuitry is the "fight-or-flight response." The primitive urge to fight when challenged may be instinctive, but unless you're a kickboxer or a professional wrestler, it is almost always unacceptable in a civilized social context. Unless our executive functions can quickly intervene like a referee with a whistle, there's a real danger that like Zinedine Zidane we'll do something we will truly regret. And yet, if we try somehow to tamp down our instinctive emotional response, the damage we do may not be quite as spectacular, but it can be nearly as detrimental—and even more dangerous to our long-term health.

For the most part, our bodies are more inclined to protect us from threats than to seek out rewards. When you think about it, this makes evolutionary sense. Although pursuing rewards can be advantageous and pleasurable, our very survival can depend on dealing with threats. We may think of stress primarily as a bad thing, but there's no escaping this fact: You are alive today because your ancestors had a threat response that didn't let them down when they needed it most.

"We Have Met the Enemy and He Is Us"

The famous line from the Sunday comic strip *Pogo* is truer than cartoonist Walt Kelly may have ever realized. Although poisonous plants and animal predators have always shifted us into threat mode, from an evolutionary perspective, our biggest enemies are other people. Granted, we may not always consciously feel this way, but our unconscious is wired to respond with a high level of suspicion to anyone we perceive as an outsider.

The explanation dates back to the dawn of humankind. In fact, until relatively recently, humans lived in small groups, typically fifty people or fewer. It was a difficult and dangerous world, and our lives frequently depended on maintaining good relationships with the people in our particular tribe.

Then, just as now, not everyone got along all the time. If you discovered that someone within your group had taken a particular disliking to you, it could put you into a potentially life-threatening predicament. After all, the next time your tribe was attacked by an enemy tribe, you might find yourself next to your nemesis. Rather than coming to your aid, he could betray you. Or he might simply choose to run away to save his own life, leaving you at the mercy of your enemies. Then again, he might set aside old grudges and join with you in beating back the attackers. Which path would he take? Our ancestors were frequently faced with this sort of dilemma. It could be difficult to predict but essential to determine. For the sake of your own survival, you needed to be acutely aware of even the subtlest cues to decide whether you had someone you could trust by your side.

Modern conflicts may be more civilized and sophisticated, but we've retained the primitive wiring that makes us extra sensitive to small potential threats from the people around us. And our suspicions aren't limited to the battlefield. This explains why telling your spouse once in twenty years that you love her is unlikely to gain you a two-decade grace period, especially if in the meantime you overlook a key anniversary, throw out a beloved souvenir, or make the classic mistake of responding honestly to the question, "Does this outfit make me look fat?"

This tendency to place greater emphasis on threats than rewards is more than just stressful or annoying. It can be devastating to long-term relationships. In fact, University of Washington psychologist John Gottman claims to be able to predict the success or failure of a marriage with an astounding 83 percent accuracy, simply by analyzing a fifteen-minute conversation between the couple. Gottman's research points to a "magic ratio" of 5 to 1, which suggests that for every negative feeling or interaction between partners, there must be five positive feelings or interactions to offset them in order to ensure a successful marriage.

Of course, married couples aren't the only people with threat and reward circuits. We all have them. The extra weight we give to threats also explains why your boss's many heartfelt compliments about your performance can be overwhelmed by a single offhand remark about an area that "needs improvement." Rewards are intense but short-lived. A threat never forgets.

Stress Ate My Brain

If it isn't obvious already, our brains are largely a product of the distant past. Although we may have evolved somewhat since then, our tools for responding to stress have not. We've spent a lot more of our time on earth running from danger than running for the bus. These days most stress no longer protects you as it was originally designed to do. Ironically, it is more likely to put you at risk. According to data provided by the American Institute of Stress, a nonprofit organization, 75 to 95 percent of all visits to the

Our brains are largely a product of the distant past.

doctor are for stress-related conditions. When our threat response reacts to sudden and genuine danger, it can literally be a lifesaver. But this fight-or-flight reaction was designed to be acute, not chronic.

If your body remains on constant alert, it leads to a physiological and neurological state called *allostatic load*, which is damaging to your health and cognitive performance. There is an almost immediate reduction in working memory capacity, but even more ominously, prolonged high levels of the stress hormone cortisol in the bloodstream lead to shrinkage of the hippocampus, which is essential for long-term memory and the intake of new information. At the same time that stress is flooding your bloodstream with cortisol, it is reducing the level of the neurotransmitter serotonin in the brain, which can lead to depression and burnout.

While it's feeding on your hippocampus, stress is also feeding on itself. The more stress we perceive, the more anxious we become. The focal point of the fight-or-flight response, a region of the brain called the amygdala, becomes overactivated. As a result, chronically stressed people become hypersensitive to any potential stressor, real or imagined. This can lead to a vicious cycle of responses that make things even worse. Feeling pressure from work unfinished, we skip a trip to the gym to spend more time at our desks. Once home, we sit like zombies in front of the television, clutching a glass of wine or a bottle of beer along with a greasy snack we swore we'd never eat again, and then finally head to bed for a night of restless sleep before starting the process all over again. In short, the people most likely to feel stress are the people who are already stressed.

THE REWARD CIRCUIT: FEELIN' GOOD

Luckily, the fight-or-flight response isn't the only primitive system that we inherited from an older version of our brains. A second set of circuitry, the reward response, plays a role that's nearly as important—although not quite—as our threat mechanism. As with the threat circuit, the ultimate goal of the reward circuit is your survival, although it takes a slightly more roundabout route. Unlike fight-or-flight, which operates according to fear, the reward response deals in gratification. Our urges to eat, to mate, and, within limits, to play well with others are all driven by this response. The reason satisfying these urges feels good is because it helps to keep us and our descendants safe and alive. The reward circuit is the driving force behind emotions such as love, lust, happiness, loyalty, empathy, and trust. When the brain is in the reward state, dopamine, the novelty neurotransmitter, so important to peak performance, is released, which leads to positive sensations. The same circuitry also reacts to the consumption of drugs. And just as with drugs, over time you require more positive experiences to release the same amount of dopamine. This explains why you typically need a higher bonus this year than the one you received last year. Now if only your boss could understand this!

OUR WARRING BRAINS

In a sense, the story of the brain is the story of warring brains. Although the oldest part of the brain, the brain stem, pretty much operates on its own, serving as the usually dependable life support system, the brain's more recent parts, the midbrain and the cerebral cortex, are often at odds. This dynamic is at the crux of emotional regulation. The challenge is to develop a way for the brain's more sensible system to step in before your primitive brain gets you in trouble. By the way, trouble typically comes in two basic forms: 1) the emotional outburst that everyone notices and 2) the more subtle inhibitory response when the cerebral cortex intercedes and attempts to hold down the brain's angry dinosaur before it does permanent damage.

Ironically, the latter approach, although seemingly more civilized, is more likely to do long-term damage to your body and brain. It may not embarrass you in front of your colleagues or get you arrested for assault (or worse), but it can raise your blood pressure to dangerous levels, physically shrink crucial regions of the brain you depend on for reasoning and memory, jeopardize your immune system, or leave you with any number of maladies, everything from chronic teeth grinding to life-threatening heart disease.

Why in the world would we consciously put ourselves at risk in this way? The short answer is that we don't—not consciously, at least. That's precisely the problem. Without deliberate changes to our behavior, our self-destructive reactions are largely outside the realm of our conscious cognitive control. The key to emotional regulation is to protect yourself by strengthening your ability to handle stress and to train your brain by teaching its weaker but more sophisticated conscious regions how to outsmart the stronger but more primitive unconscious parts.

PROTECT YOURSELF

You can bolster your resistance to emotional imbalance by creating overall life conditions that promote balance. The tried-and-true recommendations of exercising, eating well, and getting plenty of sleep may sound like tired clichés, but they are cited again and again for good reason: They work. Few things can better build your resilience in facing oncoming stress than this trio. And if you can do your exercising outdoors in nature, then so much the better.

Sleep on It

Nobody's fool, the legendary physicist Albert Einstein reportedly got ten hours of sleep a night. Although you don't have to be a genius to recognize that sufficient sleep can have a restorative effect, recent research indicates that it also plays a key role in your emotional regulation.[1] Unfortunately, roughly 30 percent of working Americans get by on less than six hours of sleep daily. Making matters worse, far too many executives wear sleep loss as a badge of honor. It's often, though not exclusively, a macho thing, implying that only tough guys can get through their day on a minimum of sleep.[2]

Awaking Your Primitive Side

Matthew Walker, director of the Sleep and Neuroimaging Laboratory at the University of California, Berkeley, is intrigued by how sleep loss impairs emotional regulation and seems to roll back certain evolutionary developments in the brain: "It's almost as though, without sleep, the brain had reverted back to more primitive patterns of activity, in that it was unable to put emotional experiences into context and produce controlled, appropriate responses."[3]

When you go without sleep, the amygdala, the seat of the brain's fight-or-flight response, appears to shift into high gear, interfering with more deliberate, logical reasoning as well as impairing the release of certain neurochemicals that would normally aid in calming you down.[4] Sleep loss is more likely to leave you short-tempered, impatient, and moody. It can cause you to overreact to negative situations and to perceive neutral situations as negative.

Sleep loss does more than just interfere with your own internal emotional regulation. A study done at UC Berkeley found that sleep deprivation diminishes your ability to judge the emotions in other people's faces. This impairment was especially pronounced among women.[5] It also interferes with your decision making, harms your productivity, and, most ominously, increases your risk of cardiovascular and gastrointestinal problems.[6]

We All Go a Little Mad Sometimes

You'd be crazy to do without sufficient sleep. According to UC Berkeley's Walker, ". . . even healthy people's brains mimic certain pathological psychiatric patterns when deprived of sleep."[7] And what would those pathological psychiatric patterns entail? According to recent research, people who experience insufficient or disrupted sleep are more susceptible to bouts of depression and even have a higher risk of suicide.[8] Just how much of an emotional basket case can sleep loss make you? According to Walker's findings, "The emotional centers of the brain were over 60 percent more reactive under conditions of sleep deprivation than in subjects who had obtained a normal night of sleep."[9] That's a pretty significant effect—and it's entirely within our control.

The Benefits of Sleep

Of course, the story of sleep isn't simply about averting disaster. Sleep loss interferes with your ability to maintain your composure, but getting sufficient sleep can do wonders to help you withstand many of life's inevitable stresses and aggravations.

Many of us spend far too much of our present reliving stressful memories of our past. Simply recalling social slights, workplace confrontations, and nerve-racking assignments can be enough to reactivate the threat response. Luckily, adequate sleep has been shown to take a lot of the sting out of stress. During the all-important phase of our sleep cycle known as REM (rapid eye movement) sleep, the brain is able to remove noradrenaline, the stress-related neurotransmitter, from processing recent events, before storing them as long-term memories. This means you'll still be able to recall these incidents without dredging up the emotional baggage that may have traveled with them when they first occurred.[10]

Adequate sleep has been shown to take a lot of the sting out of stress.

More and more companies are realizing that workers who are well rested are better adjusted and more productive. In fact, in addition to encouraging employees to get sufficient sleep at night, high-profile companies such as Google, Nike, Time Warner, and the *Huffington Post* not only permit napping during the workday but actually encourage it.[11] A number of companies, including Nike and thyssenkrupp, have quiet rooms where employees can nap or even meditate. Perhaps not surprisingly, Google's approach is even more innovative. Special "nap-pods" are located throughout the corporate campus. Looking a bit like a cross between a lounge chair and a giant Ping-Pong ball, these pods provide privacy and play soothing sounds for workers who feel the need to catch up on sleep or simply chill out.[12]

Of course, sleep doesn't operate in isolation. Regular vigorous exercise can improve the quality of your sleep, while poor nutritional choices can make sleep more difficult. In fact, obesity is a major contributor to the epidemic of sleep-disrupting apnea.[13]

The Exercise Advantage

As numerous studies have shown, when compared to couch potatoes, people who engage in a regimen of regular exercise improve their cognitive test scores. They are superior in long-term memory, reasoning, attention, problem-solving and fluid-intelligence tasks (which involve reasoning quickly), thinking abstractly, and improvising off previously learned material in order to solve new problems.[14] In short, they are in better control of their brains. And if your goal is emotional regulation, then control is just what you need. In fact, the benefits of exercise can be so dramatic that if it were bottled, it would probably be seen as a wonder drug. Consider some of the evidence of the exercise advantage:

- When you engage in some sort of physical leisure activity, especially aerobic activity, your risk of dementia is cut in half.[15]
- Taking a twenty-minute walk every day reduces your chance of stroke by even more: 57 percent.[16]
- Exercise regulates the release of serotonin, dopamine, and noradrenaline. All three are associated with the maintenance of mental health.[17] Evidence now indicates that exercise can be used to alter the course of both depression and anxiety.[18] In a study published in the *Archives of Internal Medicine*, men and women suffering from depression were divided into three groups. One group participated in an aerobic exercise program, another

took a well-known antidepressant, and a third group did both. After four months, depression had eased in all three groups.[19]

- Exercise can also give you a better memory. It increases blood volume in the dentate gyrus, an important component of the hippocampus, which deals with the formation of memories.[20]

Exercise not only provides long-term protection and enhanced health but is also a powerful short-term solution to the damaging effects of stress. No natural remedy provides a more effective way of flushing the stress hormone cortisol out of your bloodstream. A short run, a vigorous walk, or a challenging game of tennis—in fact, almost anything that gets you up and moving—can wipe the slate clean of the day's accumulated tension and leave you feeling refreshed, ready to face the rest of the day, or pleasantly relaxed for a leisurely evening and a sound night's sleep.

Take It Outside

By itself, exercise offers ample protection against stress, but exercise outdoors can be even better. Exposure to nature of almost any kind has been shown to have a healing effect. Numerous studies have found that time spent in nature can improve emotional regulation and provide a potent antidote to stress. A study headed by Dr. Peter Kahn at the University of Washington measured the heart rates of three groups of students. One group performed a mildly stressful task in a windowless room. Another performed the same task by a window that had a view of the university's Drumheller fountain. The third group viewed a real-time image of the fountain on a plasma screen. The students who viewed nature through a window saw the biggest drop in heart rate, while the effect on heartbeat between the students who stared at a blank wall and those who saw nature via a plasma screen was negligible.[21]

Other research done before and since seems to underscore the benefits of the natural world in moderating our emotions. In a *Wall Street Journal* article, University of Oregon professor emeritus Michael Posner, a recognized expert on focused attention (see chapter 3), was quoted as suggesting that taking a walk in a park "could do wonders" in dealing with stress.[22]

Of course, people in urban areas don't always have easy access to more bucolic settings. Not to worry, says University of Michigan's Marc Berman, who found that even looking at photos of nature in a quiet room was more beneficial than walking down a cacophonous city street. On the other hand, if the street is relatively tranquil and well landscaped, it can be nearly as helpful as getting out of town.[23] "A quieter city street with interesting natural elements to look at, such as containers of plants, could do the trick, too," he told the *Wall Street Journal*.[24]

There may be a slight disparity in their results, but most of the studies seem to have reached the same basic conclusion: When it comes to reducing stress, green is good.

Food and Stress

Although exercise is generally well accepted for its role in stress reduction, busy executives who dutifully seek to stay in shape with regular trips to the gym often overlook the dramatic effects that good nutrition can have on promoting emotional regulation.

One passionate advocate for this food-stress protection connection is Holger Stromberg, Michelin-starred chef and official chef for the World Cup–winning German national soccer team. When we spoke to him recently in Munich, he was adamant about the role that a proper diet plays not only in helping players meet the physical demands of a soccer match but also in aiding both athletes and executives to stay at the top of their mental game.

Stromberg told us how he's personally witnessed remarkable changes in mental fitness that came from better nutrition. How can he tell? By the way his clients look. The toll that stress takes on the body isn't always invisible. To a skilled observer, changes to your hair, your skin, and your eyes can often provide clear visual signs of insufficient or inadequate nutrition. When he's not serving delicious, nutritious meals to elite athletes, Stromberg uses his expertise to reduce the stress and improve the overall health of top business leaders. "I have given individual advice to some of them," he told us. "A few months later they not only *feel* the change. You can actually *see* it!"[25]

Typically, when we hold seminars devoted to brain-based strategies for improving performance, we work with professional nutritionists as part of the program and serve participants "brain food" that has been created especially to enhance their rational and emotional well-being. Executives who attend our seminars often incorporate this new diet into their daily lives. Many are amazed at how tasty and easy to prepare this healthy food is and, even more important, by how much better it makes them feel.

What sorts of dishes do we serve? Unfortunately, specific menus are beyond the scope of this particular book (although they may well take center stage in a future one!), but if there's a key takeaway from the role of nutrition in building your protection against unwelcome swings in emotions, it's that nutritious food should provide you with enough energy so the fuel your brain depends upon for proper functioning is available whenever you need it. For the most part, you can't go wrong with a diet that includes a lot of nutrient-rich vegetables and fruits as well as some protein, along with some healthy fatty acids, such as olive and canola oils. Proteins are important because amino acids act as building blocks for neurotransmitters. For example, tryptophan (found in everything from chicken to chickpeas to chocolate) is a precursor for serotonin and melatonin and can't be naturally produced in the body. Although some people are militant about completely avoiding carbohydrates, we don't advocate anything that extreme. In fact, there is some evidence that low-carb diets inhibit the transportation of serotonin to your brain, which could lead to depression.[26] Simple carbohydrates may supply energy to your brain, but they have little or no nutritional benefit, which means you may be forced to consume excess calories just to get the nutrients you need. Incorporate some tasty whole-grain complex carbohydrates into the mix instead, and you should be fine.

TRAIN YOUR BRAIN

There's nothing inevitable about the way your brain responds to a particular situation. Your brain may be smart and powerful, but it's also surprisingly naive and impressionable. You can often defuse a variety of stressful situations by using your body to fool your brain, by approaching them from a positive angle, or by deflecting the considerable strength of a stress response and using it to your advantage instead.

Lead with Your Body

Although everything from smiling to stress demonstrates how the brain drives the body, the truth is it's a two-way street. Time and time again, psychologists have proved not only that emotions influence the body but that the reverse is true as well: The body can influence emotions. By "acting as if," that is, by assuming the expression and posture of a happy and successful person, you can often trick your brain into believing.

The Botox Effect

According to recent statistics from the American Society of Plastic Surgeons, an estimated 6.1 million patients received treatments using botulinum toxin type A, better known as Botox. The vast majority of patients presumably receive Botox to feel better about themselves, but psychologists discovered a surprising wrinkle in the effect of these frown-line-reducing injections on their recipients' overall dispositions.

A study of forty women who were asked to respond to statements before and after Botox treatments yielded results that made both psychologists and plastic surgeons smile. Although the subjects' reactions to happy statements were unchanged, their reactions to sad or angry statements were noticeably slower after receiving their injections. According to the "facial feedback hypothesis," our physical expressions send signals to our brains to produce the appropriate emotional response. In other words, although we smile when we are happy, sometimes smiling can actually *make* us happy. This may be due to the "frozen smile" that Botox can sometimes produce. The results from the Botox study were so intriguing that psychologists have been researching Botox as a possible remedy for depression.

Is That a Pencil in Your Mouth, or Are You Just Happy to See Me?

Other studies have been conducted that used ordinary pencils and even chopsticks instead of Botox. In the pencil study, researchers asked one group of subjects to hold a pencil lengthwise between their teeth while rating the humor of a series of cartoons. The other group viewed the identical cartoons while holding the pencil between their lips but without touching it to their teeth. Try it yourself and you will see the difference. The first grip forced each subject's face into a smile. The second generated a frown. Even though the subjects weren't consciously aware of the facial expressions they were assuming, those expressions had a measurable effect on their reactions to the cartoons. The smilers enjoyed the cartoons far more than the frowners.

Although the pencil study seemed to prove the effect of positive expressions on our emotions, the chopstick study went a step further, making a direct connection between smiling and our resilience when we're exposed to stress. In this case, one group of subjects held a chopstick in their mouths, producing smiles that were similar to those in the pencil study, while the other group assumed a neutral expression. Both groups were subjected to minor stressful events, such as plunging their hand into a bucket of ice water. In each instance the researchers measured the subjects' heart rates before, during, and after the event. The heart rates of subjects who were smiling (even though they didn't realize it) recovered more quickly than the heart rates of those who maintained a neutral expression.

The Power of Posture

Facial expressions aren't the only things that influence your attitude. A study done at two prestigious business schools found that posture has a greater effect than even a promotion on your overall behavior. Subjects who assumed a so-called expansive posture—spreading out by crossing their legs instead of keeping them together and by draping an arm over the back of a chair instead of placing their hands under their legs—were found to exhibit a greater sense of confidence and power than subjects who sat more submissively but had been granted a superior role. The results were so decisive that they surprised even those who had conducted the study. "Going into the research, we figured role would make a big difference," said Li Huang, a PhD candidate at the Kellogg School of Management. "But shockingly, the effect of posture dominated the effect of role in each and every study."[27] In a subsequent study, headed by Harvard psychologist Amy Cuddy (author of the book *Presence*), that simulated a job interview scenario, candidates who struck a "high-power pose" were judged as performing better and were more likely to be hired.[28]

How 'Bout a Hug?

Whereas smiles can cheer you up and a powerful pose can increase your feelings of confidence, a simple gesture can have an almost miraculous effect on calming you down. Giving or receiving a hug can trigger a huge release of oxytocin, which is popularly known as "the cuddle hormone." In fact, physical contact in general releases oxytocin, which has been found in studies to be more effective than even soothing words to reduce levels of stress. In one study, husbands accompanied their wives to a stressful test. One group offered words of encouragement. The others simply massaged their wives' shoulders. The latter group saw a decline in stress levels associated with testing. The former did not.

Granted, in some circles, hugging your business colleagues or massaging their shoulders may be frowned upon—and in some situations can even trigger a threat response from the recipient. (Just ask German chancellor Angela Merkel, who in 2006 received an unsolicited and clearly unwanted back rub from then-president George W. Bush!) Luckily, there are other, more socially acceptable ways to get your oxytocin fix. Cuddling with a pet or a partner can release oxytocin and, although its effects may not be quite as dramatic, so can simply shaking hands with a client or colleague.

Because our brain operates according to a negativity bias, our initial response when meeting someone new is to treat that person as a foe instead of a friend until we're led to believe otherwise. Handshake to the rescue! This custom not only has a historical purpose—proof that you're not holding a weapon—but it also has a neurological one: to reduce the threat response and generate a greater sense of connection by releasing a modest squirt of oxytocin.

Switching off Stress

Now that abundant scientific evidence shows that changes to your body can influence reactions in your brain, it seems increasingly clear that one of the most effective strategies for controlling stress begins with altering your physical behavior.

Your autonomic nervous system, the mechanism that operates largely without your conscious assistance to keep your body running, has two main channels: the sympathetic and the parasympathetic. It is the sympathetic channel that activates the fight-or-flight response, while the parasympathetic is responsible for what are sometimes called "rest and digest" or "feed and breed" activities.

There are some exceptions, but in general, when one

channel dominates, the other is dormant. When we are feeling under stress, for example, we are usually unable to properly rest and digest. In order to put your body in the best position to respond to a threat, your sympathetic nervous system temporarily shuts down all nonessential functions, including digestion, reproduction, and, perhaps needless to say, relaxation. You don't usually want to be taking it easy when your life is in danger!

Although it isn't quite as straightforward as a light switch, it's close. Learning to relax involves developing the ability to shift from the sympathetic nervous system to the parasympathetic one, that is, to switch off stress and switch on relaxation. Most of the popular techniques for relaxation rely on the same simple but often elusive principle: finding a way to flip your own switch.

DEEP BREATHING. Normally, no one has to tell you to keep breathing. You do it continuously every day throughout your entire life, largely without thinking. Deep breathing, also known as belly breathing, not only gets you to focus on your breathing, but it also encourages you to change the way you breathe—slowly inhaling through your nose rather than your mouth and using each new breath to expand your abdomen (belly) instead of your chest. Then when you exhale, you do so through your mouth, breathing out slowly as your abdomen deflates. Most of us have experienced the fast, shallow breathing that comes with anxiety or stress and the deep, leisurely breaths we take when we're feeling pleasantly sleepy or relaxed. Deep breathing turns this process on its head, using your breaths to define your mood instead of the other way around.

PROGRESSIVE MUSCLE RELAXATION. Developed by physician Edmund Jacobson in the early twentieth century, progressive muscle relaxation is exactly what it sounds like. It involves methodically moving through your body's muscle groups, tensing and relaxing each before moving on to the next group. The technique not only provides systematic relaxation throughout your body, but it also increases body awareness of what each muscle group feels like when it's tense and when it's relaxed. This will often strengthen your ability to recognize and remedy any feelings of stress you may experience throughout your body.

AUTOGENIC TRAINING. Back in the 1930s, German psychiatrist Johannes Heinrich Schultz developed a relaxation technique called autogenic training. It involves sitting or lying quietly for fifteen minutes—preferably two or three times a day—and repeating a set of visualizations that are intended to induce relaxation. Some thirty years later, American cardiologist Dr. Herbert Benson picked up where Dr. Schultz left off and adjusted the instructions slightly, encouraging patients to sit comfortably and quietly and focus on a sound, word, or phrase, or gaze at a specific object. Over time, this practice increases your awareness and control of your autonomic nervous system, enabling you to switch from your stress-laden sympathetic nervous system to the more soothing parasympathetic system, what Dr. Benson calls "the Relaxation Response."

Changing your body can change your brain.

Although the instructions for each of these techniques vary, they share a fundamental idea. Changing your body can change your brain. Hundreds of peer-reviewed studies support this powerful conclusion: By consciously focusing on relaxing your body or by directing your attention to a simple sound or object, you can cause your brain to switch off its stress response.

You can use these established techniques, or you can try something a little more informal. If you're mired in what seems

Let your body lead the way, and your brain will usually follow.

like an endless meeting, simply shifting your posture can often have a noticeable effect on your outlook. If you're sitting at your desk feeling low, sometimes the fastest way to change your emotional tune is to get up and move around. Let your body lead the way, and your brain will usually follow.

Think Positively

For the bulk of the past century, a wide variety of motivational speakers have advocated so-called positive thinking with an almost evangelical intensity. The speakers may have had hundreds of thousands of adherents, but naturally skeptical scientists still viewed their sunny attitudes with understandable suspicion. After all, positive thinking was more of a philosophy than a science, and scientists above all are dependent on data. Now, thanks to scientific innovations such as functional magnetic resonance imaging (fMRI), we finally have that data. And although the positive thinkers probably had more than their share of charlatans and naive but well-intentioned advocates, their underlying message—that changing your attitude can change your life—is now borne out in hundreds of peer-reviewed, number-heavy studies.

You Gotta Believe

But first, the bad news. There are some wildly popular self-help approaches that still aren't supported by solid neuroscientific evidence. The best known among these is the idea of positive affirmations.

When legendary boxer Muhammad Ali proudly told the world, "I'm the king! I'm the greatest!" he was doing more than simply reminding his audience what they already knew. He may also have been helping his performance in the ring. Ali's pronouncement followed a proud tradition of positive affirmations, the idea that by combining an optimistic attitude with a strong positive statement you can achieve almost any goal.

The problem is that for every Muhammad Ali who used positive affirmations to help him succeed, there are tens of thousands of needy and well-intentioned individuals for whom these affirmations actually make matters worse! Empirical data show that these quick-fix attempts to redirect your life can work, but only if you already have a healthy self-esteem. In fact, when self-affirmations were used in a stressful testing situation, they worked *against* subjects who had low self-esteem. If you don't have a positive sense of yourself, the first thing you'll need to do is change your core beliefs about who you are.

Blame It on the Basal Ganglia

Like our ability to ride a bicycle, our sense of self-worth is embedded in a part of our brain called the basal ganglia. These ganglia, not surprisingly, are located in close proximity to both your threat and reward circuits. If you tell yourself you're lovable but deep inside you're convinced you are not, the result is a debilitating and stressful cognitive dissonance, in which your conscious brain is at odds with your unconscious.

So what happens if you don't have a positive self-image? Are you doomed to lead a life of missed goals and mediocrity? Absolutely not. Your self-image, like your brain in general, can be compared to a muscle. If your legs are fat and flabby and you want to have muscles that are strong and well toned, the solution is usually obvious: exercise. By the same token, if your tendency toward optimism is underdeveloped or has atrophied, what you really need is a workout. Counting your blessings, building on your successes, and reestablishing your identity can all be used to strengthen your self-image.

Every Day Is Thanksgiving Day

It's no coincidence that most of the world's major religions place a major emphasis on gratitude. Gratitude is not about suppressing or inhibiting. That not only doesn't work, but it's been proved again and again to be detrimental. Instead, it's about redirecting your attention. Although it doesn't have to be religious or spiritual, gratitude therapy shifts the focus away from affirming beliefs you may not even have to being grateful for those things you do have.

THE SCIENCE OF GRATITUDE. In numerous studies, the results of this shift have been dramatic. Just three weeks of gratitude training has been shown to improve personal well-being and overall psychological health. It leads to an increase in energy and exercising and a boost in optimism, as well as better sleep and more time spent helping others.[29]

All these improvements have a cumulative effect. They influence the way you act and behave and ultimately the way you think and feel about yourself. The mounting empirical evidence supporting the effects of gratitude therapy is nothing short of miraculous. Although research has repeatedly pointed to a so-called happiness set point—a baseline for happiness that makes some people just naturally happier than others, regardless of the external circumstances—gratitude research highlights the potential for raising that home base of happiness by as much as 25 percent.[30] "It's not happiness that allows us to be grateful," explains David Steindl-Rast, a Catholic Benedictine monk who has a PhD in experimental psychology. "It's gratefulness that allows us to be happy."

A GRATITUDE GAME PLAN. How can you put all this miraculous-sounding gratitude theory into practice? One very simple thing you can do once a day is to write down three to five things you are grateful for. You may want to set aside a specific time of day for doing this. Or you may prefer to add to your list while you're traveling, during a sleep-inducing meeting, or whenever you find yourself with some free time.

Although this is sometimes referred to as a gratitude diary, there's no need to keep an actual diary. If you'd prefer, you can create an innocent-looking file on your smartphone and maintain a running list. A number of gratitude apps are available to make this routine a little easier. Most of them are free, and they often provide passcode protection to keep your list away from prying eyes, as well as a notification option to remind you to add to your list, until it becomes a regular part of your day.

WHAT SHOULD GO ON YOUR GRATITUDE LIST? To better understand what gratitude is, it is important to understand what it isn't. Gratitude isn't about comparing yourself to others.[31] Recognizing that other people may not be as wealthy, as talented, or as good-looking, or that they're simply worse off than you are isn't gratitude.[32] In fact, that approach can promote a corrosive arrogance. Nor is gratitude an enumeration of your personal accomplishments, even though these are almost certainly worth celebrating.

Gratitude is directed instead at a source outside yourself.[33] It typically places an emphasis on people or things in your world that have made your life better, more fortunate, or more meaningful. This can include everything from the sight of a beautiful sunset to the taste of a delicious meal, a smile from a stranger, or the aid of a colleague, relative, or friend.

Build on Your Successes

It's difficult if not impossible to think positively if you don't have a positive assessment of your own capabilities. That's where self-efficacy comes in. Self-efficacy is a fundamental belief that you have some control over your own life and outcomes. Even though much of your sense of self-efficacy is formed when you are a child, events throughout your life can either strengthen or weaken that sense. Each new skill you acquire and each new success you achieve can conceivably bolster your sense of self-efficacy. By the same token, failures or setbacks can erode those feelings, although they don't have to. A quick litmus test for your level of self-efficacy depends on the way you approach a difficult task. People with strong self-efficacy view such tasks as challenges, while those with weak self-efficacy are more likely to characterize them as threats.

Approaching tasks as challenges rather than as threats can have a powerful effect on your life and your emotions. It can generate a chain reaction of accomplishments while reducing stress and your susceptibility to depression.[34] Few things are more effective in perpetuating a positive attitude than being able to point to a string of proven successes.

But what if you don't currently have such a string that you can point to? There are two things you can do to foster a permanent positive attitude toward your life and everything you do. First, whenever you make a mistake of any kind, dismiss it as temporary and remind yourself that you will do better next time. This is how optimists respond to setbacks. Second, whenever you experience a failure, look upon it as a temporary blip on your radar screen of life but nothing that you can't get over. Optimists see every setback as something impermanent and fleeting. They then move on to the next activity.

Stanford University psychologist Albert Bandura, a pioneer in the study of the field, points to four key factors—mastery experiences, social modeling, social persuasion, and psychological responses—that can determine your level of self-efficacy.[35] Each can be translated into a concrete action that can bolster your belief in your ability to succeed.

1. **Draw on previous triumphs.** A past success can serve as a springboard for overcoming a present obstacle. The stakes may even be higher this time, but if you can use the strength you gained from a similar challenge, then you can rely on that memory for momentum to help power you through.

2. **Compare yourself favorably to your peers.** Look to examples of others around you who have faced similar challenges. Telling yourself, "If that idiot can do it, so can I!" might seem a little harsh, but that's the basic idea, although it definitely doesn't need to be so scathing in order to be effective.

3. **Gain support from someone you respect.** The right vote of confidence from the right person can often extinguish any lingering self-doubt. Trusted mentors, relatives, or friends who have a clear understanding of your abilities can be perfect for this role. Find someone who will cheer you on and who will be on your side like a good sports coach.

4. **If you feel good, then you can do it.** Your sense of the size of the obstacle and the odds that you can overcome it can be colored by the way you are feeling. Chronically cheating yourself out of rest or relaxation, for example, can influence your emotional state, your physical reactions, and your level of stress. Optimists are often physically fit and well rested. It's amazing how a good mood can miraculously reduce a mountain to a molehill.

Conquer Impostor Syndrome

A managing partner for one of the world's top multinational professional services firms once recalled asking herself, "What are you doing here? What do you think you're doing? You're going to be found out."[36] It may seem strange, but a sizable number of people in the modern world, many of them with an impressive array of accomplishments to their credit, feel deep down that they are actually frauds, that they don't truly deserve their success. The long list of people who suffer from this feeling includes business leaders, Supreme Court justices, and Oscar-winning actresses.

Although it isn't an official diagnosis yet, psychologists generally recognize what is commonly called "impostor syndrome" as a form of intellectual self-doubt that is accompanied by anxiety and often by depression as well.[37] Almost none of us is immune to this feeling. Researchers suggest that up to 70 percent of people have felt the ache of impostor syndrome at one point in their lives.[38]

WHO SUFFERS FROM IMPOSTOR SYNDROME. People who feel this way aren't slackers or incompetents. On the contrary, they are usually highly motivated overachievers who don't feel as though they truly deserve the many accolades they often receive.[39] Instead, they are more likely to focus on the things they haven't yet achieved.[40] According to Atlanta psychologist Dr. Suzanne Imes, codeveloper of the impostor phenomenon theory, many of the adults who experience impostor syndrome grew up in households where high achievement was emphasized. Achievement then becomes inextricably linked with their general sense of self-worth.[41]

WHY IT HAPPENS. One possible explanation for impostor syndrome is that because experienced leaders often rely on expert intuition to make their best decisions (see chapter 5), these wise choices barely register in the conscious brain, making them harder to recall. What's more, the anxiety from not remembering can in turn activate the amygdala, which interferes with the ability to make conscious, rational decisions, thus reinforcing the feeling of inadequacy.[42]

So, if you sometimes find that you are unable to account for your success, that doesn't automatically mean that you're a phony. On the contrary, there's a good chance it indicates that you were able to execute important decisions unconsciously. And that is the characteristic of an expert, not an impostor.[43]

GENDER DIFFERENCES? Psychologists who first investigated the impostor phenomenon initially concluded that it was more common among women. In one study of 150 high-performing professional women, many dismissed much of their hard-earned success as simply a case of being in the right place at the right time.[44] The people who suffer from impostor syndrome may surprise you. U.S. Supreme Court Justice Sonia Sotomayor once confessed, "I am always looking over my shoulder wondering if I measure up."[45] British actress Kate Winslet, who's won an Oscar, an Emmy, a Grammy, and four Golden Globe awards and has been nominated numerous times, once described her own feelings of self-doubt: "I'd wake up in the morning before going off to a shoot, and think, *I can't do this; I'm a fraud.*"[46]

Despite candid comments about impostor syndrome from high-profile women, recent research has made it clear that men aren't exempt from the experience.[47] A key factor in feeling like a fraud appears to come from being different from the majority of your peers in some way.[48] According to Dr. Pauline Rose Clance, a clinical psychologist in Atlanta and a codeveloper of the impostor phenomenon theory, the experience is more common among minorities. Asian Americans were more likely than African Americans or Latino Americans to experience impostor feelings.[49] Nonetheless, one study found that a whopping 93 percent of female African American college students were plagued by impostor syndrome.[50]

Although women and men both suffer from self-doubt, the two genders appear to have distinctly different ways of dealing with it. Whereas women may use feelings of insecurity as motivation to prove themselves,[51] men are more likely to steer clear of further competition for fear that it will leave them feeling more vulnerable and will reveal their perceived weaknesses to a wider world.[52]

HOW IMPOSTORS THINK. Not surprisingly, people who worry they're impostors tend to be moodier, less confident, and more likely to suffer from performance anxiety.[53] When they're praised or rewarded, people with impostor syndrome are convinced they don't deserve it.[54]

Rather than alleviating some of the anxiety, each new accomplishment can actually make things worse for impostor syndrome sufferers, whose irrational worries of being revealed as frauds intensify as the stakes get higher and higher.[55] And if for some reason they're overlooked for recognition, they secretly understand.

Perfectionism is also common in impostor syndrome sufferers, who seldom seek help and yet feel that everything must be done just right.[56] In some respects, the impostor syndrome can be seen as the dark side of intrinsic motivation. If you're motivated by your own goals rather than by ones that have been set by others, in times when you don't meet your stringent personal standards, you can quickly become your own worst enemy.[57]

SURPRISING ADVANTAGES. Of course, this nagging feeling of insecurity isn't always a bad thing. It can often provide further motivation for achievement.[58] What's more, because countless studies have shown that people tend to grossly overestimate their own abilities, impostorism can sometimes be a helpful way to keep overconfidence in check.[59]

OVERCOMING IMPOSTOR SYNDROME. For those who genuinely feel they're frauds, there are a number of techniques that can help to overcome this potentially debilitating disorder.

Embrace it. The first step to overcoming impostor syndrome is self-acceptance.[60] This means acknowledging that it exists and that it is part of your personality.[61] According to Dr. Rosalyn Lang-Walker, a molecular biologist who has struggled with feelings of self-doubt in the past, acknowledging impostor syndrome is the secret to combating it: "Once you recognize it, you can always talk it down. You can say to yourself, 'I've gotten this far for a reason.'"[62]

Take inventory. Dr. Imes suggests writing down the things you're good at as well as the areas that need work. The process of creating the list can remind you how much you've achieved and shine a reassuring spotlight on your strengths.[63]

Don't compare. Stop comparing yourself to others. Doing so is always subjective, rarely accurate, and almost never helpful.[64] Recognize that the people who seem more confident are often just better actors. In private, they may be plagued by self-doubt that is as strong as or stronger than yours.[65]

Get a second opinion. If you're tough on yourself, look to outside evaluations, such as promotions, awards, and feedback from managers and colleagues, as more reliable assessments of your actual abilities. Remember that research has shown that we are poor judges of our own abilities.[66]

Stay competitive. Don't let harsh self-judgment prevent you from regularly sharpening and expanding your skills.[67] Rather than lowering the bar, set some realistic expectations that will leave you feeling slightly overchallenged instead of completely overwhelmed.[68] It takes courage to pursue goals when you run the risk of falling short and losing face.[69]

Don't clam up. If you are plagued by self-doubt, don't keep silent. Share your feelings with people you trust. You'll often find that articulating your insecurities will make it clear that most of your worries are unduly exaggerated or even baseless.[70]

Find a mentor. Supportive supervision can help to break the spell of the impostor phenomenon.[71] Attach yourself to a role model or advocate who truly believes in you, even when you may not believe in yourself.[72]

Be a mentor. Working with junior colleagues can help you realize what you've achieved and how much valuable knowledge you are capable of imparting.[73]

Say thank you. Don't dismiss or discount the people who praise you, even when you think they're mistaken. Rejecting heartfelt compliments may seem modest, but it can sometimes convey contempt for the judgment and feelings of others. On the other hand, graciously acknowledging praise is good for both the giver and the receiver.[74]

Celebrate. When you reach a minor milestone, take time out to pat yourself on the back and acknowledge your success before moving on to the next challenge. When the milestone is bigger, set aside some time to do something special as a reward and recognition of your achievement.[75]

Use Cognitive Jujitsu

Strictly speaking, stress is not the enemy. What matters is the way in which you respond to that stress. It is possible to take what would normally be considered negative, corrosive stress and transform it into something positive and energizing. A group of amorous young Canadian men unconsciously helped psychologists to prove this point.

Asked to walk across a shaky wooden suspension bridge that dangles high above the Capilano River in North Vancouver, British Columbia, the men experienced sweaty palms, a quickened heartbeat, and a number of other classic symptoms associated with elevated arousal. The source of this arousal should've been obvious. After all, crossing the bridge is exciting and scary. But when each got to the other side, something interesting happened. An attractive young researcher with a clipboard was there to meet him and to administer a short quiz. The woman's presence caused half of the men to suddenly change their assessment of the situation, mistakenly attributing their excitement not to the perils of a precarious bridge but to a mutual romantic attraction.[76]

Psychologists refer to this phenomenon as "misattribution of arousal." What this experiment provides, aside from some predictable insights into the male libido, is a better understanding of how stress really works. Rather than operating as one continuous response, it plays out in two discrete phases, each handled by a different brain function. Although our powerful and primitive limbic system is automatically activated in response to an arousal, it is the more civilized part of our brain that has the job of analyzing the data. There is a tantalizing lag between when our speedy, instinctive subconscious responds and when the slower and more deliberate region of our brain interprets that response. Making use of this tiny delay may hold the key to effective emotional regulation and to taking the sting out of stress. The important thing is not the stress response itself but how you respond to that response. And that is where what we like to call Cognitive Jujitsu comes in.

Emotional Regulation as a Martial Art

The Japanese martial art of jujitsu rests on a simple but powerful idea: When confronted with a stronger opponent, if you attempt to overpower him, you will almost certainly lose. But if you can find a way to neutralize that opponent's strength or use it against him, you have a good chance of winning.

A janitor at a company we know is also a student of martial arts. One of the strongest members of his local fight club, he was pitted against a teammate who was equal to him in strength but perhaps not in cleverness.

Carefully assessing the situation, the janitor knew he would be able to win not by force but only by outwitting his opponent somehow. Luckily, jujitsu is a martial art that permits all sorts of unorthodox tricks. As the two men grappled, the janitor suddenly kissed his opponent on the mouth. The other man was so startled by the move that he loosened his grip and the janitor was able to use this brief moment of weakness to throw him down to the mat. Although that particular move may not be found in any martial arts manual, it was a memorable and decidedly unconventional example of jujitsu.

The principle of jujitsu originally pertained to two human opponents, but it could just as easily have been describing two rival regions of the brain. Emotional regulation is a contest between your powerful limbic system and your weaker but wilier prefrontal cortex. If you attempt to counteract stress by fighting it directly, you will fail. That hasn't stopped many of us from attempting to battle stress by suppressing it, a technique psychologists call "inhibition."

Why Inhibition Doesn't Work

Our society places a regrettable premium on the ability to keep a stiff upper lip. Unfortunately, holding back your emotions not only doesn't work, it's also bad for you and for the people around you.

If you are sitting in a meeting and inhibiting stress, the effect on your brain's executive functions can sometimes be so devastating that you might as well not be attending the meeting at all. While you're silently congratulating yourself for not "losing it," you're probably losing your ability to create, innovate, plan, and remember. What makes inhibition so insidious is the fact that the toll it takes on your thinking is largely invisible to you. Everything may seem fine precisely because the part of your brain that would normally alert you if it weren't has essentially been shut down.

What's worse is that even though you may not be aware of the fact that you aren't functioning anywhere near 100 percent, it's often apparent to the people around you, even if it's only on an unconscious level. One study found that when someone inhibits stress, the blood pressure of the people around him increases. Keeping your stress under wraps is a bit like carrying a concealed weapon. Others can often sense that you're hiding something, and their threat circuits are activated as a result.

Finally, suppressed stress has an uncanny tendency to reappear unpredictably. Inhibition is so energy intensive that when your prefrontal cortex runs out of fuel, the very thing you tried so hard to keep down is often the first thing to pop up. If you're familiar with the expression "Don't think of an elephant," you already have a good sense of how this works. Deliberately resolving not to think of something may actually increase the likelihood that you think of it.

Rather than attempting to inhibit your stress, it's far more efficient—and effective—to redirect that stress, which is precisely what Cognitive Jujitsu is designed to do. The two secret weapons of Cognitive Jujitsu are *labeling* and *reappraisal*.

Labeling: How Giving Stress a Name Can Make It Go Away

Labeling is just what it sounds like. It involves giving a name or an explanation to your emotional response. If you're feeling nervous about an upcoming presentation, for example, acknowledge those feelings in words—not necessarily to others, but to yourself—by writing them down. In a meeting you want to be fully functioning. When you're feeling stressed or emotional, you're allowing your primitive brain to run the show. Labeling helps you to regain control.

Ironically, one of the reasons so many people suppress their emotions instead of acknowledging them is because they're convinced that acknowledging their stress will only make matters worse. They fear that by labeling their emotions they will be in danger of losing control. In fact, the opposite is true. Research has shown that labeling the source of your stress actually lessens the activation of the amygdala, the primary source of your fight-or-flight reaction.[77]

In a study done by UCLA psychologist Matthew D. Lieberman, thirty people were shown images of individuals with different emotional expressions. Below the picture of each face there were either two words, such as "angry" and "fearful," or two names, such as "Harry" and "Sally." In each case, the subjects were asked to label the image appropriately. In cases in which subjects were given the option of labeling the picture with an emotion, they saw a reduction in the response of the amygdala. When subjects were given names as choices instead, labeling the image produced no reduction in the amygdala's response.[78]

In a sense, labeling provides a kind of implicit self-control.[79] And that's why it's an example of Cognitive Jujitsu. You're resisting the power of your emotions, not by fighting them directly, but by redirecting their energy. According to University of Chicago psychologist Sian Beilock, author of *Choke: What the Secrets of the Brain Reveal About Getting It Right When You Have To,* "It's not just understanding emotion that helps to thwart the overreaction of emotional centers of the brain; it's actually putting these feelings into words that does the trick."[80]

Ultimately, there's a cathartic nature to labeling. Instead of keeping stressful emotions bottled up, you're releasing them but in a way that is not disruptive to the people around you.

Labeling not only defuses stress but functions as a form of mindfulness, which, as we'll see in the next chapter, can be used to improve your long-term ability to focus.[81] You're increasing your self-awareness by acknowledging your feelings. When you feel anxious or angry or under a lot of additional stress, it pays to give your feelings some space. Of course, like most worthwhile skills, labeling takes practice. If it doesn't work for you right away, don't give up. Your ability to identify and label your emotions will improve over time. And as your abilities improve, so will the power and benefits of this enhanced self-awareness.

Reappraisal: Turning Lemons into Lemonade

There are countless examples, both obscure and famous, of people who have used reframing not only to counteract stress but in some cases to completely change the course of their lives. Make no mistake: These are not people in denial; they are men and women who encounter many of the stresses, strains, disasters, and setbacks we all face (in some instances they face even more) and yet find a way to reinterpret them in a more positive light. It's best summed up in the proverbial phrase "When life gives you lemons, make lemonade." Psychologists refer to it by a decidedly less colorful label, *cognitive reappraisal* or, simply, *reframing*.

Your limbic system responds instinctively, unconsciously, and remarkably quickly to anything that it perceives as a potential threat, whether or not it deserves to be seen as a threat. By the time this threat response is activated, there is nothing you can do about it—at least not directly. What you *can* do is to influence how you *interpret* that response. That's the essence of cognitive reappraisal.

The gap between when your limbic system responds and when your executive functions interpret that response is brief, but it provides a huge potential for emotional regulation. And yet, emotional regulation isn't foolproof. You may not always be able to redirect your emotions or the emotions of others at the drop of a hat, but if you take good care of yourself and train your brain, your ability to regulate your emotions should improve over time and put you in a stronger position to control and sustain where your attention and energy are focused. And that is the subject of the next chapter.

CHAPTER 2 IN A NUTSHELL

···

KEY POINTS FROM "REGULATE YOUR EMOTIONS"

Head and heart. Two key regions compete for the control of your brain. The prefrontal cortex (PFC) is the rational "thinking part," while the limbic system is the center of emotional processing. In any battle between these two regions, the limbic system will always win.

Threat and reward. Within the limbic system there are two principal and very primitive responses: threat and reward. When you are in a threat state, your PFC temporarily shuts down. When you are in a reward state, your thinking abilities are actually enhanced.

Emotional resilience. To build up your resistance to the potential ravages of stress, you need to eat well, exercise, and get sufficient sleep.

Change your body. Change your thoughts. There are two routes to emotional regulation: changing your thought patterns and changing your response to stress.

Fake it till you make it. Although the brain drives the body, the communication channels go both ways. If you assume a confident posture or flash a satisfied smile, your brain will usually transform that made-up mood into a genuine reaction.

Don't forget to say thanks. Just taking time in each day to be grateful has been shown to raise your baseline for happiness by as much as 25 percent.

Try Cognitive Jujitsu. The best way to cope with stress is to treat it the way experienced martial artists handle their opponents. Instead of fighting it directly, deflect it, by using its strength to your advantage through labeling or reframing.

Just name it. Simply labeling a stressful response when it occurs is usually enough to temporarily disarm the limbic system and allow your rational brain to regain control.

From lemons to lemonade. A threat can be a tantalizing challenge. A sudden setback can spell an unexpected opportunity. How your brain and body handle stressful situations can be dramatically altered depending on how you choose to reframe them.

CHAPTER 3
SHARPEN YOUR FOCUS

Gain the Control You Need to Zero In on
What's Important and Leave Distractions Behind

IN April 2012, walking forty-four yards along a jittery nylon and steel tightrope known as a slackline, forty-year-old Dean Potter crossed China's spectacular Enshi Grand Canyon in a little over two minutes. The drop to the floor of the canyon below was more than a mile long.[1]

Unlike Philippe Petit, who famously walked along a steel cable stretched between New York's World Trade Center towers in 1974,[2] Dean Potter made his crossing without the aid of a balancing pole or safety leash. What he demonstrated is something we all experience from time to time: extraordinary focus. With practice, each of us can reach a state of sharpened focus—to improve performance and achieve extraordinary results.

THE GORILLA IN THE ROOM
In 1999, psychologists Christopher Chabris and Daniel Simons shot a brief video of two groups of students weaving

around in a circle while passing two basketballs back and forth. Half the students wore white T-shirts. The other half wore black. The students in white shirts passed the basketball back and forth between each other. The students in black T-shirts did the same.

Once the video had been shot and edited, subjects were given a simple task: to silently count the number of times that the team in the white shirts passed the basketball.[3]

As is so often the case in psychology experiments, the official assignment was merely a cover story. Chabris and Simons were actually testing something other than their subjects' ability to count basketball passes. About twenty seconds into the video, another student, dressed in a gorilla suit, walks right into the center of the basketball-passing students, stops, beats her chest, and then resumes walking until she's out of the frame.

After the volunteers counted the number of basketball passes, they were asked first if they had noticed anything unusual about the video and then if they had noticed anyone other than the players. Finally, those who answered no to the previous questions were asked whether they noticed the gorilla. *The what?!* Approximately half of the volunteers, most of whom watched the video intently in order to count the number of passes, responded with utter disbelief. They had completely overlooked the entrance of the student in a gorilla suit.[4]

Hearing about the gorilla experiment and, even more so, getting to try it out themselves often surprises and even alarms people. "How could I have possibly missed that?" they wonder. And yet, except in certain circumstances, your ability to overlook the gorilla can actually be a good thing. It demonstrates that you are capable of focusing on what's important, even when there is a dramatic distraction competing for your attention.

A LIGHTBULB GOES ON

A variation on this phenomenon occurred in one of our seminars. We were working with an audience in a small conference room one late afternoon. The facilitator was standing up at the front of the room just a few feet away from a floor lamp. As the room grew darker, he reached over and switched on the lamp. It didn't work, so without missing a beat, he continued with the seminar despite the growing darkness.

About ten minutes later, the light suddenly came on. "It's like magic!" said the facilitator, who seemed genuinely amazed that the lamp was now working. Many in the audience laughed heartily at this remark. When the facilitator looked perplexed, someone in the audience explained. A staff member from the conference center had come in, stood just a few feet away from the facilitator, and repaired the lamp, all without the facilitator's noticing. Although the staff member who fixed the light was reportedly not wearing a gorilla suit, the facilitator was so intensely focused on his audience and on what he had to say that he failed to notice the entire electrical operation.

The surprised response from subjects who failed to notice the gorilla only underscores our obliviousness to our own attentional shortcomings. So if you think that you can perform two cognitive tasks simultaneously without any adverse effects on either, your answer is not only wrong but also quite predictable. Your brain is too overloaded to notice. That failure to notice is, in effect, the gorilla in the room.[5]

In the spirit of cognitive reappraisal (see chapter 2), there's an upside to overlooking the gorilla in the room. In each instance, the gorilla and the electrician were overlooked because they were largely irrelevant. In the case of the electrician, you could argue that he actually *was* relevant, given the effect that his work would have on the light in the conference room. But watching the electrician while he worked would've been about as effective in repairing the lamp as looking hopefully down the subway tunnel is in causing your train to arrive faster. The facilitator had enough experience and cognitive control to be able to direct his attention to where it was needed most and to sharpen his focus by eliminating all but the most important elements in the room. His attention wasn't drawn to the lamp until it was illuminated again. Only then was the change relevant.

Episodes like these cause us to challenge the traditional image of the absentminded professor, who's routinely ridiculed for being unable to focus. The truth is that what is often perceived as distracted behavior by outsiders is actually an indication of the exact opposite! It's a sign of intensely *focused* behavior. Your brain has allocated nearly all its resources to solving one specific problem and has deliberately and efficiently shut out any stimuli that are considered irrelevant to the task at hand. Instead of a weakness, extreme focus can be a strength. It's a breathtaking demonstration of the power of the rational brain and truly a triumph of deep concentration. (We concede that it can still be annoying if you happen to be the professor's spouse!)

UNDERSTANDING FOCUS

When you pause to think about it, the fact that you are able to focus at all is pretty amazing. You may take for granted, for example, that you're reading this book, but there are dozens of other stimuli around you, all simultaneously clamoring for your attention instead—sounds, smells, and a wide variety of visual stimuli that include virtually every item in the room you're currently in. And then there are the sensations: your awareness of whether it's too hot or too cold, whether or not your shoes fit, and the feeling of the paper on your fingertips each time you turn another page or the heft of your e-reader in your hands.

Two different mechanisms in the brain combine to make focusing on this book possible. One enhances the attended channel (in this case, our book) while another is used to inhibit the signals you want to ignore. It is the job of the prefrontal cortex to either boost or attenuate each of these signals.[6]

FOCUS STARTS WITH THE PREFRONTAL CORTEX

Chances are if you're like most of us, you were hired primarily because of your prefrontal cortex, or PFC. In fact, you probably wouldn't be a leader if it weren't for a well-functioning PFC, which, among other things, is the part of the brain that determines your IQ.

The PFC is responsible for rational processing. It handles what are often referred to as the brain's "executive functions," such as reasoning, strategizing, and problem solving. It's also the home to the working memory, the staging area where new information rests while you decide what to do with it. From an evolutionary perspective, it is the youngest part of the brain. It wasn't fully developed until about half a million years ago, and it is the region that distinguishes us from most animals.[7]

Interestingly enough, the PFC is also the last part of our

brain to mature. In fact, for some people it can take until they're in their twenties until it's fully developed. Anyone who's raised a teenager can appreciate the consequences of this delay in the brain's capacity for rational processing!

In general, whenever we think about thinking, we're thinking about the PFC. As German-born neuroscientist Arne Dietrich explains, "It's where we take simple ideas and add all kinds of layers of complexity to them."[8] Comparatively small but energy intensive, it's like a MINI Cooper that gets the gas mileage of a Cadillac Eldorado.

For such a relatively small region, the PFC has a lot of responsibilities. It helps you weigh alternatives and think up a brilliant strategic plan. When you are deciding whether or not to order a second glass of wine at lunch, it is the PFC that makes the final call. The PFC is responsible for higher-order thinking like planning and decision making, as well as focus, or what psychologists commonly call *attention*.

THE RECIPE FOR ATTENTION

Attention occurs when the PFC has the right mix of neurotransmitters, hormones, and other chemicals released by the body.[9] Several of the names will sound suspiciously familiar. The DNA of Peak Performance—dopamine, noradrenaline, and acetylcholine—not coincidentally, is also the recipe for attention. Noradrenaline is constantly on the lookout for any unusual activities. When something catches your attention, acetylcholine zeros in on its location and identity. And finally, dopamine helps you to determine what to do about it. Unfortunately, dopamine and noradrenaline operate like double agents in a spy thriller: They can both strengthen and sabotage your attention.

When your dopamine levels rise, the reward feeling you

receive drives you to keep doing more of what you're doing in order to get even more dopamine. The result is often focus. But as your attention flags (for whatever reason), your fickle brain starts seeking out new experiences that will trigger another burst of the neurochemical.[10] In other words, the same neurotransmitter that led you to focus in the first place may be responsible for your subsequent distraction.

Noradrenaline suffers from a similar capriciousness. You can count on it to attract your attention, but you can't rely on it to maintain your focus. Any potential threat (and that includes a challenging task) will prompt you to zero in on it with great intensity in order to determine which of the three classic options you'll pursue: fighting, fleeing, or freezing. But this response is intended to be a quick reaction, not a sustained campaign. Unless you take action, both dopamine and noradrenaline will keep you searching for the next distraction.

DEFEATING DISTRACTIONS

In many ways, the brain can be seen as a distraction detection machine. Although survival influences it to notice any changes to your environment, both internal and external, your brain's instinctive tendency to attend to new and novel stimuli can have a detrimental effect on your ability to focus. One influential study showed that subjects were distracted from the task at hand almost 50 percent of the time.[11]

Distractions are handled by your limbic system, which responds to potential threats and rewards, real or imagined. The PFC is slower, weaker, and more resource intensive than the rest of the brain.

The best way to sharpen your focus is to eliminate factors that disrupt it and cultivate skills that encourage it. Consciously attempting to inhibit distractions might seem like the proactive approach, but because it tends to aggravate your more powerful limbic system, conscious inhibition rarely works. Instead, it usually makes matters worse, draining the limited cognitive resources that could otherwise have been used for focusing.

Rather than attempting to ignore distractions, it is best to minimize or eliminate them whenever possible. On the other hand, one way to make focusing far more difficult and work less productive is to multitask. Although it might seem like the pinnacle of productivity, multitasking is the archenemy of focus. That's because, unlike the many disruptive sights, sounds, and smells you often can't control, multitasking is a voluntary distraction. You're deliberately diluting your brainpower and blurring your focus.

Multitasking is the archenemy of focus.

Minimizing Multitasking

Colorful comparisons between the brain and a computer are plentiful and appealing. It's nice to be able to think that the organ inside your head is just an older, squishier version of the laptop on your desk. It's nice, but wrong. It may come as a surprise to some people, but our brains aren't computers. In most cases, they're far superior to computers. But in at least one way, computers have a decided edge. The term "multitasking" was originally a computer term used to describe an operating system that was capable of running more than one application simultaneously. Because we spend so much of our time using computers, multitasking leaped from the computer world into the human world and seemed to be an apt description for our tendency to attempt to work on several things at once. There's just one little problem: We can't actually multitask.

The Multitasking Myth

Although nearly everyone knows someone who appears to be able to multitask successfully, most examples are situations in which one of the activities is performed by a different part of the brain. Strictly speaking, this isn't multitasking. After all, we don't brag about our ability to simultaneously breathe and keep our heart beating. When we talk about multitasking, we're talking specifically about activity in the prefrontal cortex, the home of most of your planning, ruminating, and reasoning. And in the PFC, true multitasking is impossible. Your brain may be amazingly coordinated, but your prefrontal cortex is a bit of a klut; it can't walk and chew gum at the same time. When you think you are multitasking, what you are probably doing is *sequential task switching*, shifting your focus rapidly back and forth between multiple activities. Sometimes the switching happens so quickly that it truly feels as though you are performing two tasks at once. Trust us, you aren't. Besides, all this speedy shifting comes at considerable cost.

The True Cost of Multitasking

Whenever you shift from one activity to another, say, writing a presentation to checking your e-mail, your brain goes through a four-step process. It makes no difference how quickly you shift your attention; the process is still essentially the same. 1) To begin with, blood rushes to the anterior prefrontal cortex, which notifies the rest of your brain that you're about to work on your presentation. 2) This all-points bulletin to your brain has two parts. First it searches for the neurons that it'll need for a particular task, almost like an Old West sheriff recruiting local townspeople for a posse, and then it notifies those neurons that they're needed. These neurons, most of which are capable of taking part in a variety of tasks, are then temporarily deputized to participate in the process of writing your presentation. This entire search and notification routine is fast, but it still takes a few tenths of a second. 3) Then, when you decide to stop writing your presentation and check your e-mail, your brain must first disengage from the current task before moving on to the next. This process is speedy, but as we'll soon see, it's not nearly rapid enough. 4) The final step is the same as the first, only this time the anterior prefrontal cortex, instead of telling your brain that you plan to write your presentation, will notify it that you intend to check e-mail. Once again, a few tenths of a second are required.[12]

The whole process of shifting from one task to another takes about half a second. That might not seem like much until you realize that this process is repeated *every single time* you shift from one task to another. Those half seconds begin to add up quickly. What's more, each time you shift, to some extent you're starting over. If multitasking were advertised like a soft drink, its slogan would probably be, "Now where was I?"[13]

If you remain unimpressed with the prospect of wasting time in half-second increments and aren't all that concerned about constantly having to reorient yourself, perhaps some additional statistics will make a stronger impression:

- People who are interrupted take an estimated 50 percent longer to complete a task and have been found to make up to 50 percent more errors.[14]

- Although it takes just a few seconds to shift from one task to another and then back to the original task, researchers at the University of California, Irvine, found that it requires an average of twenty-three minutes to get fully back on track, even after a brief interruption.[15]
- Constantly texting or checking e-mails—a mainstay of multitaskers—has been shown to temporarily reduce your IQ by as much as 15 points.*[16]
- And finally, academic studies have found that most of us are interrupted—or interrupt ourselves—an average of roughly every three minutes![17]

Granted, some interruptions are unavoidable. But the thing about multitasking is that it's interruption by choice, not by chance. Why would you knowingly reduce your efficiency, deliberately increase your odds of making mistakes, and intentionally make yourself less intelligent? Now that you've read this, maybe you'll no longer multitask. The decision to stop multitasking is not just smart, it could even save your life.

Multitasking Can Be Deadly

In 2008, a Los Angeles commuter train collided with a freight train, killing twenty-five passengers, including the train's engineer, who was texting at the time and failed to notice a red signal as a result.

---

* Given that IQ tests essentially measure the ability to use your PFC, stimuli that monopolize this comparatively small area are going to diminish that capacity. Research has shown that if you are given an IQ test while you are distracted, your score will drop. Although this doesn't mean that multitasking makes you permanently stupid, it can make you stupid temporarily!

He received his last text message approximately eighty seconds before impact.

Many people now recognize the dangers of phoning or texting while driving and have addressed the problem by putting down the cell phone and using a "hands-free" device instead. Unfortunately, the main issue with calling while driving isn't the handheld device; it's the social dimension. "It's very difficult for your brain to ignore social input," says Paul Atchley, a psychologist in the Transportation Research Institute at the University of Kansas. Social cues get high-priority treatment from our brain. And if they happen to come just as another car is making an unexpected swerve into your lane, it can prove to be a problem.[18] Of course, the vast majority of people who use cell phones while driving will do so without getting into an accident—that is, until they do get into an accident.

Why would anyone take such a risk? Perhaps the allure of multitasking is just too great. After all, the myth persists that multitasking can make you more productive, when the evidence points to exactly the opposite conclusion.

Multitasking Is Counterproductive

Despite our best intentions, multitasking actually harms productivity and takes more—not less—time. As Steven Kotler, author of *The Rise of Superman*, explains, "By trying to improve performance by being everywhere and everywhen, we end up nowhere and never."[19] Multitasking increases both errors and stress, leads to mental fatigue, and ultimately is no fun.

Multitasking Harms Your Brain

Multitasking not only fails in the short term, but it can cause problems in the long run. The attraction to distraction that drives most multitasking can be hard to shut off. As a result, you may find it difficult to focus even when you aren't multitasking. Also, evidence suggests that multitasking uses a different, less flexible kind of memory that may harm your ability to create and retrieve long-term memories. Furthermore, a recent study suggests a vaguely ominous connection between media multitasking, that is, the simultaneous use of multiple media forms, and a decrease in the gray matter of your anterior cingulate cortex, a region associated with error checking.[20]

Why We Still Multitask

Given the mounting evidence against multitasking, why do we still do it? The common explanation—to save time and improve productivity—may describe our motivation, but it's at odds with the outcome. As we've seen, multitasking actually *wastes* time and *harms* productivity. By now, most of us know this. We have read innumerable articles about the dangers and pitfalls of multitasking, and yet we continue to ignore the evidence. Why?

WE'RE ATTRACTED TO NOVELTY

The probable answer is a familiar one: Blame your brain. We multitask because our brains are driven by a powerful search for novelty. Responding to a distraction provides us with a squirt of dopamine. According to Stanford professor and psychologist Russell Poldrack, despite its reputation as a "feel good" neurotransmitter, dopamine is actually a "gimme more" neurotransmitter.[21] The habit quickly becomes addictive. Without it, we're likely to feel bored.[22]

As usual, survival lies at the root of this trait. When our ancestors were fixing a meal or building a hut, the sudden appearance of a potential threat would quickly shift their attention away from these more deliberate tasks and onto more immediate concerns, such as staying alive. Unfortunately, the chime of incoming e-mail functions the way the roar of a ferocious lion once did. Your brain is a distraction-detection device, and your e-mail program or smartphone is a novelty-generating machine.[23] But the chronic nature of these distractions makes them less like lions and more like the arcade game of Whac-a-Mole, in which a plastic rodent keeps popping up unpredictably out of a series of holes and you get points for each one you can smack with a plastic mallet. That's doubly bad. An e-mail alert is not only disruptive but, according to research done at the University of California, Irvine, it's also stressful.[24] At first we might respond to the chirp of an incoming e-mail like a child on Christmas morning, but it doesn't take long for the thrill to subside even though the compulsion continues. Although multitasking is initially driven by the desire for novelty, as with most addictions, the effect of any rewards gained from it will steadily diminish over time.

WE IMITATE OUR ROLE MODELS

Another reason we multitask is that we have multitasking mentors, men and women who convey the impression not only that they are succeeding but also that multitasking is a key to their success. Most of us know someone who appears to be able to multitask. In fact, the "ability" to multitask is often viewed with a certain level of awe and respect. If you have a boss or an especially successful colleague who's a chronic multitasker, you're liable to get the impression that multitasking is the source of her success, when in fact she's probably successful *in spite* of her multitasking and would almost certainly be even *more* successful if she focused on just one task at a time.

WE THINK WE'RE GOOD AT IT

Most of us grossly overestimate what we are able to do while we're multitasking. If the mounting number of stories of accidents that occurred while people were attempting to send text messages while driving leaves you scratching your head wondering, "Why in the world would they do such a thing?" the answer is relatively simple: They thought they had everything under control.

But study after study proves that they were fundamentally—and sometimes fatally—mistaken. In a recent study, the people who rated themselves expert multitaskers were actually really bad at it.[25] Ironically, the people who routinely tackle multiple tasks simultaneously are worse at multitasking than people who aren't used to juggling jobs but are called upon to multitask. According to research done at Stanford University, heavy multitasking is more likely to increase your susceptibility to distractions.[26] Habitual multitaskers are "suckers for irrelevancy," explained Clifford Nass, the professor who led the Stanford study.[27]

But Women Are Different, Right?

If there's one factoid that everyone seems to cite about multitasking, it's that women are better at it than men. Unfortunately, like many factoids, it doesn't hold up to scientific scrutiny. Despite the rash of breathless headlines in popular magazines, the verdict on multitasking is decidedly mixed. There is nothing conclusive that gives either gender the advantage.[28]

Even so, it's a rare workshop when there isn't at least one

executive who proudly claims, "My wife can definitely multi-task better than I can!" As the saying goes, "The plural of anecdote is not data."

The widely popular notion that women are better at multitasking manages to misunderstand both women and multitasking. Despite decades of reported advancement, women with full-time jobs often wind up doing the lion's share of the cooking, housecleaning, and child rearing. Therefore, it's still not unusual to walk into a household where Dad is sitting on the couch watching TV, while Mom is in the kitchen cooking dinner, talking on the telephone, and tying Junior's shoes.

It's almost certainly not Mom's first choice to be juggling all these tasks. Nor is it truly multitasking that she's engaged in. Multitasking refers to activities that compete for real estate in the limited space of your prefrontal cortex. If you iron a shirt only once a year, then you're probably relying on your PFC for the job. That's why it's difficult if not impossible to iron and chat at the same time without running the risk of burning your shirt. On the other hand, if you are used to ironing a certain number of shirts every week, then you're probably outsourcing that ironing to another part of your brain. That's what makes it easier to carry on a conversation while you're working. There's nothing uniquely feminine about this phenomenon. Any man who's accustomed to ironing shirts should be able to do the same.

Luckily, habitual tasks are less cognitively demanding and make use of other parts of your brain, primarily the basal ganglia, instead. That doesn't necessarily make life any less busy for Mom, but it does give her PFC a bit of a break. All that practice rapidly shifting between household chores has unwittingly turned her into an expert.

Despite the understanding that experience is not the same as multitasking, it may still turn out that women truly have a special knack when it comes to rapidly switching between tasks. But for now, the jury is still out. We really don't know for sure. Besides, additional experiments with multitasking seem to indicate that spatial ability rather than gender may be the deciding factor when it comes to multitasking. In two recent experiments conducted in Sweden that measured the abilities of men and women to multitask, males actually outperformed females. The research concluded that executive functions such as working memory and spatial ability were the deciding factors for multitasking ability and that only spatial ability was influenced by gender. In that area, males held the edge.[29]

STRATEGIES FOR STAYING FOCUSED

As we've seen, staying focused isn't easy, and multitasking makes it even harder. The best ways to avoid succumbing to distractions are still pretty straightforward: Instead of deliberately attempting to shut them out, make every effort to eliminate them. At the same time, do your best to ensure that the most interesting and enjoyable stimulus is the very activity you're focused on.

Prepare for Each New Task

Reduce internal distractions by clearing your head before embarking on difficult tasks. Take time to settle and focus before engaging in a particular activity.[30]

Find Some Fun and Interest in What You're Doing

Emotions can make focusing easier. If your task is novel and fun, you're less likely to look elsewhere for stimulation. If the task you're saddled with seems dull or routine, see if you can't find a way to make it more interesting.

If your regularly scheduled meeting is suffering from a growing malaise, try changing rooms—or just changing seats. Switching from one chair to another, from one meeting to the next, or even from one topic to another can literally and figuratively provide everyone with a fresh perspective. If the discussion has descended into the doldrums, encourage everyone to stand up and walk around for thirty seconds. Or try standing by the window during the next topic. A highly successful German kitchen company decided to move its regular Monday-morning board meeting from a conference room to the field outside its headquarters. Instead of sitting around a table as usual, they all took a refreshing stroll. The walk freed them from the normal distractions of the work environment and stimulated the creativity of all in attendance. According to one of the board's members, satisfaction and efficiency increased remarkably as a result.

You can apply similar strategies when you're working on your own. Clear off your desk before you begin focusing on a specific task. Work on one task at your desk and then pick up your laptop and move to a different location before starting the next task. The subtle change in your work environment will provide a signal to the brain that you're tackling something new. Take a five-minute walk or grab a cup of coffee. The trip to the café or the coffee machine (along with the caffeine) should invigorate you. After you complete one assignment and before you move on to the next, devise a ritual of walking ten steps to the next task. Stop and stretch slowly or do a few exercises at your desk. Recite a little poem. Sing or listen to a song before moving on. Even the smallest signs of novelty, exercise, or fun can provide the breakthrough you need to keep going.

Eliminate Potential Distractions at the Outset

It takes valuable space in your prefrontal cortex to resist potential distractions. Furthermore, it's stressful. We tune out a tremendous number of stimuli on a regular basis. This takes brainpower. Some distractions are beyond your control. Others are well within your control. Don't waste thinking power by stacking the deck against yourself. It's easier and more energy efficient simply to clear distractions out of the way. Remove pictures, paper, knickknacks, and any other potential distracters from your field of view. If you have family photos in your work area, consider putting them on a shelf behind your chair instead of on the desk in front of you. Close your door if you have one. Try using earbuds or noise-canceling headphones if you don't.

It's better to store a potential distraction in a desk drawer or leave it at home than it is just to vow not to fiddle with it until after you've finished writing a presentation. Self-discipline may be an admirable trait, but it depletes valuable brainpower at an alarming rate.

Establish Concentration Time

Depending on the nature of your job, you may not find it possible to completely shut yourself off from the rest of your colleagues. However, in all but the rarest of cases, you should be able to carve out some "concentration time" during the course of the day, when your door is closed, your phone is turned off, and everyone who works with you is aware that you are unavailable. No one questions the fact that you are unavailable when you're already in an important meeting, but there's often an unspoken assumption that when you aren't in a meeting, you're free. And yet when you need to focus, you *are* in an important meeting—with *yourself*.

Let your colleagues know the times when you don't want to be disturbed. The "open-door policy" is noble and can encourage interaction and cooperation when the motive is teamwork. But when the goal is concentration, it's an unmitigated disaster.

If you have a job in which there are constant and often unpredictable demands for your attention, it doesn't hurt to impose a little bit of control. An executive we know who worked in a company where an open-door policy was the norm found that although this ideal of openness was inspiring in theory, in practice it was wreaking havoc on his productivity. So he came up with a simple, ingenious routine. He attached a flip chart outside his office door. When his door was closed, coworkers were free to jot down their names and their desire to meet with him. His assistant, who had a desk nearby, would periodically go through the chart, figure out a time when her boss was available, add it to his schedule, and then send out a calendar invitation to the person who had written down the original note on the chart. In many cases, the two were able to meet within the same day. The arrangement not only improved the executive's ability to focus and with it his locus of control, but it also increased the locus of control of the coworkers, who were virtually assured of a meeting with their manager, just not on the spur of the moment.

Work in Manageable Blocks of Time

If you find it difficult to work on a single task to the point of completion, try the "20-minute rule." Rather than rapidly switching back and forth between multiple tasks, devote twenty minutes exclusively to one before shifting to another.[31] The satisfaction of completing each time block should give you a dose of dopamine, as will the prospect of facing the next "new" task. Also, the modest pressure to spend each time block efficiently should help to raise noradrenaline levels and bring you closer to your performance "sweet spot."

For those who simply can't resist the allure of chirping electronic devices, psychology professor Larry Rosen of California State University, Dominguez Hills, recommends "tech breaks," in which you stop work every fifteen minutes or so, spend two minutes texting, surfing Web sites, or posting, and then return to fifteen more minutes of undistracted work. If you start with a modest length of time, you should find that you can gradually extend the periods you remain disconnected.[32]

Use Your Brain Wisely

Recent evidence suggests that even something as innocuous as walking can interfere with your cognitive functions. You may be able to walk and chew gum at the same time, but if you're performing a task that requires your concentration, the steps you're taking may be decreasing your productivity and increasing your chances of making mistakes.[33] As for whether background music is a help or a hindrance, the verdict is pretty much a mixed bag. If you're engaged in a highly repetitive task (such as working on an assembly line), then music can be a boon to your productivity. Likewise, repetitive ambient music can occasionally improve your performance on certain higher-order cognitive activities, such as reading. But in general, the popular music that many of us listen to in our spare time—particularly when it has lyrics—can definitely interfere with functions like reading comprehension and information processing.[34]

Of course, there's also plenty of evidence to support the positive effects of both walking and music on the brain. So where does that leave us? It's safe to say that music and walking can influence our emotional state in a positive way. A little bit of preliminary music can pep you up for tackling a challenging assignment, while walking has been found to dissipate pent-up stress. But if your livelihood depends on the productivity of your brain, it's best to save music and walking for those times when you're not actually working.

Keep Your E-mail Habit Under Control

E-mail fits the classic complaint: "Can't live with it. Can't live without it." Typical professionals spend 23 percent of their workday dealing with e-mail.[35] When Gloria Mark and Stephen Voida of the University of California, Irvine, asked thirteen employees at a nearby corporation to go without e-mail for five days, they found that the workers were less stressed and able to focus on a single task much longer before switching screens.

Obviously, it's pretty unrealistic for most of us to go without e-mail for an extended period of time. What Mark and Voida suggest instead is that you develop a routine of checking e-mails at scheduled times during the day and that you leave your e-mail notification off for the rest of the time. Consciously designating on and off periods for e-mail and texts should give you a clearer sense of the extent to which these devices can dominate your day. Becoming mindful of the role that smartphones and e-mail play in distraction is the first step in improving your self-control.[36]

Fighting Fire with Fire

There are certain situations in which you can actually combine our natural attraction to distraction with the power of deep concentration to help make a bogged-down meeting run more smoothly and efficiently. Almost all of us have been stuck in meetings where one member's obsessive attention to detail has brought all progress to a grinding halt. For get-togethers where the goal is to sketch out the broad strokes of a strategy instead of haggle over mind-numbing specifics, a detailed memo or spreadsheet can come in handy. Simply hand it to the stickler to carefully scrutinize and you will usually discover that he or she becomes completely engrossed in the document, oblivious to the meeting's main conversation, which will now magically pick up in pace. Often by the time the demon for details has finally returned to general awareness, most of the key decisions will already have been made and any nagging from the naysayer is no longer a problem. Of course, in the interest of harmony, you can usually welcome Mr. or Ms. Fine Print back into the fold at the end, and it's likely that the meeting will conclude with everyone feeling a sense of satisfaction and accomplishment.

CALMING A RESTLESS MIND

Even if you closed your door, inserted earplugs, pulled down your window blinds, took all the pictures off your walls, and cleared your desk of everything but a pen and a clean sheet of paper, there's still no guarantee that you'd be able to focus. Why? Because the single most tenacious source of distraction, more powerful than sights, sounds, smells, or other external sensations, is your own wandering mind. In fact, a recent Gallup survey found that 71 percent of American workers reported that they were either "not engaged" with or "actively disengaged" from their jobs. And for those who are highly educated, the forecast for focus was even worse. Of those respondents who had done postgraduate work or earned a postgraduate degree, only 27 percent were engaged in the work.[37] This is bad news—and not just for bosses. Mind wandering not only occupies roughly half our waking life, but it's also associated with lower levels of happiness.[38]

Exactly what happens when your mind wanders? Top neuroscientists including Judson Brewer and Jonathan Schooler now have a pretty good idea. A wandering mind is the domain of neuronal circuitry known as the default mode network, or simply the default network. The default network, as the name suggests, is the network your brain uses by default during most of your waking moments. It is associated with planning, pondering, and daydreaming. It's active when you think about yourself as well as about other people. It's sometimes called the narrative network because you take in information through your personal filter and then use its implications to construct your own narrative interpretation of things that have happened and things that you anticipate. In fact, the one conspicuous area where the default network falls short is in focusing on the here and now. And as you can imagine, that can be a bit of a problem if you're supposed to be paying attention. Two things can help to keep your mind from straying: happiness and cognitive control.[39]

HOW TO STAY FOCUSED WITHOUT HAVING SEX

A number of years ago, Harvard psychologists Matthew Killingsworth and Daniel Gilbert used an iPhone app to contact people at random intervals to ask them what they were doing, what they were thinking, and how they were feeling. Out of more than 2,000 people surveyed and more than a quarter of a million responses, the verdict was clear: The people who were happiest were the ones who were having sex. On a scale of 0 to 100, sex, at a score of 90, ranked an average of 15 points higher than the second-happiest activity, exercising. The people who were least happy were typically engaged in personal grooming, getting to or from work, or work itself.[40]

What does sex have to do with focus? When the subjects having sex were asked where their thoughts were, less than 10 percent reported that their minds had wandered to other thoughts. In other words, they were strongly focused on the activity they were engaged in. Not so with other activities, which were accompanied by wandering minds from 30 percent to as much as 65 percent of the time. The overall average found that people's minds were wandering 47 percent of the time.[41]

Focusing on Happiness

The correlation seems clear: The more enjoyable the activity, the less likely it is to be accompanied by a wandering mind. While this conclusion is easiest to understand in the case of sex, the fact is that, regardless of the activity, subjects were found to be happier when they focused on what they were doing instead of on extraneous thoughts. Actually, whether or not their minds wandered was a greater predictor of over-all happiness than the activity itself.[42] And when we're happy, our brains release a number of neurochemicals, including do-pamine, which greatly increases our ability to learn and re-member. What's more, when the mind ceases to wander, we tend to feel better because we're no longer on high alert for the next potential threat.[43]

All of us can relate to the role that happiness plays in our ability to stay focused and interested in the task at hand. But how about cognitive control? When your mind still strays in spite of it all, what can you do to bring your thoughts back and refocus your attention? For the answer to that question, we turn to what may seem like an unlikely authority: an American football team.

CULTIVATING MINDFULNESS

If a single word could be used to describe what transpired at New Jersey's MetLife Stadium on the evening of Sunday, February 2, 2014, that word would be "decisive." It was the largest margin of victory in twenty-one years of America's most popular sports ritual and the most-watched TV program in U.S. history.[44] After an eight-year hiatus, the National Football League's Seattle Seahawks returned to the Super Bowl and trounced the Denver Broncos by a score of 43-8, the third most lopsided outcome in that championship's history.

As expected, professional analysts and armchair quarterbacks freely offered a wide variety of opinions on the secret of Seattle's decisive success, but there was one intriguing factor that made the Seahawks unique among professional football teams. The typical professional football team has more than two dozen coaches and trainers. Beginning in 2012, the Seahawks added an unusual member to their staff: a mindfulness coach.[45]

Most of us have been in the embarrassing situation in which we seem so obviously distracted that someone finally feels compelled to point it out to us. "Sorry," we sheepishly reply. "I guess my mind must have been elsewhere." Although the people around us may not always notice it, the startling fact is that for most of us, our mind is elsewhere almost half the time that we're awake. That can be annoying and counterproductive if you spend your day working at your desk or sitting in meetings, but it can be dangerous and even deadly if you earn your pay on a football field or a battlefield.

A wandering mind, as we'll see in chapter 5, can sometimes have its benefits but only when it's used deliberately and strategically. Mindfulness is the antidote for a wandering mind.[46] It involves observing your thoughts and feelings from moment to moment, nonjudgmentally. By doing so, you learn to become an outside observer of your own thinking process, a skill that gives you greater control over those times when your thoughts are focused and prevents you from constantly heading down the path of each new distraction.[47]

The key brain regions associated with mind wandering are found to be less active in experienced mindfulness meditators. At the same time, those regions associated with self-monitoring and cognitive control are more strongly coupled, and not just when subjects are meditating.[48]

The common definition of mindfulness, "being present," may be simple and perfectly satisfactory for some people, but it makes others a little squeamish because it conjures up images of meditating monks. Although it's true that variations on mindfulness are an integral element in most of the world's major religions, you don't have to have faith to gain focus. An alternate, secular definition of mindfulness is "restful awareness": "awareness" because you're paying attention and you know you're paying attention, and "restful" because unlike a situation in which you're creeping silently through your house in the middle of the night in an attempt to catch a burglar in the act, your awareness is acute but not stressful. You're alert without being alarmed.

One night we were having dinner with a client who was struggling to grasp the concept of mindfulness. The classic introductory mindfulness exercise, which involves focusing intently on a single raisin, seemed utterly bizarre to him. So did our preferred approach, the "shower exercise," which asks leaders to pay close attention to the way they typically wash and then encourages them to consciously strive to perform the ritual in a slightly different way. Neither exercise made any sense to him. As it happens, the man was a wine connoisseur, and so he ordered an expensive bottle with our meal. We watched with great interest as he raised his glass to carefully examine the deep red color of the liquid in the light. Then he held it beneath his nose and breathed in its exquisite bouquet with an expression of sublime intensity before finally taking his first tentative sip, savoring all the complexity of the wine's many flavors. After he'd finished his taste, we told him that he had just engaged in mindfulness. His initial expression of surprise changed to one of sudden comprehension. At last he understood what we had been getting at. It was a lesson he never forgot.

What's truly astounding about mindfulness is that it not only changes your thoughts, but it also physically changes your brain.

Build Stronger Connections

Richard J. Davidson, professor of psychology and psychiatry at the University of Wisconsin–Madison, is among the researchers who have made a discovery that is both shocking and extremely exciting. "It is clear," he told an audience at Google's Mountain View, California, campus, "that the intentional deployment of specific mental training strategies can induce plastic changes in the brain, which endure and which can transform our cognitive and emotional styles."[49]

In other words, you can alter the overall makeup of your brain without surgical intervention or the use of pharmaceuticals. Mindfulness has been shown to physically change several regions of the brain in as little as eight weeks.

Mindfulness thickens your frontal cortex and posterior cingulate cortex, which increases not only your capacity for attention but also your memory and processing power.[50] This enhanced cognitive control allows you to respond more rationally and enables you to more easily deflect inappropriate emotional responses. Meditators have been found to have greater gray matter in the right orbitofrontal cortex, a region of the brain associated with emotional regulation.[51]

Mindfulness also strengthens the connections to your insula, which is responsible for body awareness.[52] Body awareness is helpful for intuition and, in turn, for decision making (as we'll see in chapter 5). You become better at "listening to your body," catching small signals and picking up subtle warning signs. You don't get sick as often because you are more likely to notice early on when something is wrong. Additionally, you may be able to exert greater cognitive control over your emotions, a key factor in determining whether a stimulus is distracting.[53]

While the insula is associated with your own body awareness, another region, the temporal parietal junction (TPJ), plays a role in your awareness of others. Like the insula, the TPJ has been shown to gain in gray matter after mindfulness training.[54] This increase seems to improve social relationships and make people more empathetic.[55]

Mindfulness enhances the brain's capability to dynamically rewire itself.

Not all the changes to the brain are marked by increases. Mindfulness actually leads to a decrease in density in at least one area, the amygdala, the region of the brain most associated with emotional reactivity and fear.[56]

Overall, mindfulness enhances the brain's capability to dynamically rewire itself, a phenomenon commonly known as neuroplasticity, which, as we'll see in chapter 6, improves your mental flexibility and your ability to learn.

Gain a Sharper Focus

Just as chronic multitaskers seem to have trouble focusing even when they're limited to a single task, seasoned meditators appear to have greater control over mind wandering even when they aren't engaged in meditation.[57] Mindfulness training has been found to strengthen the brain's ability to pay attention by increasing your capacity to ignore both internal and external distractions and to focus instead on what is happening in the moment.[58]

To strengthen focus you need to increase activity in the prefrontal cortex and the parietal cortex. The PFC is critical for maintaining attention, while the parietal cortex points your attention at a specific target.[59] Studies by Davidson have shown that longtime practitioners of mindfulness meditation show higher activation of the PFC and parietal cortex when focusing on an object.[60]

Finally, mindfulness also strengthens connections between the PFC and the amygdala, which enables you to prevent the negative thoughts we all experience from time to time from spiraling out of control.[61]

Make Mindfulness a Habit

The best way to employ mindfulness over the long term is to dedicate some time every day to mindfulness practice. Make it a part of your daily routine, like brushing your teeth or flipping the switch on the coffee machine. Most of us don't have to schedule such things; they simply become a habit.

Practicing Mindfulness

Because mindfulness involves tuning in to your direct experience and tuning out extraneous thoughts, you can practice it in a wide variety of situations, such as while you're eating, walking, showering, going for a run, or simply taking a break at your desk.

The best approach is to zero in on a particular sense, such as the rhythm of your breathing or even the feel of your feet on the floor, and then to repeat the process often, preferably daily, so you become increasingly adept at focusing on this single sensation at the expense of all others.

STOP: A Quick-Fix Approach to Mindfulness

An informal way of using mindfulness to decrease stress and anxiety in daily life is encapsulated in the acronym STOP, which outlines a very simple and effective method for bringing the body and mind back into balance:

S = Stop

T = Take a breath

O = Observe

P = Proceed[62]

The idea behind STOP is simple but powerful. Periodically during your day, just call a quick time-out and take a deep breath. Observe what you were doing at that moment, and think about how it makes you feel as well as how it might make others feel. Are your shoulders tense? Are you feeling hungry or tired? Are you brooding about something in the back of your mind? Is there anything you would like to change? Could the current situation be handled differently?[63]

If you can't think of a different way of handling the situation, proceed as before. If you can, strive to make changes—either small or big depending upon the circumstances—to your behavior, attitude, mind-set, or how you feel about the situation in general. This basic act of reflection—psychologists call it "metacognitive awareness"—can lead to potent, positive, and often permanent changes in your thinking patterns and physical responses.

The great thing about STOP is that you can put it into practice right away and do it practically anywhere, even surreptitiously in the midst of a stressful meeting. It's a wonderful way of periodically checking in with yourself and asking, "How am I doing?" Some executives like to use the technique before specific activities or when they're tense or upset. Others rely on alarms in their calendar software to remind them to take a quick inventory of their mood and awareness throughout the day.

Unlike other, more elaborate techniques, STOP is easy to use and remember: There's no mantra required, no special posture you need, and no meditation class to sign up for. More important, it can help you to increase your own self-awareness. You may discover that there are predictable times during your day when you're feeling good and others when you're feeling not so good. By increasing your awareness, STOP enables you to identify these times and make appropriate adjustments when needed.[64] Like any skill, mindfulness requires practice. The longer you work at it, the better you'll get at it.

Silence Is Golden

In high-pressure meetings, what many participants desperately crave are just a few minutes of silence to gather their thoughts and to sharpen their focus. Yet in far too many meetings, the atmosphere is exactly the opposite: A couple of outspoken attendees battle each other to establish the most airtime. There is no silence. People might even be talking over each other. As a result, instead of gaining sufficient time for thoughtful analysis and reflection, the majority of the meeting's participants are continually flooded with distracting cues.

Although that may be a familiar dysfunctional model in most company meetings, there are some intriguing alternatives. One of the companies we work with, which is very well known for its sustainable success, has an unwritten rule for its boardroom meetings: The time spent in silence should be equal to or greater than the time spent speaking. In other words, after input of two minutes, there is a pause of two minutes or more in which everyone has an opportunity to digest what has just been said.

As consultants who were participants in this unusual process, we must confess that we found it a little disorienting at first. To be honest, some younger colleagues were even making fun of it. Let's face it: In these times of relentless competition, lightning-fast communications, and an unprecedented flood of information, most managers would find an extended period of silence to be utterly intolerable. In fact, few can tolerate *any* amount of silence. Nearly all our clients would see this as a complete waste of time; the quiet would make them very uncomfortable. Frankly, it even made *us* uncomfortable. That is, until we saw the results.

After participating in the third meeting that used this unconventional format, we began to notice three remarkable effects. First, all the participants had sufficient time to digest every opinion and to align them with their own state of mind.

Second, although fewer things may have been said, everything that was said carried more weight and more value, and earned more careful consideration because everyone was listening and everyone was focused. Unlike in typical meetings where the distraction levels are high and participants are often ignoring the speaker while they plan out their own responses, here everyone was compelled to pay close attention to what was being said. Finally, the mutual respect was significantly higher than in typical meetings. The pauses encouraged emotional regulation and discouraged any shouting matches. As a result, instead of behaving like rivals, participants had a clearer sense that they were all on the same team. By the way, the total meeting time at this client's company was much lower than what we witnessed at comparable organizations, while the outcome in terms of truly committed decisions was significantly higher.

The Power of a Pause

The group we consulted with was by no means an anomaly. Cutting-edge companies are putting mindfulness theory into powerful practice.

Uli Heitzlhofer, global people development program manager at Google, reported the recent creation of a Mental Pause Team with the goal of reducing distractions that can often plague meetings at critical moments. An example is a two-minute meditation pause prior to starting team meetings in which key decisions are made. To aid in this guided meditation, the team can either call a specialist from the Mental Pause Team or get detailed instructions for how to lead this meditation themselves. Early feedback has been overwhelmingly positive.

Meanwhile, just down the road from Google at enterprise

software giant SAP, the company recently introduced its Ambassadors of Mindfulness. This position is taken so seriously that individuals who bear the title can proudly list it on their business cards.

FROM FOCUS TO FLOW

It may seem like it's been a long time coming, but workplace practices that once were dismissed as kooky or counterintuitive are changing the course of cutting-edge companies. Thanks to decades of solid research by neuroscientists, more and more leaders are coming to the realization that reducing distractions, discouraging multitasking, and encouraging mindfulness in the workplace are putting their employees on the path to the most satisfying and productive form of focus: flow.

GETTING TO FLOW

Something almost magical happens when you are able to shut out distractions, focus on the task at hand, and simply enjoy what you're doing. A few hours later after you have had breakfast, answered a few e-mails, and chatted with your colleagues, you close your office door, forward your calls to your assistant, and concentrate hard. Within a few minutes, you start whipping up a brilliant strategic presentation for the meeting with your key customer later in the afternoon. You feel challenged but also confident that you can come up with actionable solutions to the issues your client has been facing. You have gathered all the relevant numbers to make a strong case. You can nail this one. The ideas seem to pop up in your head, and you hardly notice that nearly three hours have passed since you sat down to work on the presentation.

According to positive psychologist Mihaly Csikszentmihalyi, behaviors associated with mastery and control are as important to human nature as the drive to reproduce.[65] In fact, it was Csikszentmihalyi who coined the term "flow" to describe the supreme and most rewarding form of concentration that is popularly known by a variety of nicknames, including feeling "in the zone," "in the groove," and "centered."

What Flow Feels Like

Flow is a subjective state in which you are completely involved in something to the exclusion of everything else.[66] People experiencing flow often report a loss of self-consciousness.[67] They feel a sense of control but seem unconcerned about losing that control. They maintain a vague awareness of distractions without feeling distracted. Likewise with time, which seems to lose any importance or urgency, subordinated by the activity itself.

Often the most successful people in their fields, everyone from athletes to entrepreneurs, are able to reach this flow state almost at will. On the other hand, surveys indicate that between 15 and 20 percent of adults in the United States and Europe never experience flow. A similar percentage reports experiencing it every day.[68] The difference between a leader in flow and a leader who isn't is far from trivial.

Productivity increases fivefold when top executives are in flow.

In fact, it's nothing short of breathtaking. According to a decade-long study conducted by McKinsey, productivity increases fivefold when top executives are in flow.[69]

What Makes Flow Go

Rather than depending on some sort of external reward, flow is typically driven by intrinsic motivation. It originates with the nucleus accumbens, the brain's reward center and dopamine pathway.

The paid employees who produced Microsoft's Encarta encyclopedia software were unable to compete with Wikipedia, an online encyclopedia created by people who were doing it for free and for fun. In this case and many others, it was probably flow that made the decisive difference. Microsoft discontinued Encarta in 2009, whereas Wikipedia is still going strong, the sixth most popular Web site in the world.[70] If you aren't having fun, you probably aren't in flow.

Achieving Flow

To achieve flow, you need a well-defined goal, an optimal challenge, and clear, immediate feedback. The goal supplies acetylcholine to help maintain your focus,[71] the challenge triggers noradrenaline, and the feedback provides you with a rewarding burst of dopamine.

Well-Defined Goal

Simply working is unlikely to put you in a flow state. You have to be working toward something *specific*, and you need to have a strong sense of where your efforts are leading. A group of application developers who are challenged to make their software easier to use may have a noble goal, but it's also pretty vague. But when that goal is reframed as something more specific, such as taking an operation that once required five clicks and reducing it to just three, they will suddenly find themselves in the zone.

Visualizing your goal can sometimes make a huge difference. A team given what seems like a straightforward task, such as "double revenue within two years," may still struggle to focus until they go beyond those numbers and visualize themselves in a photo labeled "team of the year" in the CEO's office. That's when the flow kicks in.

Once your goal is clear, it becomes easier to differentiate between distractions and those things that are essential to reaching your target. According to author Steven Kotler, "The point is this: when the brain is charged with a clear goal, focus narrows considerably, the unimportant is disregarded, and the now is all that's left."[72]

Having a clear goal not only sharpens your focus, it also improves your mood. According to Csikszentmihalyi, "Without a task to focus our attention, most of us find ourselves getting progressively depressed. In flow there is no room for such rumination."[73] Nor is there room for multitasking. The divided attention that grows out of attempting to accomplish two or more things at once robs the productivity and satisfaction that come from pursuing a single purpose.

Optimal Challenge

Although skills and challenges should be in balance, the best situation for flow is when you are feeling slightly overchallenged. When your challenge and skill level are well matched, you should be able to stay focused on the task at hand.

If the challenge outweighs your skills, then you are likely to feel anxious.[74] After all, it's difficult if not impossible to feel in control when you are feeling like you're in over your head.[75] When you shift out of flow and into the threat response, levels of noradrenaline will push you beyond the peak of the performance curve (see chapter 1), and the resulting stress will wrest control away from the moderating influence of the PFC.

On the other hand, when your skills outweigh the challenge, you lack the noradrenaline and dopamine you need to reach your peak and are likely to grow bored.[76]

It's important to note that your chances of experiencing flow increase in proportion to your abilities. The higher your skill level, the more likely the occurrence of flow. Therefore, the concert pianist will experience more flow than the first-year piano student—even if both are feeling slightly overchallenged. The more skilled you are, the easier it becomes to have fun!

Clear, Immediate Feedback

It is highly encouraging to know how well you're progressing and whether you need to adjust or maintain your present course of action. Video game manufacturers have long used this principle successfully. Note how the most popular games are almost always divided into levels. Each time you achieve a milestone you receive another rewarding burst of dopamine that helps you to stay focused and encourages you to keep going. As Erik Gregory, executive director of the nonprofit Media Psychology Research Center in Boston, once explained, "Placing players in flow is the key to video gaming's universal appeal."[77]

Using Flow Strategically

Flow rarely works if you try to use it all the time. In fact, attempting to maintain a flow state for a prolonged period can lead to burnout. To willfully enter the flow state, you may need to deliberately increase the challenge. Concert pianists, for example, are constantly testing their limits by learning and playing progressively more difficult pieces. This keeps them in flow. In other cases, entering flow may entail acquiring new skills. It's helpful to be aware of those conditions or situations in which you have experienced flow in the past. This may include the time of day, the environment, your mood, and even the people you are working with. In a team situation, you may be able to pick and choose tasks that are more likely to put you in flow and share or delegate those that leave you feeling either anxious or bored.

Flow represents the pinnacle of peak performance. It marks the culmination of optimal emotional regulation and a sharpened focus. It helps you find and reach the sweet spot that is essential for sustained excellence.

DEAN Potter's heart-stopping crossing of China's Enshi Grand Canyon took him less than three minutes and was just one feat in an impressive career filled with daredevil highlights.[78] In Steven Kotler's inspiring book about peak performers, *The Rise of Superman*, Potter explained how his mother, a yoga instructor, and his father, an army colonel, helped to shape his personality: "I think yoga gave me my first taste of the zone," he said, "but I definitely got a runner's high . . . out training with my dad and the troops."[79]

According to Beaver Theodosakis, the founder and president of prAna, a climbing apparel company that has sponsored Potter, "Dean holds that zone for hours on end, when the mind can't wander, when you can't second-guess, when you have to be so confident and deliberate in your moves."[80]

"Imagine in everyday life," Theodosakis mused, "if we could go to the office like that and not be distracted."[81]

Imagine.

Eventually, and perhaps inevitably, Dean Potter proved that even imagination and focus have their limits. On May 16, 2015, he and fellow climber Graham Hunt both died in an accident at Yosemite National Park.[82] Potter's unflinching ability to focus may have saved his life time and time again, and his lifelong reliance on mindfulness may have provided him with precision cognitive control, but ultimately, it is the sublime feeling of flow—a feeling that can be generated in a meeting room as well as on a mountaintop— that supplied him with the drive to keep testing his limits and the power to keep achieving his goals.

CHAPTER 3 IN A NUTSHELL

KEY POINTS FROM "SHARPEN YOUR FOCUS"

Executive functions. The ability to plan, delay gratification, and maintain sustained, focused attention all originate from the prefrontal cortex (PFC).

Driven to distraction. The PFC may be powerful, but it is also very sensitive to a variety of disruptions. Two of the primary culprits in the workplace are constant, unexpected interruptions from a variety of sources, and, above all, multitasking.

Multitasking mythology. Rather than promoting productivity, multitasking undermines it. It can make tasks take 50 percent longer and with 50 percent more mistakes. A number of devastating accidents have been blamed on multitasking.

So you think you can multitask? True multitasking, which relies entirely on the PFC, is impossible. Instead, your brain switches rapidly back and forth between tasks, a highly inefficient process that comes at great cost to both concentration and productivity.

Don't resist distractions. Get rid of them. Consciously attempting to ignore distractions can be as big a drain on your brain as multitasking. The key to successful concentration is to clear your mind and your desk of any potential distractions before you turn your focus toward an important task or problem.

Schedule a regular meeting of one. One simple strategy for sharpened focus is to regularly set aside a block of time when you close your door, silence your devices, and focus exclusively on a few minutes or hours of undistracted thinking time with yourself.

The mindfulness miracle. There is mounting scientific evidence to support a powerful mental training technique called mindfulness. Mindfulness can change the wiring of your brain to improve your performance and increase your ability to focus.

The pinnacle of performance is "flow." Characterized by complete and focused attention, flow occurs when your skills are in balance with the challenge you face. Highly skilled people who feel slightly overchallenged are far more likely to be able to enter the flow state when they need to.

PART 2
CHANGING YOUR BRAIN

CHAPTER 4
MANAGE HABITS

··

Take Advantage of Your Brain's Ability to
Operate on Automatic Pilot

PRESIDENT Barack Obama and actress Jennifer Aniston seem like an unlikely pair. Yet the two have something curious in common. Sure, they're attractive, intelligent, and talented, but there's something more: Over the course of their lives, each has struggled with an addiction to cigarettes.

Aniston, who established her acting reputation on the popular TV show *Friends*, was frequently photographed smoking on the set of the sitcom. In 2002, she vowed to "eventually quit smoking." Yet, almost ten years later, when asked about her noticeable weight gain, Aniston claimed the extra baggage was an unwelcome side effect of recently kicking the nicotine habit. "It's just I quit smoking," she explained in October 2011, "so I've gained a couple of pounds."[1]

Fans who'd been keeping a close watch on Aniston's career as well as on her personal life heaved a smoke-free sigh of relief, applauded the decision, and speculated that the long-delayed end to her habit may have been due to the positive influence of her relatively new boyfriend (now husband), actor Justin Theroux.[2]

But apparently not even boyfriends can work miracles. In February 2013, while celebrating her birthday in the company of Theroux as well as a host of other movie and television luminaries, Aniston was photographed smoking a ceremonial cigarette.[3]

It's unclear exactly when Barack Obama had his first cigarette, but he has admitted that he was already a smoker by the time he entered Occidental College as a freshman in 1980.[4] Since then, his efforts to kick the habit have been an ongoing saga. Although he certainly wasn't the first smoker to live in the White House, the pressure to set a good example in an era when the dangers of cigarettes are largely uncontested increased as the presidential election progressed. Even so, six months into his presidency, Obama publicly acknowledged in a news conference that he still indulged in an occasional cigarette.[5]

In early 2010, the chief executive's doctor, navy captain Jeffrey Kuhlman, told Obama that he should stick with his "smoking cessation efforts," advice that made it obvious to anyone reading between the lines that the president still hadn't managed to kick the habit.[6] As 2010 drew to a close, when asked about the president's on-again, off-again relationship with cigarettes, former presidential press secretary Robert Gibbs told reporters, "I've not seen or witnessed evidence of smoking in probably nine months."[7] A few months later, the White House appeared to make it official: The president was no longer a smoker.

During an interview in the days following the announcement, First Lady Michelle Obama insisted that her husband had finally quit so he could look both of his daughters in the

eye and tell them in all honesty that he didn't smoke.[8] The
president, however, provided a slightly different reason when
overheard chatting about it with United Nations special rap-
porteur Maina Kiai in a conversation that was picked up by
an open mike. He confessed to Kiai that he had quit "because
I'm scared of my wife."[9]

Why is it that so many people, many of them wealthy,
talented, and highly intelligent, find it so difficult to quit
smoking, even when faced with ominous and indisputable evidence of the detrimental effect that cigarettes have on their
health? Some point to the physically addictive nature of nicotine as the reason. Yet Jennifer Aniston and Barack Obama
both provide compelling anecdotal evidence that the urge to
keep smoking continues long after the symptoms of physical
addiction have subsided. The reason that smoking maintains
such a tenacious hold on some of us is relatively simple: It's a
habit.

Although occasionally frowned-upon activities like smoking, drinking, gambling, drugs, and even nail-biting typically
spring to mind when we hear the word "habit," the fact is
that we spend most of our days engaged in one habit or another. And for the most part that's a good thing. According to
University of Southern California psychologist David Neal,
habits of one sort or another account for roughly 45 percent
of daily life. During these times, rather than relying on reason or motivation, we shift into automatic pilot and depend
instead on context, automated actions, time pressure, and
yes, even low self-control to provide the engine for our
behavior.[10]

There's a good reason for this: Our brains would quickly
become overloaded if everything we did had to be done consciously. Good habits make life easier by using our brains

more efficiently. Bad habits make life harder and in some cases can be harmful or even deadly. The automatic nature of habits is what makes them hard to control or change. Whether they are good or bad, old habits are attractive to your brain because they require less energy. That's why developing new habits can be difficult. They initially force your brain to work harder and less efficiently than it would like. But once you manage to sufficiently strengthen and establish a new and rewarding habit, your brain will automatically choose it instead of the old one.

THE SURPRISING CHALLENGE OF COUNTING TO THIRTY

Here's a game we call Evil Number Seven. If you are of a certain age, you may even remember a variation of this from when you were in elementary school.

We divided the participants into two groups and had each group sit in a circle. At first their assignment seemed relatively simple: Go clockwise around the circle, counting from number 1 to 30. The first person would say "one," then the person to his or her left would say "two," and so on all the way up to 30. Pretty simple.

There were, however, certain exceptions. And this is what made the game interesting. Anytime you reached a number that contained the numeral 7 or was divisible by 7, instead of saying that number, you had to stand up, clap your hands, and sit back down again. Then the person next to you would pick up where you left off, counting "eight" in the first instance, "fifteen" in the next, and so on.

And did we mention that this was a competition? While you and your group were trying to race to 30, being sure to stand and clap at all the right times, the other group was watching your every move and delighting in each mistake your team made.

Oh, and one more thing. If anyone skipped a number or failed to stand and clap for a number that contained or was divisible by 7, the entire group had to start all over again. As luck would have it, the greatest stumbling point would often come just as the group was nearing 30. In most cases, the person who had the number 27 would correctly stand up and clap. But what about the person who had 28? The fact that 27, which contains the number 7, is immediately followed by 28, which is divisible by 7, seemed to trip people up again and again. And so just a few numbers from the finish line, they were forced to start over.

We tried this several times. Our hunch is that most participants found this to be the most stressful case of counting to 30 that they'd encountered since they were kids first mastering their numbers.

But we weren't quite done even then. As you might expect, many of our clever participants were calculating in advance what number they'd have next and silently getting ready, especially for cases in which they'd have to stand up and clap. So we added an extra wrinkle to the rules. Each time someone stood up and clapped, the counting would have to change directions. So if the group was moving clockwise when it reached the number 7, it would then shift and continue counterclockwise until someone clapped at number 14, signaling yet another change in direction.

Needless to say, the race to the number 30 took even longer this time.

This little game not only demonstrates how difficult and disruptive it can be to break out of well-established, deeply ingrained habits, but it also teaches us a lot about how two important parts of the brain operate: the prefrontal cortex and the basal ganglia.[11] We already know about the prefrontal cortex from the previous chapter. But it's the golf-ball-size basal ganglia region that normally does the work when we're counting. Most of us learned to count so long ago that we can do it almost unconsciously. But what happens when we take something we know "by heart" like counting to 30 and add an extra requirement? Suddenly, a task we normally take for granted requires some additional conscious effort.

Although counting's not the same as riding a bike, the basal ganglia handle both activities. These are the things we've committed to long-term memory and can engage in with relative ease. Our brains may be smart, but they're also kind of lazy. From the brain's perspective, each habit in our basal ganglia functions like a dishwasher or an electric can opene: It's a labor-saving device.

Our brains may be smart, but they're also kind of lazy.

Habits as Macros

If you're a computer power user, you probably know that many types of productivity software provide you with the option of creating and storing routines for functions you use regularly. In Microsoft Word and Excel, these are known as macros. Many Macintosh-based applications use something called AppleScript. In Adobe's Photoshop and Illustrator, they're called Action Scripts.

The names may be different, but the basic idea is the same: A procedure you follow regularly that may involve dozens of steps is stored as a single routine that can be initiated by a single command. From that point on, whenever you need it, you select a menu item or push a button to activate the routine instead of painstakingly repeating each step.

Habits work in a similar fashion. Take a moment to think about all the steps involved in putting on and tying your shoes. Listing each step in the process makes it look rather intimidating. Yet you probably run through the entire procedure at least once a day without even consciously thinking about it. When it comes to habits, all of us are power users. The basal ganglia provide storage for your brain's equivalent of computer macros.

Understanding the components of a habit can make it easier to change bad habits and establish good ones. A typical habit has three components: a cue, a routine, and a reward. The cue is a specific stimulus or combination of stimuli. A cue can be practically anything: a place, an emotion, a time of day, a thing, or even a word or phrase. The cue is what triggers the routine. The routine is the habit itself. The nature of the routine can vary from extremely simple—a grimace, for example—or relatively involved or complex, such as the way you tie your necktie or the route you take each morning to work. Initially, it is the anticipation of a reward that drives the routine and ensures its storage in the basal ganglia. The reward might be food or drugs or simply a feeling of relaxation, accomplishment, or satisfaction.[12]

CHANGING HABITS
Establishing good habits or getting rid of bad ones involves the same basic skills: 1) goal setting and motivation, 2) getting started, and 3) staying on track.

Goal Setting and Motivation

How can you tell when you've reached your destination if you don't know where you're going? Goal setting supplies that destination. It provides the needed focus for initiating a new habit or getting rid of an old one. Most successful goals share two key qualities: 1) there is an emotional basis for the motivation, and 2) the goal setter is able to visualize not only reaching that goal but also, and more important, the process involved in achieving it.

Establish an Emotional Connection

Changing a bad habit or adopting a new one rarely works simply because it's the right thing to do. That approach may look good on paper, but it seldom plays out in practice. If the goal you set doesn't make your eyes light up when you think of it, or if you feel no fear at the possibility of failing to reach it, then it probably isn't a good goal for you.

The reward and threat circuits that provide the basic infrastructure for our emotional wiring are essential when it comes to successfully pursuing and achieving a goal (see chapter 2). A goal without emotion is a goal that is almost guaranteed to fail.

The intensity of the accompanying emotion often influences the speed at which a new habit is adopted. The goal you set should be specific, personal, and written down. In addition, you should have a set of action items that mark the steps leading to the goal's completion. It's no coincidence that a key component of successful habit change is also a major factor in flow (see chapter 3). When the goal is clear, the outcome becomes easier to determine, and the reward is usually easier to obtain. This combination increases the level of motivation.

Visualize Your Goal

Most offices hold periodic emergency drills, in which everyone learns to evacuate the building in a calm and orderly fashion according to a carefully planned route.

Visualizing the steps you plan to take in pursuit of your goal is a bit like practicing an emergency drill. It lays down the track for a neuronal pathway you can follow to achieve your particular goal. Then, when the time comes to pursue that goal, not just in your head but in the real world, the route you're going to take has already been established. Your brain says in effect: "Don't worry. I know the way. Let me take over from here."

In general, visualizing the path to your goal is more powerful than imagining its completion, just as thinking about the route you would take to escape a fire is more practical than simply seeing yourself safely out of reach of the smoke and flames. Even so, it can still aid motivation to envision yourself reaching your destination as well.

When it comes to visualizing a positive outcome, whether that means escaping a burning building or delivering a successful presentation, psychologists make a key distinction between positive *fantasies* and positive *expectations*. Positive fantasies can sometimes be entertaining as a means of relaxation and escape, but their value in goal setting is limited and even detrimental. After all, a vivid image of success can sometimes trick your brain into believing you've already reached your destination before you've even taken the first step. The strength of positive expectations is that your confidence carries an additional message: You don't simply feel you can do it; you also know *how* you're going to do it. Instead of celebrating prematurely, the brain releases dopamine and increases your motivation in anticipation of impending success.

Getting Started

Of course, even with clear goals, great expectations, and a carefully plotted plan, many of us who seek to develop new habits or jettison old ones run into an immediate obstacle: getting started, which is one of the most difficult parts of changing. That's why the best time to start is right away. Procrastination is the principal impediment to initiating a habit change. Large goals can seem intimidating unless broken into manageable steps. *Kaizen*, the practice of using small steps, can help you to avoid the threat response that frequently drives procrastination.

One Lap at a Time

A colleague who wanted to get in shape decided to start a swimming regimen at his local pool. Having attempted new fitness plans in the past, he was concerned that this one might lead to another failed routine. What's more, if he tried to start swimming regularly and failed, the fact that he passed the pool every day on the way to work would serve as a constant visual reminder of that failure—a truly discouraging prospect. The pool was quite small and nowhere near Olympic size, so he realized that he'd have to swim at least twenty to thirty laps to get sufficient aerobic exercise. That goal seemed both monotonous and out of reach. Instead, he started out by swimming five laps a day (which took him about five minutes) and by imposing a very simple rule: He was free to swim more than five laps at any time, but once he increased his total, he could never swim fewer laps from that point on. In theory, he could've stuck with five laps forever. But human nature being what it is, he gradually upped his total over time. Within a few months, he had gone from five laps a day to more than seventy, almost imperceptibly—and in good weather and bad. It had become an ingrained habit.

Our colleague may not have been aware of it at the time, but his regimen for developing a swimming habit was an excellent example of kaizen. Although the kaizen technique is strongly associated with Japan, it actually originated with the U.S. military. Using the mantra of "continuous improvement," the idea was to make modest but steady alterations in how the Japanese businesses were run. The approach, which came to be known as kaizen in Japanese, was implemented widely and embraced enthusiastically by industries in the island nation, who would ultimately use it to transform Japan into an economic powerhouse admired throughout the world for the efficiency of its production and the quality of its products.[13]

How did kaizen change the course of Japanese industry? It operated using six basic principles, all of which placed an emphasis on "small."

1. **Ask small questions.** Kaizen's "small questions" provide a powerful way of programming your brain. Unlike bigger questions, which tend to trigger a threat response, small questions can often be fun. If your goal seems too large or intimidating, simply ask yourself, "What is one small step I can take toward reaching that goal?"[14]

2. **Think small thoughts.** Now that you've answered your question, it's time to visualize yourself acting on it. The principle of "mind sculpture" suggests that the brain learns better in small increments instead of large doses. If you've ever stood still at the ocean's edge and watched as the waves slowly bury your feet in sand, you've witnessed the effect of these small but steady changes. If you isolate a task that you are afraid of or that makes you uncomfortable and then gradually—very gradually—visualize

yourself beginning to work on it, over time your mind's attitude toward the once-dreaded task will be reshaped.[15]

3. **Take small actions.** Small questions and small thoughts ultimately require small actions. The executives we coach frequently ask too much from their direct reports. The goals they set for their employees are often too large. As a result, both parties wind up disappointed and demoralized. Never make target agreements like this: By the end of the year, you'll regularly make ten phone calls a day to customers. Instead, here's what we typically advise: Ask the employee to make *one* call per day in the first week, two calls in the second week, and so on. Meet regularly to see how things are going. It should be easy to add one call per week, every day. The key is to continue making steady progress.[16]

4. **Solve small problems.** Ask yourself if there are ways in which you irritate your family, friends, coworkers, or customers. Strive to do so without punishing yourself. Negative self-talk will rarely be successful in convincing you to make changes. On the other hand, your new awareness alone should reduce the probability that you will make this mistake again. While you're at it, ask yourself whether this mistake is part of a bigger problem. If you can peg the error to a larger issue, you'll give yourself further incentive to work on it.[17]

We were coaching a top executive whose team claimed that he didn't truly care about them. Although this perception was creating a huge amount of tension in the group, it was obviously a large and rather ambiguous complaint. It would've been unrealistic to expect that we could transform him into Mr. Empathetic overnight. Instead, we started by pinpointing the smallest possible problem for him to solve: his habit of checking e-mails during meetings. It was a simple change that he found easy to make. Yet it had a dramatic effect on the team's attitude. They definitely noticed the difference. With momentum on our side, we found fifteen other behaviors that had contributed to the problem, including failing to look his employees in the eye while talking to them, breaking off conversations abruptly and prematurely, and holding sensitive discussions in the presence of the entire team when they should have been conducted one-on-one. The motivation for change was high. After a few months of making these incremental improvements, the problem was gone.

5. **Give small rewards.** As we now know, most of the habits we engage in were originally triggered by the expectation of some sort of reward. The small reward you choose for habits you are attempting to change or develop should be appropriate to the goal. For example, a square of chocolate is a fine reward for an onerous task but is probably not suitable for someone who is trying to develop healthier eating habits. Although it may sound counterintuitive, small rewards can often be a greater source of motivation than large ones.[18] In fact, a team of researchers, led by author and psychologist Dan Ariely, found that higher rewards can actually have a dampening effect on motivation.[19] Besides, they may not even be what the employee truly wants. A busy management consultant

Small rewards can often be a greater source of motivation than large ones.

we know, who was fairly well paid but who put in grueling hours crisscrossing the continent, placed a much higher premium on a day off or even a chance to go to the gym than she did on receiving yet another cash bonus.

6. **Identify small moments.** The little things can sometimes mean a lot. Often people who notice what seem like inconsequential details find that those details can lead to dramatic results.[20] During the late nineteenth century, the San Francisco Mint would burn its carpets every four years, recovering an estimated $3,200 in accumulated gold dust in the process.[21] With today's prices, the value of that dust would amount to more than $200,000. The former CEO of an American airline famously discovered that he could save the company an estimated $40,000 a year simply by removing a single olive from the salads that the company used to furnish its passengers for free.[22]

But small moments aren't all about money. Sometimes they come down to the little things you do—or don't do. Psychologist John Gottman's study of couples found that in successful relationships positive attention, what he refers to as "turning toward," outweighed negative attention ("turning against") by a ratio of 5 to 1. What constitutes positive attention? You'd be surprised. It doesn't mean treating your partner to a lavish dinner or a Mediterranean cruise (although both are nice). It's more likely to involve the seemingly minor, day-to-day interactions, like sharing in the grocery shopping or sending an encouraging voice mail when you know your partner is facing a rough day.[23] These small gestures support the notion that you're working together instead of apart. Negative or positive, the little things we tend to overlook can often loom large.[24] Like the drip, drip, drip of a faucet you ignore as you drop off to sleep, only to wake up and find your entire bathroom is flooded, or the token amount of money you set aside each month that turns into a formidable retirement fund, these little things truly add up.

These small moments can have a major impact at work as well. In the factory of one of our clients, the workers were upset by the inaccessibility of their boss. They complained that they never knew when he was in and were annoyed that they always had to go through a secretary to speak to him, even for trivial matters. What we discovered was that he was using a separate entrance to get into his office each day. That maneuver may have saved him about twenty yards of walking, but it rendered him virtually invisible to his employees. We suggested that he lock the back entrance of the office so he was compelled to walk the extra distance through the factory floor every day in order to get to his desk. This small change had a huge impact on company morale. Each day began with pleasant greetings and smiling faces. The boss was frequently able to solve little problems and provide quick advice as he headed to his office every morning. Taking a different route may have added five to ten minutes to his walk, but the investment in time paid off dramatically in the next worker satisfaction survey.

Why all the emphasis on small? Wouldn't it have been faster and more efficient to make larger changes from the outset? To understand why big changes often don't work, we need to return to the brain's threat and reward circuitry. All of us are aware of things that take us out of our comfort zone, but few of us have an understanding of the neuroscience that underlies this response. If you've tried to make a fundamental change in the way things are done at your company, you may have been genuinely surprised by the level of resistance you've encountered from some of your colleagues. People can get extremely defensive in such situations. "That's not the way we do it," some may say. "The old system worked fine." "Why do we have to learn a whole new procedure?" Although these misgivings will occasionally have genuine merit, the responses are almost always visceral. Your well-meaning improvements have bypassed the more reasonable prefrontal cortex of your colleagues and gone straight to the amygdala, the principal region of the notorious fight-or-flight response. In other words, your changes are perceived as a threat. Maybe not as threatening as a wild animal or a marauding enemy from a rival tribe, but on a fundamental level the brain doesn't make much of a distinction between a violent attack and an unexpected change in project management software. Under certain circumstances, a seemingly innocuous comment like "May I make a suggestion?" can be treated as though you had asked "May I kidnap your spouse and your children?" instead.

Surprisingly enough, this response is natural. Unless the prospect of a reward is clear and imminent, our brains are evolutionarily conditioned to respond to most changes as threats. From the standpoint of your brain, threats aren't simply things that put your life in immediate danger, although those are certainly the most dramatic type. They can also be anything that the brain perceives as a misallocation of resources. As you grow accustomed to a certain way of doing things, the process becomes habitual and energy efficient. Changing almost any routine, whether it involves how you do your work, the way you structure your day, or even what you eat at mealtime, requires additional conscious effort and, with it, additional energy. Aroused from its comfortable complacency, your brain sounds the alarm by awakening the watchdog of your limbic system, the amygdala, which triggers your threat response.

The secret of kaizen is that it operates below the radar of your brain's threat response. Touch a warm surface and your fingers will sense the temperature, but you're unlikely to experience any dramatic reaction. Touch a red-hot surface, however, and your hand will jerk back reflexively before your conscious brain has even had a chance to realize what happened. Similarly, you can usually continue working even when someone nearby is whispering. But if someone breaks the silence of the office with a sudden shout, most of us are likely to jump. Kaizen works like a warm surface instead of a red-hot one, like a whisper instead of a shout. The actions you take are so small, so incremental, and so seemingly inconsequential that as psychologist Robert Maurer, author of *One Small Step Can Change Your Life: The Kaizen Way*, explains, they "tiptoe right past your amygdala."[25]

Staying on Track

Making new habits stick can be difficult if not impossible if you try to use inhibition and willpower. Of the estimated 50 percent of Americans who make New Year's resolutions, 92 percent of those people fail.

Although it may seem tempting and even admirable to rely on "mental toughness" to stick to your resolution or plan, it's extremely energy inefficient and almost guaranteed to fail. It's like resolving to drive across the United States on a single tank of gas. Not even the flattest route and the best of intentions will be enough to get you from one coast to the other. It's a simple matter of energy: When you're out of gas, you're out of gas. Your conscious brain uses glucose for gas, and like a classic Cadillac or a gargantuan Hummer, it's a notorious guzzler. Making decisions, devising plans, remembering a phone number, and sticking to your diet all rely on the same region of the brain and consume the same limited fuel.

The key to keeping your resolutions is to increase their energy efficiency. You do this by transforming them into habits. After all, most of us don't need to resolve to switch on the coffee machine when we get up, to brush our teeth after breakfast, to log on to the company network every morning, or to add a cc list of essential team members to important e-mails. In the words of a famous manufacturer of athletic shoes, equipment, and apparel: We just do it.

Some of the resolutions we make at the start of the year aren't that much more ambitious, and yet the overwhelming majority of us fail to stick with them. What's the difference?

Resolutions work best when they become automatic, triggered by a cue that provides a recognizable signal to your unconscious that tells it to activate a particular routine. With most ingrained habits, we've long since forgotten the cue. In the case of the coffee machine, the cue could be setting foot in your kitchen first thing each morning. As for the routine of brushing your teeth, you may trigger it by walking into the bathroom after breakfast. Your brain has long since learned these cues and established the routines that go with them. The problem with resolutions is that they often lack the cues that make our daily habits seem so effortless. We actually have to think about them. A resolution without a cue taxes the brain's limited supply of willpower.

Habits can rarely be stopped—or started—with brute force. As chapter 2 has already shown us, attempting to go head-to-head against your powerful unconscious is destined to be a losing battle. A more successful long-term strategy is to rely, once again, on Cognitive Jujitsu, that is, working *with* your unconscious instead of against it. In this case, it involves consciously manipulating the three-part cue, routine, and reward that provide the habitual framework. A strategy called implementation intentions can help you stay on track by artificially reproducing the three elements of most habits. With implementation intentions, you consciously choose a cue, routine, and reward.

Use If/Then Plans to Create Your Own Habits

Known informally as "if/then" or "when/then" plans, implementation intentions are remarkably flexible. You can use them to change an old habit by attaching a new routine to an existing cue or to create a new habit by linking some sort of cue to a desired routine. For example, instead of resolving to keep your expense records up-to-date, an admirable goal that is nonetheless likely to go the way of most resolutions if you rely on your memory and your willpower, create an implementation intention that gradually turns the resolution into a homemade habit. You might say, "During the time when my computer is booting up in the morning, I will gather my latest receipts and put them in an envelope." Now you have a trigger, starting up your computer, that stimulates you to engage in a routine, gathering your receipts. You can even follow up this implementation intention with another to complete the process: "On my daily walk to the canteen, I will drop off my receipts at the accounting department." Do this enough times deliberately, using your computer start-up time and your walk to the canteen as cues, and it will actually begin to feel odd if for some reason you forget to turn in your receipts. Eventually, like most habits, the implementation intention will become automatic.

Establishing implementation intentions can be a huge help

for planned change of behaviors in development dialogues between superiors and their employees. In fact, we've found that when commitments of personal change are supported by concrete implementation intentions, the probability of achieving specific objectives doubles.

In one instance, an employee and his manager met and both agreed that he needed to be "more active" in meetings. That's a noble goal, but what exactly does it mean? Most companies are content to describe this sort of development target as a so-called SMART goal, which stipulates that the behavior must be *s*pecific, *m*easurable, *a*ttainable, *r*ealistic, and *t*imely. In the case of the employee who needs to speak up, if the meeting has six participants, he might commit to a goal of expanding his speaking time in sixty-minute team meetings to at least ten minutes.

Unfortunately, although this clearly defines the goal, it doesn't provide any concrete guidelines for implementing it. Exactly when should the employee speak up or contribute to the meeting? It's possible that he could go into the meeting with every intention of playing a more active role and yet still wind up silent by the time the meeting is over.

This is where implementation intentions come in. In the case of the bashful employee, we suggested an if/then plan that would use a simple cue to remind him to chime in. Every time the superior intentionally clicked his pen, it served as a signal that it was time for the employee to speak up. By creating this cue, the *routine* of speaking up was established. This small change made a big difference, improving not only the employee's participation but also his general focus on the discussion. What's more, instant group feedback after each meeting ensured the improvement of both the quantity and the quality of his contributions over time.

Once this basic template is understood, it can be expanded into all sorts of areas with relative ease. There are many ways to use implementation intentions to develop individual habit changes in teams. For example, an acoustic signal that occurs every twenty minutes can remind you to call a client, or you can develop a routine of reducing stress by standing up and stretching after each phone call. We have a colleague who used to be driven to distraction by stop-and-go city traffic. Now, whenever he's stuck at a stoplight, he uses it as a cue to do some belly breathing. The new routine is a win-win. It distracts him from the aggravation of urban gridlock and allows him to engage in a practice that is a proven technique for encouraging relaxation.

The results from these simple changes can seem almost miraculous. The magic, according to UC Santa Barbara psychologist Jonathan Schooler, lies in the *strict and rigorous if/then link* that simply has to be mechanical; it doesn't need to be content related. For example, every time you close an office door, you recall the five company values. And every time you finish reading a chapter of this book, you lean back and think about its three most important points.[26]

3-D Habit Change

Some habits are so stubborn that they seem impossible to break. Many of us are plagued by certain compulsions, such as biting our nails, constantly checking e-mail, and yes, like Jennifer Aniston and President Obama, smoking.

Dr. Jeffrey Schwartz, a research professor of psychiatry at UCLA, created a four-step process for habit change that was specifically designed for patients with obsessive-compulsive disorder.[27] While most of us don't have habits that rise to the level of OCD, we've streamlined and adapted Dr. Schwartz's four steps into three simple but powerful processes that we call "3-D habit change": describe, distract, and delay.

Describe. The first step in kicking a deeply ingrained habit comes with recognizing and acknowledging the trigger when it occurs. "I'm feeling nervous. That always makes me want to chew on my fingernails." Or, "I'm having a beer. That always makes me want to light up a cigarette to go with it." Or, "I'm feeling stuck on this project. That always makes me want to check my e-mail."

If this step sounds a little familiar, it should. It relies on the same cognitive technique as labeling, which is explained in chapter 2. Like labeling, describing your habit trigger leads to *metacognition*, or "thinking about thinking." It takes a normally unconscious process and shifts it into the realm of your conscious. It also taps into the power of mindfulness (see chapter 3) by enhancing your overall awareness of the here and now. This provides a window of opportunity that enables you to regain conscious control over an unconscious response and sets the stage for the next step.

Distract. Now, instead of trying to outmuscle your impulse with energy-intensive, brain-draining self-control, use Cognitive Jujitsu (see chapter 2). Redirect that energy toward something different. If you feel like lighting up a cigarette to go with your beer, try eating some pretzels instead. If you find yourself tempted to chew your fingernails or check your e-mail, develop a competing ritual, such as adding tally marks to a sheet of paper, that will momentarily divert your attention from your original compulsion.

By the way, the most effective distracters are pleasant ones. They put you in a reward state, triggering a burst of dopamine, which makes your brain more receptive to change.

Unfortunately, many people sabotage their attempts at habit change by choosing truly unappealing distracters, almost as though they deliberately want to punish themselves. If, for example, you choose to distract yourself from consuming a delicious dish of chocolate ice cream by eating a raw Brussels sprout instead, you don't have to be a trained neuropsychologist to realize that this particular strategy is doomed to fail!

Like describing, distracting shifts the energy from the unconscious regions of the brain that drive most habits and back to your prefrontal cortex, the focus of conscious attention.[28] And just as describing is similar to labeling in chapter 2, distracting has a lot in common with the cognitive reappraisal technique from the same chapter. Resisting a habit directly is no more effective than inhibition is in attempting to tamp down an unwelcome emotion. In fact, in both cases, it's more apt to exacerbate the situation than improve it. In each situation, Cognitive Jujitsu, that is, skillfully using the power of the unconscious by deflecting instead of opposing it, is more likely to lead to a successful outcome.

Sometimes even a momentary distraction is enough to break the bad-habit circuit. Dr. Andrew Weil, a physician and well-known advocate of alternative medicine, mentions a mild form of aversion therapy that involves wearing a rubber band around your wrist. When you catch yourself engaging in a bad habit, such as biting your nails, snap the rubber band against your wrist so you feel a slight sting—not so it really hurts but with enough of a smack that it alerts you to your habit and reminds you to literally snap out of it.[29]

Delay. Once you've found an effective alternative to your old bad habit behavior, the key is to sustain it. In some instances, sustaining your behavior refers to its duration. This is particularly important with compulsions. If you're always tempted to check e-mail, for example, the longer you can last without "giving in," the more ingrained the new neuronal pathway will become. In other cases, sustaining your new behavior may refer to repetition. The more times you engage in the alternate behavior, the stronger it will become and, more important, the weaker the old bad habit will get. As the two routines vie for supremacy, you'll need to keep the new habit in your conscious mind until it catches up with and eventually overtakes the old unconscious routine. When that finally happens, the new habit, just like the old one it replaced, should become second nature.[30]

ALTHOUGH no one but close friends and family can probably say for sure, it seems apparent that President Obama finally managed to kick the smoking habit. As for Jennifer Aniston, that's a little more uncertain. What is certain is that smoking provides a sobering example of just how tenacious habits can be.

Habits provide a dramatic demonstration of the power and utility of our unconscious. But the role of the unconscious doesn't end with habits. Although the old saying about using only 10 percent of your brain isn't true, there *are* ways we can learn to use our brains more effectively. In fact, that's the subject of the next chapter.

CHAPTER 4 IN A NUTSHELL
....

KEY POINTS FROM "MANAGE HABITS"

Habit change is hard. Our brains prefer the path of least resistance. In order to trailblaze a new neuronal pathway, the brain must be convinced that all that extra effort is worth it.

Changing habits. Establishing good habits and getting rid of bad ones involve the same basic skills: 1) goal setting and motivation, 2) getting started, and 3) staying on track.

Putting your heart into it. Goals that look good on paper have no guarantee of succeeding. In order to be successful, your goal must be emotionally relevant.

What's in it for me? People who don't have an emotional stake in the process are unlikely to change. Unless they can anticipate a meaningful reward or threat, they might go through the motions but fail to make the necessary effort that a change requires.

The first step is always the hardest. The biggest obstacle to getting started is procrastination. The way to outsmart the brain's natural aversion to change is to use kaizen, which involves taking very small steps. That enables you to steadily make progress without setting off your brain's evolutionary alarm bells.

Sustainable habits depend on triggers. If you want to make a change that lasts, good intentions aren't enough. You need to attach your new routine to a trigger. These trigger/routine combinations are technically referred to as implementation intentions but are better known as "if/then" or "when/then" plans.

CHAPTER 5
UNLEASH YOUR
UNCONSCIOUS

....

Sometimes the Fastest and Best Decisions Are Made
Without the Direct Participation of Your Conscious Mind

MOST of the men were relaxing when the alarm suddenly shattered the silence and echoed against the walls of the fire station: *Probable kitchen fire in a single-family house.*

When the trucks arrived on the scene and the lieutenant led a hose crew into the house, he immediately sensed that something was odd. The living room was far hotter than it should've been for a fire that was supposedly coming from the kitchen. The fire was also much quieter. Fires make noise, and extra-hot fires make a lot of noise. More troubling was the fact that attempts to extinguish the flames rising out of the kitchen weren't succeeding.[1]

The lieutenant had seen enough. Something about this fire just didn't *feel* right. He ordered his men to evacuate the house immediately. Seconds after the last man left, the entire living room floor collapsed. Had they remained a minute longer, some, and perhaps all, of the firefighters might have perished.

For years, the lieutenant was convinced that some sort of extrasensory perception had alerted him to the impending danger. He was mistaken. Although scientists still debate whether anyone can have ESP, the firefighters who escaped were saved by something we all possess: a powerful unconscious mind.

UNCONSCIOUS POWER

The most powerful and underappreciated part of your brain is the part that by definition you're unaware of: your unconscious. According to Wolf Singer, former director of the Max Planck Institute for Brain Research in Frankfurt, Germany, our unconscious accounts for a major part of our decision-making activity. In fact, whenever we take action, our conscious brain is often the last to know. There's a good reason for this. Our unconscious is designed to work faster in order to ensure our survival. After all, if a wild animal confronts you, you don't have time to ponder the pros and cons of your best course of action. By keeping your heart pumping and by allowing you to continue breathing without having to think about it, the unconscious is literally keeping you alive. Plus, unlike the working memory, which typically has room for just four pieces of information at a time, the capacity of the unconscious is practically limitless.

Analysis Paralysis

Although much of the thinking we do takes place in our conscious mind, two key factors—the limited capacity of our working memory and the risk of what psychologists sometimes call analysis paralysis or decision fatigue—can make it an inferior approach for activities that require complex evaluation.

Your working memory may be clever, but its capacity is small. In fact, it's next to impossible to make a complex conscious decision using just your working memory; it simply doesn't have enough room or resources to accommodate all the variables. When your working memory runs out of energy, you experience decision fatigue. Decision fatigue doesn't lead to a reduction in total brain activity. Instead, it causes an increase in activity in some regions of the brain and a decrease in others. The brain becomes more focused on short-term rewards and less interested in long-term prospects.[2] Did you buy a car that had a questionable safety record because you liked its color? If so, you can probably blame decision fatigue.

Strange as it may sound, thinking less can lead to a smarter answer. Often, a lack of time, a lack of conscious information, and reduced activity in the prefrontal cortex, the "thinking part" of our brains, can result in better decisions as well as better actions and outcomes. Although this can apply to everyone in certain cases, it can be especially true when you're an expert in the area where action is needed. In some instances, the more we think, the further we stray from the optimal outcome.

Thinking less can lead to a smarter answer.

When the Unconscious Is the Key

Skilled decisions, just like skilled tasks, are often performed without conscious awareness. It's one thing to be unaware of brushing your teeth or making coffee in the morning. These are habits that are virtually identical from one day to the next. It's different when the task requires you to respond to new and changing information. In one eye-opening experiment conducted by cognitive psychologists at Vanderbilt and Kobe universities, skilled typists were shown an image of a blank computer keyboard and asked to supply the correct letter each time a key was highlighted. For most of the subjects, their knowledge of the key locations was surprisingly incomplete or inaccurate. Although they managed to correctly identify slightly more than half the key locations, they misidentified nearly 23 percent and omitted almost 20 percent. Keep in mind that these were experienced typists. They typed at a mean speed of more than 76 words per minute with a mean accuracy of close to 95 percent. Yet, despite this obvious expertise, on average they were able to explicitly identify only slightly more than half the keys. These people were speedy typists not because they consciously knew the locations of the keys, but because they knew them all unconsciously.[3]

Failing Grades

When it comes to information, more is not always better. In one study, guidance counselors were bombarded with a wealth of facts about high school seniors in order to predict their grades during their freshman year in college. The data included transcripts, test scores, application essays, the results of personality and vocational tests, and even in-person interviews. Meanwhile, a mathematical formula made the same prediction using only two factors: each student's GPA and just one standardized test score. The predictions made by the simple formula proved to be far more accurate than the careful assessments from the guidance counselors.[4] The late Nobel Prize laureate Herbert A. Simon, who devoted much of his career to the study of decision making, explained it succinctly: "A wealth of information creates a poverty of attention."

No Choking Matter

One of the more dramatic and yet most common illustrations of analysis paralysis is "choking," a phenomenon most closely associated with sports but that can occur in almost any high-pressure situation, including the business world.

Interestingly enough, choking is almost the reverse of a failure of emotional regulation, such as the notorious amygdala hijack that prompts a person to forgo common sense and act impulsively or even destructively. In an amygdala hijack, our threat response gets the better of us, and our more thoughtful and reasonable conscious brain is taken off-line.

With choking, the prefrontal cortex hijacks the unconscious brain. A professional golfer suddenly gets the yips when he starts thinking about the individual elements of his stroke, causing a normally smooth follow-through to be disrupted by unnecessary analysis.

The fact that professional golfers are more likely than amateurs to suffer from a case of the yips points to an intriguing reality. There's a key distinction between the intuition of an expert and that of a novice, or the putting of a pro golfer and that of an amateur. While beginners benefit from thinking more, experts can actually be hampered by it.

While beginners benefit from thinking more, experts can actually be hampered by it.

A classic demonstration of this phenomenon occurs in a tennis match in which the inferior player compliments her opponent on a brilliant backhand return. "Wow! How did you do that?" she asks with feigned admiration. "Did you shift your grip slightly or turn your elbow out a little more?" Even if the opponent fails to answer the question adequately (and if she's an expert, she probably can't), there's a good chance the damage has already been done. Her next backhand won't be nearly as effective as her previous shot. That's because the player who asked the question has made her opponent think consciously about something she normally does unconsciously. This is usually enough to disrupt a smooth process and throw the player's rhythm off. Nearly all athletes have had the unpleasant experience of choking, but it typically happens without outside intervention. In this case, however, a devilishly clever question has caused the choke to occur.

When you're learning, practicing, and perfecting a new skill, your conscious brain is essential for organizing, analyzing, and reflecting on what you're learning. You need to think about keeping your feet shoulder-width apart, adjusting your grip, or keeping your elbow bent just so. But by the time you're an expert, that information has long since become part of your procedural memory. You're no longer using your conscious brain to get the job done. Your stroke is smoother, more assured, and more accurate. Likewise, your decisions at work are made quickly and with confidence. Thinking about what you're doing, rather than simply being unnecessary, can actually become disruptive.

Whether you're a pro golfer or a seasoned executive in an international firm, the solution is to reduce the burden on your prefrontal cortex whenever possible by relying more heavily on the brain's secret weapon, unconscious intuition.

Placing an emphasis on using your unconscious brain can increase the speed, efficiency, and accuracy of your performance. The unconscious can play a starring role in how we make decisions, solve problems, and take creative approaches.

INTUITIVE DECISIONS

When Captain Chesley "Sully" Sullenberger's commercial jet-liner was critically disabled in 2009 by Canada geese that were abruptly sucked into the engine, he acted quickly and was able to make an emergency landing in the Hudson River. All 155 passengers on board survived. Although the incident turned him into a nationally recognized hero, Sullenberger was more circumspect: "One way of looking at this," he told CBS news anchor Katie Couric, "might be that for forty-two years, I've been making small, regular deposits in this bank of experience, education, and training. And on January 15 the balance was sufficient so that I could make a very large withdrawal."[5]

THERE was nothing particularly imposing physically about Wayne Gretzky, arguably the greatest hockey player of all time, and yet he seemed to have an uncanny knack for being in the right place at the right time. According to Gretzky, "To be a winner, you don't skate to where the puck is, but you skate to where it will be."[6] Thanks to his extraordinary use of what fans call "hockey sense," no player in NHL history has more career points than Wayne Gretzky. He's also the only player to total more than 200 points in a single season. And he managed to reach that milestone four separate times.[7]

NEITHER Captain Sullenberger nor Wayne Gretzky had the luxury of time. They both had to make their decisions quickly and intuitively. Although there's a common misconception that intuitive decisions are random and signify a lack of skill, the exact opposite is true. Intuitive decisions are often the product of years of experience and thousands of hours of practice. They represent the most efficient use of your accumulated expertise.

A FLIP OF A COIN

Among those who question the value of intuitive decision making, some worry that it's as random as flipping a coin. Ironically, flipping a coin can actually be a great way of making a decision. But probably not in the way you think. If you're torn between two choices of seemingly equal merit, flip a coin. If you're satisfied with or relieved by the decision the coin made for you, then go with it. On the other hand, if the result of the coin toss leaves you uneasy and even makes you wonder why you used a coin toss to decide such an important decision in the first place, then go with the other choice instead. Your "gut feeling" alerted you to the right decision. It took a random coin toss to make this obvious. What is this "gut feeling"? To answer that, we need to better understand the anatomy of intuition.

THE ANATOMY OF INTUITION

Two regions of your brain drive intuitive decisions: your basal ganglia and your insula. As you probably remember from chapter 4, your basal ganglia manage the stored patterns and routines that reflect your accumulated expertise. Your insula (also known as your insular cortex) handles body awareness. It is acutely sensitive to any changes in your body. It not only keeps track of vital functions like your heartbeat, but it also notices when your skin is cool or hot, when your bladder is full, or when your stomach is bloated. In short, it's helpful to have around!

When you are called upon to make a decision, your unconscious brain often begins working on it right away, even though you might not be consciously aware of it. When you finally attempt to make a conscious decision, your brain compares it to the decision your unconscious has already made. If the conscious and unconscious decisions correspond, your brain registers a subtle reward response. If the decisions disagree, it registers a threat. Both responses trigger changes in your body.

If the brain predicts a reward and the reward doesn't come, it registers surprise. The anterior cingulate cortex (ACC) handles this. Dense with dopamine neurons, it is an error detector. When an expected reward doesn't come, the ACC generates an electrical signal known as an error-related negativity. (It's sometimes referred to as the "oh shit!" circuit.[8])

Thanks to the insula, people with good awareness of their bodies feel a change. This is why intuitive decisions are often called gut feelings. We sense whether a choice is a good one or a bad one by noting the subtle change in how we feel.

Expert Intuition

Expert intuition isn't an exclusively unconscious affair. Just as Sully Sullenberger suggested, it draws heavily from your bank of experience. It begins with consciously assembling all the data you'll need to make your decision and then keeping your conscious mind distracted while your unconscious rolls up its sleeves and gets to work.

Expert intuitive decision making performs the same basic operation as conscious decision making, except it does so much faster and more efficiently, taking less of a toll on your brain's limited resources. Think of it this way: You can wash your dishes by hand. Or you can carefully load them into the dishwasher, add some detergent, close the door, turn on the machine, and then settle in to read a book or go for a run. While you're gone, the dishes will be getting cleaner faster and with much less effort on your part. Using expert intuition is like washing your dishes in the dishwasher.

One of the reasons intuitive decision making often works better is because it has more brain space. Let's say you have several hundred books at home and you want to put them all in alphabetical order. Conscious analysis is like trying to reorder your books in the cramped confines of a telephone booth. Intuition is like rearranging them on a spacious living room floor.

When psychologists Joseph Johnson and Markus Raab showed team handball players videos of high-level games, they would stop the clips periodically and ask each player to quickly choose his best possible next move. Then, before moving on, they gave the players time to think about other possible alternative moves. What the researchers found was that the first choice was almost always the best one.[9]

More so than perhaps any other competitive activity, chess is recognized as a highly analytical, brain-intensive game. Yet the true chess masters provide a surprising insight into how chess moves are really made. "Of course, analysis can sometimes give more accurate results than intuition, but usually it's just a lot of work," said Magnus Carlsen. Carlsen should know. At age twenty-two, he passed legendary Grandmaster Garry Kasparov to become the highest-ranked chess player in history. Although chess players have a reputation for being hyperrational analysts, Carlsen's world champion method is decidedly different. "I normally do what my intuition tells me to do," he explained in an interview with the *Financial Times*. "Most of the time spent thinking is just to double-check."[10]

Why We Don't Trust Intuition

If expert intuition is faster, more effective, and more accurate than conscious decision making, then why don't more people and companies use it?

Take a moment to consider: What if you told senior management that you wanted to expand the company's business into a new market and spend large sums of money doing so all because you had a hunch? Imagine how far that would go. Scenarios like that make even people who understand the power of intuition wince a little, wondering to themselves (or even out loud), "But what if it didn't work?"

An unfortunate by-product of this ingrained uneasiness with intuition is what German psychologist Gerd Gigerenzer calls defensive decision making. In the risk-averse corporate world, executives who rely on intuitive decisions frequently feel the burden of backing up those decisions with data. This often forces them to supply a detailed explanation *after the fact* for a decision that originally grew out of a gut feeling. Similarly, experienced doctors who make an instantaneous assessment of a patient's condition may still feel compelled to conduct a series of costly and sometimes invasive tests to prove what they knew all along. Even worse, a leader may settle on a second or even a third choice simply because he knows he can provide facts and figures that appear to support it. Gigerenzer estimates that this skittish, inferior approach is used in one-third to one-half of important decisions. As he told *Harvard Business Review*, "Defensive decision making hurts the company and protects the decision maker."[11]

The common distrust of intuition stems from a number of factors: historical prejudice, biased analysis, and a misunderstanding about what intuition really means.

Historical Prejudice

For more than 250 years, rationality has been king—and with good reason. The Enlightenment ushered in an age of reason, bolstered science and mathematics, destroyed sometimes-deadly superstitions, and paved the way for modern democracy. On some matters, however, the Enlightenment was not quite as enlightened as it seemed. It had at least one regrettable casualty that amounted to cultural collateral damage: intuition. In an age where reason rules, intuition is anathema. Leaders, the vast majority of whom were male and placed rationality above all, added insult to injury by referring to "going with your gut" not only as "intuition" but as "feminine intuition," a double insult suggesting that intuition was something to avoid at all costs.[12]

And with that, the die was cast. Intuition has been working to recover its reputation ever since.

Biased Analysis

Although we like to think that we have advanced since the Enlightenment, old habits can be difficult to break. We still place a premium on conscious, rational thought over expert intuition. Another actor we can point a finger of blame at is right in the middle of our forehead: the prefrontal cortex. Is it any wonder that the seat of our conscious thought would look askance at decision making that relies on the unconscious instead?

The PFC, the same part of the brain that is the hero when it comes to concentration and analysis (see chapter 3), is working like a malicious backstabber in some royal court intrigue to convince us that intuition couldn't possibly be superior to the conscious and conscientious service it so proudly provides.

Call it an inferiority complex perhaps, but it's not surprising that a region of the brain that is explicitly conscious would be suspicious of a rival system that is explicitly unconscious.

Intuition or rational analysis? Which should it be? When you think about it, the general prejudice against intuition may be wrong, but it makes sense. After all, what part of your brain is deciding which method is superior? Your conscious brain, of course! Would you trust a Most Beautiful Baby pageant in which the one and only judge has his own infant entered in the contest? Of course not! Your conscious brain is naturally biased in favor of—you guessed it—your conscious brain! As author and neurologist Dr. Robert A. Burton once described it in his book *A Skeptic's Guide to the Mind*, "hiring the mind as a consultant for understanding the mind feels like the metaphoric equivalent of asking a known con man for his self-appraisal and letter of reference."[13]

One of the chief characteristics of intuition is that we can't always articulate what led us to make a particular decision. Our gut reaction and subsequent decision are the only elements of a complicated process that come into consciousness. This explains why the fire lieutenant attributed his decision to ESP. At the time, he was unable to supply a more satisfactory explanation. He just *felt* that it was the right thing to do. You can imagine why this would create problems for our conscious brain, which, rather than being about feeling, is more about explaining. In fact, neuroscientist David Eagleman sometimes likes to compare the different regions of the brain to a "team of rivals." The regions may work together, but each has a slightly different agenda. Intuition seems like a direct attack on the agenda of our rational brain.[14]

Or is it? One of the common complaints against intuition

is that it's "too emotional." Officially, we tend to place a premium on cold, calculated decision making. Unfortunately, that shows a fundamental misunderstanding of how the rational decision-making process actually works.

One of the better-known patients in modern neuroscience is known as EVR. He had a brain tumor in a specific part of his frontal lobe known as the ventromedial prefrontal cortex, or vmPFC. Although the tumor was removed successfully and EVR seemed superficially normal, he became professionally and personally unreliable. He often showed up late for work, failed to complete tasks, and seemed utterly incapable of making even the simplest decisions. The damage to his vmPFC hadn't harmed either his memory or his intelligence. What it had done, however, was to sever a vital connection between the thinking and feeling parts of his brain.[15]

Choices are made with goals in mind, and goals in turn are attached to our reward and threat circuits. In other words, each decision we make—even something as trivial as deciding what task to tackle next or what to order for lunch—has an emotional component. Emotions don't just color our decisions; they are an essential part of the decision-making process. According to neuroscientist Antonio Damasio, on one level even rational decisions are gut decisions.

On one level even rational decisions are gut decisions.

Without an emotional component, we are unable to keep goals in mind. And without goals, it becomes virtually impossible to decide what information is relevant to making a decision and what is immaterial. In EVR's case, this meant that his brain was flooded with trivia, rendering it incapable of making even the simplest choice.[16]

We Don't Understand What Intuition Means

If we say our intuition tells us that soccer superstar Lionel Messi is going to score a goal on this next corner kick, that's really not intuition. That's a glorified wild guess. If someone looks at your palm and says you're going to meet a tall dark stranger, that's not expert intuition, that's twenty-five dollars you could've spent on dinner or a movie instead. If you have a traumatic experience in a particular town or neighborhood, you may get a "bad feeling" when you return there. But that isn't intuition. That's an oversensitive threat response.

In this book, when we refer to intuition, we mean "expert intuition," a speedier way of analyzing information using accumulated expertise. But the expertise needs to be there or intuition won't work. What we don't mean is taking a wild guess. Unfortunately, that's what many people think of when they hear the word "intuition." If you're new to a subject or a business, then using intuition is unwise and probably irresponsible. But if you've accumulated expertise over time, then intuition may be the best way to go.

One of the problems with properly investigating intuition is that over the years it has acquired an unscientific reputation. In fact, if you do an Internet search on the word "intuition," you will find a garbled mixture of legitimate neuroscience and magical mumbo jumbo.

In reality, there's nothing magical about expert intuition. It is based on solid, mainstream neuroscience. The product of accumulated expertise and practice, intuition operates by combining past experience with external cues to arrive at a decision that registers on the unconscious level and then is interpreted by a body response that we commonly refer to as a "gut feeling." According to decision-making expert Herbert Simon, "intuition and judgment are simply analyses frozen into habit."[17]

These gut decisions aren't typically as instantaneous as they may seem. On the contrary, your unconscious mind often lays the foundation for an answer well before you've even had a chance to pose the question.[18] In fact, throughout your life, your unconscious is building a veritable encyclopedia of experiences. Former Disney CEO Michael Eisner agrees: "Gut instincts are the sum total of those experiences— millions and millions and millions of them. And that sum total enables you to make reasonable decisions."[19]

While it's true that lightning-fast intuitive decision making is occasionally susceptible to manipulation, it's equally true that time-consuming (and often budget-busting) rational decision making can be prone to massive misjudgment as well.

Why We Shouldn't Always Trust Rational Decision Making

Few business fiascos in recent history match the 1985 introduction of New Coke, the meticulously thought-out reformulation of the iconic soft drink brand designed to beat archrival Pepsi in the famous taste test known as the Pepsi Challenge. Although the Coca-Cola Company had oodles of encouraging data to support the change, the new drink's debut was an utter disaster. In fact, in order to quiet substantial public outcry, Coke was compelled after just seventy-nine days to bring back the "old" Coke under the name Coca-Cola Classic. Most loyal Coke drinkers could determine with a split second of "gut instinct" what Coca-Cola was unable to fathom with months of research and a mountain of data: "Why would I want to drink a new Coke that tastes more like Pepsi when I can drink Pepsi instead?"

OK, so intuition isn't perfect, but then neither is rational decision making. The Coca-Cola saga is just one high-profile example in which rational decision making turned out to be wrong, wrong, wrong. And there are plenty more.

Clayton Christensen's classic best-selling business book, *The Innovator's Dilemma,* tells the tale of how established industries were confident that upstart rivals posed no threat. Department stores weren't concerned about the prospect of discount stores. Nor were mainframe computer companies worried about the rise of personal computers. Manufacturers of cable-actuated earthmoving machines saw no reason to fear the introduction of hydraulic-powered equipment. Why weren't these companies worried? Because they'd carefully done their homework and had the numbers to prove it. They each made a rational decision to stay the course and continued on a path that would prove to be a collision course.[20]

Although the once-mammoth Xerox Corporation dominated the photocopying market, to its credit, the company appreciated the importance of research and development, and with that in mind started Xerox PARC, the Palo Alto Research Center, in the early 1970s. Unfortunately, the tools that were being developed at PARC—including the mouse, the graphical user interface, and the laser printer—started to make management a little nervous. Concerned that some of the innovations might undermine the company's core business of copy machines, Xerox kept the ideas under wraps. But that didn't discourage visitors to the center, including a couple of youngsters named Bill Gates and Steve Jobs. Years later, Jobs looked back on that monumental visit with disbelief. "They just had no idea what they had," he said.[21] Without the tools developed at PARC, computing in the Internet age would be almost inconceivable. Yet rational decision making prevented Xerox from taking advantage of them.

When in Doubt, Delegate

Given the potential for failure that both intuition and rational decision making hold, what's a leader to do? A time-honored management strategy also applies to individual decision making. The optimum way to use your brain in many decision-making scenarios is to delegate the lion's share of the work to your unconscious brain and rely on your conscious primarily to monitor and vet the unconscious decision-making process. The unconscious excels at getting the job done quickly and efficiently. The conscious is best at double-checking to make sure that it has been done right. There's a reason why the key activities inside the prefrontal cortex are commonly called executive functions!

Tips for Increasing Your Intuitive Decision-Making Skills

Although some people are naturally more intuitive than others, intuition can be improved and refined by increasing your expertise and enhancing your body awareness.

1. **Pave a path toward expertise.** The best intuitive decisions arise from when you unconsciously tap into a considerable wealth of experience and expertise. But if you're not currently an expert in a particular subject, then you're better off using analysis.
2. **Improve your body awareness.** So-called gut feelings are a key component of expert intuition. Mindfulness (as discussed in chapter 3) has been found to thicken gray matter of the right anterior insula, the region that drives your body's recognition of small warning signs.[22]

3. **Learn when—and when not—to trust your intuition.** Intuitive decisions based on accumulated expertise are effective and usually reliable. Decisions based on ingrained stereotypes or prejudices are not.

The unconscious plays a key role not only in effective decision making but also in problem solving. Although there's still a vital role for rational, consciously calculated decisions to play, some of the world's most innovative ideas are the product of creative insights. They have arisen in a flash of inspiration and have come as a result of a wandering mind. Learning the factors that lead to creative insight can be crucial in setting the stage for innovation.

RATIONAL PROBLEM SOLVING

There are many instances in which rational problem solving is sufficient and even superior and other instances in which it's your only option. Almost any mathematical problem, even if you use a calculator, is solved rationally. No matter how hard you try, the sum of a long column of figures is unlikely to pop into your head in a sudden aha moment.

Here's a classic example of a problem that requires rational problem solving. After a nearby house was robbed, police were able to round up four suspects—A, B, C, and D—and take statements from each of them.

- A said, "C did it."
- B said, "I didn't do it."
- C said, "D did it."
- D said, "C lied when he said that I did it."

As it turns out, only one of the four statements was true, and only one of the suspects committed the crime. Can you figure out who told the truth and who committed the crime? (The correct answer is at the bottom of the page.*)

It is virtually impossible for the solution to this particular problem to suddenly pop into your head. You need to logically think through the possible scenarios to arrive at the correct answer. Rather than tapping into the capacious space of your unconscious, rational problem solving uses the constrained confines of your prefrontal cortex to consciously analyze, compare, and rearrange information.

Other problems can be solved both ways—either rationally or with creative insight. Scrambled word puzzles provide a good example. Some people can look at the following characters and immediately unscramble them:

ARNIB

Those who do are using creative insight. The speed at which they arrive at the answer is a testament to the power of the unconscious. Others may find it necessary to methodically try out various letter combinations until they finally arrive at the correct answer. That's an example of rational problem solving. It may be conscious and systematic, but because it uses the limited space of the prefrontal cortex, it's also a lot slower. (By the way, the answer to the scrambled word is BRAIN.)

---

* D told the truth. B committed the crime.

CREATIVE INSIGHTS

Ancient Greek scholar and mathematician Archimedes finally arrived at a method for assessing the purity of metal while he was soaking in the tub. If the story is to be believed, he was so excited by the discovery that he ran naked through the streets of Syracuse shouting, "Eureka," which is Greek for "I've found it." More than 2,000 years later, boy wonder and television pioneer Philo Farnsworth suddenly figured out a way to generate a video image while he was methodically mowing the fields of hay on his family's farm.[23] As the well-known legend of Archimedes and the lesser-known story of Philo Farnsworth both demonstrate, some of the world's greatest discoveries have come from a burst of creative insight.

The Anatomy of Creative Insights

Thanks to a number of key technical innovations from the past twenty-five years, neuroscientists finally have a pretty good idea of how these creative insights occur. In general, they work in three stages: the impasse, the moment of insight, and the confirmation.

The Impasse

We all know the feeling of an impasse. We have a problem to solve. We've been racking our brain for hours, perhaps even days, and have been unable to find an answer. In these situations, your brain usually brings out the big guns, the regions of your prefrontal cortex, in order to put the full force of your cognitive ability into it.

Paradoxically, the harder you strive to consciously solve the problem, the harder it is to solve it. (We are all familiar with this on a more mundane level, with the so-called tip-of-the-tongue syndrome, when we know we have the answer but just can't seem to articulate it.) After all, this is not a problem of pure calculation. You're not adding a long column of figures or translating an obscure text from an ancient language. Although we often have a hard time realizing it in these situations, more is quite often less. Normally our ability to concentrate intensely is an advantage. But in this case it actually limits our ability to make the kind of connections that lead to creative insights.

As we've already seen, your intense focus relies on the three key neurotransmitters—dopamine, noradrenaline, and especially acetylcholine—to shut out all extraneous stimuli. But what constitutes extraneous when it comes to a creative insight? Ah, there's the rub. Unfortunately, this is a case in which the prefrontal cortex actually does too good a job of shutting out extraneous material. Possible avenues for solving the problem are dismissed out of hand. In fact, this quite often happens unconsciously, so you aren't even aware that they ever were options. Dysfunctional teams often have living, breathing versions of the prefrontal cortex. You know the type. They're the ones who, when someone makes an unconventional suggestion, reflexively say, "Nah! That'll never work!" and often succeed in shutting down all further discussion in that area. That's what creates the impasse in creative insight, the prefrontal cortex's overly strict elimination of distractions that may not be distractions after all.

To measure the activity in our brains that leads up to a eureka moment, neuropsychologists often use what are known as insight problems. Here's a typical example:

Rachel and Rebecca were born on the same day of the same month of the same year. They share the same mother and the same father, and yet they aren't twins. How is this possible?

In general, less than 20 percent of the people tested on problems like this arrive at the solution. Yet those who do often know right away that their answer is correct.[24]

If you need to better understand the sort of tunnel vision that leads to the initial impasse in creative insight, you need look no further than the first three words of the problem: Rachel and Rebecca. Your PFC, in a well-meaning but wrong-headed effort to streamline your problem-solving process, probably jumped to the conclusion that the two girls are twins. Thus, when you reach the end of the problem and are told that they *aren't* twins, it's too late. Your PFC is already trapped in its previous mind-set.

The reason the impasse is critical is because your conscious mind takes it as a signal to give up. The PFC basically says, "You mean I did all that work to eliminate distractions and you *still* haven't solved the problem? I'm going out for a beer. You're on your own."

And with that, the PFC releases the tight grip it had on the incoming stimuli that could've bombarded you with brain-draining diversions. Suddenly, they all rush in. It's almost as though you've been wearing earplugs and a blindfold and have now removed both. The sounds seem more intense, and the normal room light momentarily makes you squint. Things that you ignored become almost impossible to discount. Your PFC is off having a beer and has left the unconscious parts of your brain holding the fort back at work.

That is when the magic happens.

The Moment of Insight

Creative insights come from a region of the brain located just above your ear called the anterior superior temporal gyrus (aSTG). Whereas concentration is all about precision, creative insight is all about making connections.

Suddenly it dawns on you that twins aren't the only children who can be born on the same day of the same month of the same year. Rachel and Rebecca have another sibling who was born the exact day that they were. They aren't twins. They're triplets!

One of the key predictors of an imminent insight is a steady emanation of alpha rhythms from the right hemisphere.[25] Alpha waves signal a departure from goal-oriented and intentional thoughts and are a sign of deep relaxation.[26] They appear to shut out visual stimuli that might serve as a distraction to the problem solving.[27]

Three hundred milliseconds before you arrive at the answer, there is a spike in your brain's gamma rhythm, its highest electrical frequency.[28] Gamma rhythms are believed to come from the binding of neurons. Your brain is almost literally connecting the dots.[29]

What's key is that the mental calculations that lead to creative insights are unconscious. "If Archimedes had consciously monitored his own thoughts in the bath," neuroscientist Joydeep Bhattacharya of Goldsmiths, University of London, explained, "he never would have shouted 'Eureka.' "[30]

The Confirmation

One of the peculiar elements of a creative insight is the strange sense of certainty that you feel when you finally arrive at the solution. The prefrontal cortex lights up in recognition of a correct answer, even when we don't arrive at the answer ourselves.[31] The PFC in effect has been operating behind our backs, surreptitiously involving the regions of the brain that are necessary for solving the problem and only informing us after they've successfully arrived at the right answer. By the time the solution bursts into consciousness as an aha moment, it may be exciting enough to drive us to run naked through the streets of Syracuse, but as far as your PFC is concerned, it's already old news.[32]

Conditions for Creative Insights

Although you can't consciously trigger creative insights, you can do some things to help set the stage for them. When it comes to aha moments, some conditions are more conducive than others. We demonstrate this in our seminars when we divide attendees into two groups and give each group the same creative insight puzzle to solve.

Both groups are supplied with six pencils and asked to devise a way to create four equilateral triangles from them. Initially the problem seems insoluble since there don't appear to be enough pencils. Believe it or not, the problem has a very elegant solution.

Always one step away from diabolical, we prepare the two groups a little differently. Each is unaware that the other has received a slightly different context, although the goal of both is identical. With the first group, we try to foster an environment that would encourage aha moments. With the second, we do the opposite by attempting to set conditions that would actually discourage creative insights.

Setting the Stage for "Aha!"

When confronted with a problem that requires creative insight, a number of factors can increase your odds of experiencing an aha moment.

1. **Make it fun.** People are usually more likely to generate creative ideas when they are happy and laughing.

2. **Throw away the box.** Don't just think outside the box; get rid of it. Creativity almost always thrives on an absence of restriction and structure.

3. **Shift gears.** After working on the problem for a few moments, take a break and do something completely different, such as singing or exercising. (If the activity seems silly, so much the better. See number 1.) Focusing exclusively on a problem can be bad for creativity because you shut out the rest of the brain, which might otherwise be able to assist in finding the solution.

4. **Listen to yourself.** Pay attention to your own feelings, and be mindful of your inner awareness. Quiet provides the ideal atmosphere for this approach. Feel free to close your eyes if it helps. It is the individual brain itself that has the eureka insight. You can't have this kind of insight when you are focusing on what other people are doing.

5. **Hold your tongue.** Wait before you verbalize. Talking has no measurable effect on analytical problem solving, but it can be disruptive to the intuition you need for insight problem solving.[33] Granted, your clever idea will eventually have to be shared, but too much half-baked chitchat can interfere with the incubation of creative thoughts—not just yours but those of your colleagues as well. For insight problems, silent groups find the solution more than 60 percent of

the time, while verbal problem solvers find the solution only slightly more than 30 percent of the time.

FIVE SIMPLE THINGS YOU CAN DO TO DISCOURAGE CREATIVITY

Although these methods aren't foolproof, if you're dead set on squelching any creativity in your team, these simple rules should help you drastically reduce the chances of an insightful breakthrough.

1. **Dampen the overall mood.** Bad news, finger-pointing, or even a free-floating tirade should help to start things off on the wrong foot.
2. **Create a lot of stress.** Luckily, bad moods and high stress often go hand in hand. If your team seems grumpy but still strangely relaxed, turn up the heat by reminding them that failure isn't an option and by setting an unreasonable deadline.
3. **Follow a strict set of guidelines.** A straitjacket of structure should help to keep any pesky creative urges safely under wraps. Come up with a script and stick to it!
4. **Keep everyone's eye on the ball.** Clear the meeting room of anything that seems extraneous or fun and demand that people pay close attention at all times.
5. **Encourage chaos and cross talk.** Silence may be golden but not when your goal is to torpedo creative impulses. Call for a lot of chatting and insist that everyone do his or her thinking out loud.

Secretly using these two lists as our guidelines, we set up one group according to the five keys for cultivating creativity and the other one using principles designed to deliberately discourage creative insight. Time and again, our results have sent a powerful message to the participants of both groups.

There are clear steps you can take to improve your odds of arriving at creative insights. Of course, creativity doesn't always come in a flash. People in a wide variety of professions still manage to think creatively without waiting for the lightning bolt of inspiration.

THE CREATIVITY CONNECTION

When Swiss inventor George de Mestral returned from a hunting trip in the mountains, covered with ornery little burrs, he wondered whether the principle that made the burrs attach so securely could be used to create a fastener that didn't require buttons, snaps, or zippers. The result of his creative curiosity was Velcro. De Mestral's original idea grew out of his ability to look beyond the obvious and make connections that most other hikers would have missed.

Whereas creative insight is using the power of your unconscious to solve a particular problem, creativity is characterized by openness to options in all directions and the ability to tap into your unconscious to make innovative links, associations, and discoveries that might not otherwise have occurred to you.

That Reminds Me: How Creativity Works

Creative people have an increased capacity for what is known as *divergent thinking*, the ability to come up with a lot of responses to an open-ended probe. This process of making connections arises from the association cortices, which synthesize information the brain receives, attempting to make sense out of a variety of stimuli, both internal and external.[34] The association cortices are most active when the default network (aka the narrative network) is dominant (see chapter 3), which explains why we are typically at our most creative when we allow our minds to wander.

"I Know. You're Working."

When he was still a teenager, a writer we know was sitting motionless on a living room chair, staring into space, apparently brooding. When his mother walked by, she said softly, "I know. You're working."

Perhaps it helped that her husband, our friend's father, was also a writer, but it turns out she was absolutely right. Our friend had a creative assignment and had encountered an impasse.

Creativity isn't like making sausages or chopping wood. Turning the crank even faster or swinging the ax with increased ferocity and strength is unlikely to improve your production. Now, thanks to neuroimaging, psychologists have confirmed what artists and scientists have long suspected: Creativity depends as much on your unconscious mind as it does on your conscious. And for that, it requires conscious downtime.

Notice that we qualified that word "downtime" with "conscious." That's because it doesn't mean you stop working. It just means that you're no longer consciously aware that you're working. Typically that means directing your conscious away from the task at hand so that your unconscious can deal with it undisturbed. If you have a clear-cut task to complete, a set of directions to follow, a mountain to climb, even a book or a magazine article to finish reading, the best course of action to follow is to focus on it, full strength. But if the problem or assignment is a creative one, then focusing on it can often be the worst course of action.

Focusing on being creative is a fundamental contradiction. Whereas focusing involves eliminating all but the most relevant information, the purpose of creativity is to establish unique connections from information that may have seemed irrelevant at first. When you think creatively, you don't focus. You blur.

Throughout history, our instincts have served us well. And as scientific evidence has made increasingly clear, expert intuition, creative insight, and creativity in general are all the product of our powerful unconscious brain.

DESPITE what he may have originally thought, the firefighter who evacuated his colleagues from a burning house just seconds before the floor collapsed wasn't seeing into the future. He was relying on expert intuition.[35]

The heat of the living room, the comparative silence of the flames, and the fire's apparent resistance to water were all inconsistent with a kitchen fire. That's because the fire wasn't in the kitchen. It was coming up from the basement. That's why the living room floor was so hot and why the sound of the fire seemed quieter than normal. And because the flames that had come up through the kitchen were just the tip of the fire, it also explained why the water was so ineffective in extinguishing them.[36]

The lieutenant had no conscious awareness of any of these details. Yet thanks to years of firefighting experience, he had a powerful feeling that something was wrong. And, as it turned out, he was right.[37]

There's nothing random or lucky about arriving at a decision through intuition or solving a problem through creative insight. Although the unconscious is fast-working and powerful, you still need to do your homework first. As Louis Pasteur once said, "Chance favors only the prepared mind."

The clearest path to the kind of preparation you need is through learning, which, not coincidentally, is the subject of the next chapter.

CHAPTER 5 IN A NUTSHELL

KEY POINTS FROM "UNLEASH YOUR UNCONSCIOUS"

Your unconscious runs the show. Even when you make what seems to be a conscious decision, your unconscious brain does most of the deciding.

Unleashing your unconscious. When given limited time and limited information, experts often make better decisions. The tight restrictions force the brain to tap into the power, speed, and calculating capacity of the basal ganglia, where acquired expertise is stored.

Trust us. We're experts! Because they rely on the stronger, speedier basal ganglia, intuitive decisions made by experts are often superior to rational conclusions arrived at through conscious calculation.

Beginners need more time. Unlike their expert colleagues, less experienced leaders typically need more time, require more information, and will usually have to do a lot of the processing with the help of the slower and less capacious PFC.

Don't force experts to explain their decisions. The fact that experts frequently make their best calls unconsciously can make it difficult to explain just how they arrived at them. Forcing an expert to supply an after-the-fact justification for an intuitive decision may lead to hesitation and second-guessing that could undermine the original action.

Taking the analytical approach. To optimize conditions for rational processing, find a quiet corner, minimize distractions, and concentrate on the problem, solving it logically step-by-step.

Creating conditions for an aha moment. If the problem you have is a creative one, your overall mood, your level of focus, and the atmosphere around you can all play a role in triggering a sudden flash of creative insight.

Smile and it may come to you. Research has shown that a sunny disposition can increase the likelihood of an aha moment. So if you're confronted with a creative conundrum, try to make sure that you or the problem-solving team are in a good mood.

CHAPTER 6
FOSTER LEARNING

....

It May Be True That "You Can't Teach an Old Dog
New Tricks," but Then, We Aren't Dogs

WHILE driving back from Mexico to his home in California, thirty-year-old David was involved in a terrible traffic accident that left him in a coma for five weeks. Although he had to have his right arm amputated and had suffered a severe trauma to his head, when he finally regained consciousness, his parents were greatly relieved that he seemed to exhibit no deterioration in his mental capacities. Moreover, the doctors saw no obvious signs of any psychosis or other emotional disturbances.

No *obvious* signs.

Much to their shock, what his parents soon discovered was that David no longer recognized them. It wasn't that he didn't know what his parents looked like. He knew *exactly* what they looked like. But he was convinced that the two people who said they were his parents were just very clever impostors. "He looks exactly like my father, but he really isn't,"[1] he told the doctor, admitting that although the man who claimed to be his father seemed nice, he just wasn't his dad.

The woman who insisted that she was David's mother found herself in a similar predicament. One evening when she made him a dinner that he didn't enjoy, David told her, "You know, that lady who comes in the morning, she cooks much better than you." But of course the lady who had fixed him the dinner he didn't like and the better cook who had come to the house that morning were one and the same.[2]

After two months of this disturbing behavior, David's parents finally sought the help of world-renowned neuroscientist V. S. Ramachandran.

Ramachandran was able to quickly identify David's strange behavior as something called Capgras delusion. Named after the French psychiatrist Joseph Capgras, who first described the disorder in 1923, Capgras delusion is characterized as "delusional misidentification syndrome."[3] Although it is found most often in cases of paranoid schizophrenia, it also occurs in patients who have experienced brain trauma or are suffering from dementia. Perhaps because Capgras himself was a psychiatrist, the syndrome was initially thought to be Oedipal in nature. In fact, the predominant Freudian theory suggested that a patient might be attempting to resolve the intense anxiety caused by a sexual attraction to his mother by branding both parents as impostors.

As a neuroscientist, Ramachandran was understandably skeptical of this psychiatric interpretation, pointing to documented cases in which Capgras patients believed that even the family dog had been replaced by an impostor. It seemed clear to him that something else was the cause.

There was yet another wrinkle to the story that made an already strange situation even stranger. One day when his father called home, it was David who answered the phone. Although he was still firmly convinced that he was living with counterfeit parents, David had no trouble believing that the person on the other end of the line was his dad. What was it that allowed David to accept his father's authenticity on the phone but left him unable to believe him in person?

As it happens, the solution to David's mystery is also the key to why we remember some things and not others, and how we can improve the odds that what we learn will stick with us for the long term.

OUR PLASTIC BRAINS

Most people, even neuroscientists, once believed that learning was limited to your youth and that your brain was essentially hardwired by the time you reached adulthood. The expression "you can't teach an old dog new tricks" has reinforced this mistaken impression, as have countless experiences of people who tried unsuccessfully to take up a foreign language later in life or who returned to college as adults and found school to be a struggle.

Contrary to the old saying and despite anecdotal evidence, neuroscience has proved that lifelong learning is entirely possible. This concept is known as *neuroplasticity.*

Rather than being frozen when you're younger, your neurons have the potential to constantly rewire themselves throughout your life. Neuroplasticity can physically change the structure of your brain, increasing the size of particular regions and the speed with which those regions communicate with each other.

One of the most dramatic demonstrations of neuroplasticity involves some taxis, some buses, and one of the world's best-known cities.

Taxi!

Getting around London isn't easy. As humorist Dave Barry once explained, "No street ever goes in the same direction or keeps the same name for more than thirty-five yards. At that point it veers off in a new direction under a new name, assuming a whole new identity."[4] Unlike Washington, D.C., which was carefully mapped out in advance, London simply evolved. Through the centuries it steadily expanded by gobbling up unsuspecting villages and towns in its path like some sort of geographical Godzilla. No wonder there's little rhyme or reason to its layout. Granted, from time to time, the city added the occasional innovation, such as the sadistic roundabout, the evil older brother of the American traffic circle, which whirls unsuspecting motorists until all but the hardiest are completely disoriented.

A genuine navigator's nightmare, London and its 25,000 streets provided an ideal laboratory for demonstrating the brain's extraordinary capacity for change. Scientists scanned the brains of a group of London cabdrivers. Then they did the same for a group of the city's bus drivers. Two years later, they scanned the brains of both groups again. What they noticed when comparing the scans was amazing. With each cabdriver, the posterior hippocampus, a region associated with spatial learning, had increased in size, while the bus drivers showed no similar change. What accounted for the difference? Unlike the bus drivers, who traveled the same route day in and day out, the cabdrivers were constantly called upon to navigate new nooks and crannies of the city's crazy geography. The challenge of finding their way around town led to the generation of more neurons. Their brains literally expanded to accommodate the new information.[5]

The ramifications of this study are startling. And they

certainly aren't limited to people who live in London or spend their days driving a taxi. What the London cabbie study shows is that we can continue to acquire new skills well into adulthood and that the cognitive regions of our brain—commonly known as gray matter—will increase in size to help make this possible.

Lifelong learning isn't simply a slogan. It's an exciting reality.

Lifelong learning isn't simply a slogan. It's an exciting reality.

Moreover, the brain's capacity to change isn't limited to its gray matter, which occupies only about half the brain. Whereas gray matter handles our thinking, computing, decision making, and, most of all, our memory, white matter provides the brain's essential connections. If you think of gray matter as the brain's computers, then white matter can be seen as the network that links them together. Increasing your white matter can be like trading in an old dial-up modem and installing a T1 line instead. As white matter expands, the rate at which one neuron can communicate with another gets faster and faster.

People who acquire a variety of new skills—everything from juggling to meditating to ballroom dancing—show an increase in white matter as they become steadily more proficient. In other words, the ease and speed with which the brain's key regions communicate gets better and better.

An Oxford study showed that learning to juggle resulted in improved connectivity in those parts of the brain that—not surprisingly—are needed to catch the balls.[6] After six weeks of training, jugglers showed increases in white matter in the parietal lobe, the region used for what we commonly refer to as "hand-eye coordination."[7] What's remarkable is that *all* the subjects showed changes to their white matter, regardless of their abilities.[8] In fact, the benefits to the brain didn't come from the juggling but from learning something new. As University of Hamburg's Arne May, the author of earlier juggling studies, told *New Scientist,* "It suggests that learning a skill is more important than exercising what you are good at already—the brain wants to be puzzled and learn something new."[9]

When you perform an activity that requires specific neurons to fire together, they release a special protein called brain-derived neurotrophic factor (BDNF), which helps to consolidate those neurons so they fire together in the future. BDNF activates the nucleus basalis, which triggers acetylcholine. Acetylcholine, the *A* in the DNA of Peak Performance, is associated with sharper focus. BDNF also encourages the growth of myelin, a thin fatty coating that provides a slick sleeve around each neuron. Myelin is kind of like cognitive Crisco, the gloppy white vegetable shortening once common in kitchens. It's a fatty material that builds up on your nerve connections and greases the skids of your neurons, making connections from one neuron to the next more efficient and faster.[10] In short, it's the stuff that makes white matter white.

As unbelievable as it may sound, neuroplasticity can even make it possible to retrain your brain's physical abilities simply by imagining an activity instead of engaging in it. In several studies, mental practice was found to produce the same alterations to the brain's motor system wiring as physical practice.[11] So in reality, that air guitar you've been playing ever since high school may actually be providing you with genuine practice.

In the best known of these experiments, subjects were taught to play a simple melody on a keyboard. The group was split in two. One group practiced the melody two hours a day for the next five days, while the other group sat in front of the keyboard for the same amount of time and simply imagined playing the melody. Amazingly, both groups showed identical changes to their brains.[12] When called upon to play the piece, the subjects who trained on a physical keyboard had a slight edge, but a single two-hour training session was all it took to bring the mental practice group up to the level of their physical practice counterparts.[13]

In another study that is bound to make couch potatoes jump for joy (assuming they don't find even *that* too strenuous), subjects who did a physical exercise for four weeks increased their muscle strength by 30 percent, while those who only *imagined* the exercise saw a 22 percent increase in muscle strength during the same period of time. When we vividly imagine an exercise, the neurons tasked with stringing together instructions for movement are activated and strengthened, which in turn strengthens the muscles when they are contracted.[14]

Practicing Practice

Harvard-educated Bill Robertie, a world-class expert in chess, backgammon, and poker, credits his extraordinary success in these three very different games to his ability to learn how to learn. "I know how to practice," he says. "I know how to make myself better."[15]

Practice makes perfect, and practice makes practice *more* perfect. Just as practicing a particular activity improves your ability in that activity, constantly learning improves your overall ability to learn. According to neuroplasticity pioneer Dr. Michael Merzenich, learning changes the structure of the brain—and in the process further increases our capacity to learn.[16] In other words, learning how to learn is a skill in itself, and it can pave the way to more successful learning in a variety of subjects.

When you're aware of how your brain acquires knowledge and have developed strategies that capitalize on that awareness—psychologists call this metacognitive awareness—you have a powerful set of tools and techniques that should make all subsequent learning easier and more rewarding.[17]

By the way, if you needed yet another reason not to multitask (see chapter 3), here it is. Dr. Merzenich discovered that paying close attention was absolutely essential to long-term change in the wiring of the brain. When monkeys performed tasks automatically—without paying attention—they rewired their brains, but those changes didn't last.[18] Long-lasting neuroplasticity depends on that now-familiar trio that makes up the DNA of Peak Performance: dopamine, noradrenaline, and acetylcholine. While noradrenaline keeps you alert, the rewards that come from learning lead to secretion of dopamine and acetylcholine, which help to ensure that any rewiring endures.[19]

Of course, neuroplasticity is not without its downside. Bad habits can change the brain as readily as good ones. That's why if you take up a new sport or acquire new information, it is important to start off on the right foot.

First Thing's First

Thinking of taking up golf? If so, your best bet might be to take lessons right away rather than waiting until you've had a chance to play a few times. Unlearning is at least as difficult as learning, and probably even more so. Anyone who has picked up a bad habit knows this firsthand.

Bad habits actually rewire your brain, making those habits increasingly difficult to unlearn. This fact underscores not only the benefits of hiring a golf pro but also the value of early education.[20] Once you've practiced things the wrong way and the incorrect procedure has been stored in your basal ganglia (for more on habits, see chapter 4), it can be tough to remove it. That hitch in your swing or that unorthodox grip you developed when you were still experimenting may prove difficult to overcome.

The tenacity of the initial learning experience explains why a number of prominent companies (including HP, IBM, and McKinsey) hire straight out of college (or grad school) so the first thing their employees learn in the working world is the company's particular way of doing things. First-time experiences have the added advantage of novelty, which triggers dopamine, helping to make your memories of that initial experience, whether it's right or wrong, even stronger and harder to unlearn.[21] Unlearning is difficult but not impossible. It just requires the right recipe.

Oxytocin and Unlearning

Unlearning isn't simply learning in reverse. Different chemistries are involved in the two processes. When we learn something new, neurons fire together and wire together, and a chemical process occurs at the neuronal level called "long-term potentiation," or LTP, which strengthens this wiring.[22]

When the brain *unlearns* associations and disconnects neurons, another chemical process occurs, called "long-term depression," or LTD (which has nothing to do with a depressed mood state). Unlearning and weakening connections between neurons is just as plastic a process—and just as important—as learning and strengthening them. It appears that unlearning existing memories is necessary to make room for new memories in our neuronal networks. If we only strengthened connections, without weakening others, those networks would get saturated.[23]

But how do we go about unlearning? Surprisingly, evidence suggests that oxytocin, the famous "cuddle hormone" (see chapters 2 and 8), plays a role in our ability to wipe the slate clean of old information. Oxytocin is produced in a region of the brain called the hypothalamus and then released into the bloodstream.

The biologist and neuroscientist Walter J. Freeman found that sheep release oxytocin when delivering their young. Moreover, if that release is blocked, they fail to bond with their new offspring. But here's the interesting part: The sheep don't release oxytocin when they deliver their *first* litter. The neuromodulator plays a role in delivery only in the *second and subsequent* litters. Yet a ewe seems to have no trouble bonding with the offspring of her first litter. Oxytocin appears to erase old bonds in order to make way for new ones. In other words, rather than simply encouraging *new* learned behavior, oxytocin aids us in forgetting *old* learned behavior.[24]

By the way, oxytocin's role in learning and unlearning doesn't appear to be limited to lambs. Anyone who has paired up with a new partner or spouse and found themselves— often to the dismay, amusement, or confusion of longtime friends—adopting brand-new tastes in music, clothes, politics, and perhaps even friends has firsthand experience with this phenomenon. It seems that oxytocin makes our neuronal pathways more malleable, enabling us to learn—and unlearn— more readily than we normally would. We become more impressionable; as a result, change becomes easier.

Old habits may die hard, but old skills can fade fast. Another pitfall of neuroplasticity is that the brain is constantly

Old habits may die hard, but old skills can fade fast.

searching for unused or neglected neurons that it can recruit for a new purpose.

The skills in your brain are like squatters. When they detect real estate that seems vacant or fields that have gone fallow, they take them over. This means that if you stop dribbling a basketball or fail to practice the foreign language you learned way back in high school, another function is waiting in the wings to take over that territory and use it for its own purposes.[25]

Many of us commonly refer to this as "being rusty." Cognitive scientists prefer to call it *competitive neuroplasticity*. Like most of our body, the brain lives by the motto of "use it or lose it." When it comes to preserving a skill, if you want to retain it, you have to maintain it.

Similar to a person who is bored and desperately looking for something to do, neglected neurons usually find other purposes, and often quite rapidly. According to Nancy Kanwisher, a professor and researcher at MIT, "Neurons seem to 'want' input."[26]

This opportunistic tendency on the part of the brain often works in our favor. When a person goes blind, for example, the occipital lobe, the part of the brain that once handled visual stimuli, doesn't simply wither away. Instead, it gets colonized by circuits used for processing sounds. Thus, it's no coincidence that sight-impaired people often have more acute senses of hearing as well as the extraordinarily sophisticated tactile skills that are needed to differentiate the raised-dot letters used in Braille. Their plastic brains have made this adjustment.[27]

Reawakening Old Skills

Although the skills you once learned but fail to maintain may slowly fade from your memory, they're forgotten but not gone. The pathways are still there, but the space they occupy and the resources they consume have been greatly reduced.

These dormant neuronal pathways are a bit like the large purple fitness ball you once used with great enthusiasm for everything from push-ups to sitting at your desk but gradually grew tired of. Perhaps it's now deflated and sitting on a shelf in your closet or garage, where it takes up less room. But if you should decide to begin using it again, you don't have to go out and buy another one. All you have to do is take it out and fill it with air, and it will be almost as good as new.

Once-established but rarely used neuronal pathways aren't purple and aren't exactly deflated. Instead, key connections called dendritic spines, which look something like the buds on a fruit tree in early spring, grow or shrink depending on whether the skill is practiced or discontinued. As a result, when you relearn an old skill, you don't have to start from scratch. The spines wake up from their winter of neglect and expand in a springtime of renewal.[28] That explains, among other things, why you can hop on a bicycle after a thirty-year hiatus and still pedal with the same skill and proficiency you first developed as a child.

LEARN WITH YOUR HEART, NOT WITH YOUR HEAD

Despite its seemingly miraculous potential, neuroplasticity depends on a secret ingredient that you can't find in a pill or buy at any store. The stereotypical image of the highly knowledgeable person who is cold and efficient is actually at odds with the way learning really works. The key to learning is that it is a fundamentally emotional process, driven by the threat and reward circuits that reside in the limbic system.

The key to learning is that it is a fundamentally emotional process.

It's no surprise that an unpleasant experience, such as burning your hand on a hot stove, leads to immediate learning. Children who make this unfortunate mistake rarely make it a second time. The same applies to traumatic events such as the attack on the World Trade Center in 2001, which triggered what psychologists call a "flashbulb memory." Images of that morning or vivid (but not necessarily accurate) memories of where we were when we heard the news are etched in the minds of people all over America as well as in much of the world.

Although they aren't as powerful as threat responses, reward responses are the more common and much-preferred driver of successful learning. It's no coincidence that children often learn best by playing or having fun. The importance of this crucial emotional element isn't limited to learning during childhood. A man who had struggled for years to master English finally found the spark that enabled him to learn when he was able to make a connection with one of his favorite pastimes.

Tanks for the English Lesson!

By the time we met him, the Spanish executive was adamant: He would never, ever be able to learn English. He insisted that we were wasting both our time and his.

We had other ideas. Rather than following in the footsteps of our failed predecessors and starting right in with a traditional English lesson, we took some time to get to know our student first. It didn't take long to realize that outside his work this man had a definite passion. He was an enthusiastic student of World War II history and was especially fascinated with tanks. He even liked to build scale models of tanks in his limited spare time.

Suddenly, we saw our opening. It was rewarding to see this fiftysomething man's face light up and his speech quicken whenever he got to talk about his favorite subject. As our first session was drawing to a close, we left him with a modest "homework assignment": Bring along one of his scale-model tanks for the next lesson, so he could explain all about it. If he could tell us about the components of his tank in Spanish, we'd return the favor by teaching him how to explain the name and function of each part in English. You could sense that this skeptical man was looking forward to his next English lesson—perhaps for the first time in his life.

Sure enough, for the next lesson, the executive brought in a lovingly constructed and meticulously painted scale model of a tank. And although it had required a little homework on our part as well, when he methodically went through and identified each component of his tank, we were able to respond to his explanation with the equivalent in English. After that, we spent the rest of the lesson discussing tanks, but only in English.

In a short time, our reluctant executive could provide a simple, English-only description of his tank and its components. With each passing lesson we pulled further away from World War II and tanks and closer to the present day and the practical English vocabulary that a business executive needs in a global marketplace.

Hot stoves, World War II tanks, and the Twin Towers all share the element of emotional impact. In general, when information moves us, scares us, pleases us, or otherwise makes a powerful impression, we are more likely to remember it. But even this rule has its pitfalls and limitations.

When Novelty Backfires

If a teacher walks into a lecture room dressed only in a Speedo or bikini, that class is almost certain to be memorable. As for the actual content of the class, it's likely to get lost in the shuffle.

Every now and then, there are well-intentioned attempts to make information more meaningful by livening up the lesson one way or another. Unfortunately, there is a common tendency to confuse emotional relevance with sheer novelty. While attending a seminar of the psychological faculty of the Ludwig Maximilian University of Munich, we heard the sad tale of how instructors in business administration tried to freshen up a stale accounting lesson by changing the traditionally generic names in a well-worn example. "Company" became "Robot Racing Company" while "Person 1" and "Person 2" were replaced with real names, such as "Brad" and "Angelina," all with the goal of making things a little more exciting.

On one level, the strategy worked perfectly. It *was* more exciting. During class, it definitely seemed as though the students were having more fun and were more engaged. But when it came time for exams, reality reasserted itself with a vengeance. Although all the students were able to correctly remember the silly name of the company as well as the names of the people in the accounting example, their test scores were abysmal. In fact, they were the worst ever!

What happened? Rather than supporting the accounting example, the creative names actually distracted from it. Students were drawn to the novelty of the names but lost the lesson in the process. The dazzling details outshone the essential information.

Because the size of working memory is limited and the stimuli that bombard your brain are practically relentless, your prefrontal cortex is often forced to make some pretty tough choices. Dopamine, the *D* in the DNA of Peak Performance, is a primary decider. Dopamine asks, "Is it new?" And if the answer is yes, there's a good chance that your PFC will zero in on the information and your working memory will begin the process of retaining it. But if the information that is merely new is at odds with the information that is truly important, the latter is likely to get crowded out, leaving you with little or no recollection of the stuff that really matters and a dubious storehouse of titillation and trivia instead.

The lesson for leaders is clear: If you seek to increase the interest in the information you convey, be sure that the embellishments you add to liven up your lesson support your core message instead of competing with it.

Does this mean no Speedos or bikinis? Not necessarily. In his book *Brain Matters*, author and molecular biologist John Medina recalls a course on the history of cinema that he took as an undergraduate. As the instructor lectured on the portrayal of emotional vulnerability in art cinema, he began steadily and deliberately removing articles of his clothing. Stripped to just a T-shirt on top, he finally reached down to unzip his trousers, which fell to his ankles. As his trousers dropped, so did the jaws of most of the students in the classroom. Mercifully, he had on a pair of running shorts underneath. He looked out at his rapt audience and said triumphantly, "You will probably never forget now that some films use physical nudity to express emotional vulnerability."[29] And perhaps now you won't either.

An Emotional Neighborhood

Sometimes things become a lot clearer once you've had a chance to take a look at a map. Given the vital role of emotion, it makes sense that the hippocampus, the key brain area responsible for learning, resides right smack in the middle of the brain's emotional neighborhood, the limbic system. Its neighbor on one side is the amygdala, which is associated with the threat response. Its neighbor on the other side is the nucleus accumbens, which is associated with rewards.

When we acquire new information, it goes to the hippocampus, which decides whether that information is emotionally relevant and, if so, whether it's relevant in a positive or negative way. The hippocampus then compares this information with other information that has already been stored in long-term memory to determine whether this "new" information is really that new.

The principle underlying learning is an evolutionary one: "Minimize danger, maximize reward." Your brain's limbic system is constantly scanning your surroundings for things that have the potential to either hurt or help you. When it discovers them, it makes mental notes that become our long-term learning and memories. Not surprisingly, most dry textbook facts don't fit into either category. We aren't evolutionarily designed to earn an MBA or even to get the most out of a weekly company meeting. The brain is very efficient and even a little lazy. If it concludes that the information is neither threatening nor rewarding, then it unceremoniously discards it without wasting precious brainpower on something it considers irrelevant.

Outsmarting Your Brain

The brain may be ruthless, but it's also easily fooled. Let's face it, not all information you absolutely need to learn is going to be emotionally relevant. That's OK. If you can trick your brain into releasing sufficient quantities of dopamine, noradrenaline, and acetylcholine, chances are that you will still manage to learn and remember. Although nothing beats learning that is emotionally relevant and fun, there are ways that you can prime your brain for what might otherwise be an unrewarding learning experience.

Don't start with a recap. Well-meaning teachers, presenters, and leaders often make the same mistake: They start with a summary of what's gone before. But recaps are old news. They're precisely the sort of information that our brains are engineered to minimize or ignore. It's novelty that gets us to sit up and take notice. Whether you're presenting to a group or learning on your own, open with something energizing and even a little surprising. In our seminars, it's not unusual for us to start by talking about the pitfalls of comparison shopping or the bad habits of Hollywood stars. Then, once we've gotten your attention, we circle back to where we left off. With any luck, the dopamine your brain releases will provide motivation and momentum to keep you fully engaged and ready to learn.

If you can't change the subject, change the setting. If you're stuck with an old or uninspiring task, try shifting to a novel setting. Sometimes this can be as simple as changing chairs. Other times it can mean shifting to another office or location. It can even help to work on a different computer— or to write in a different font. Anything you can do that will send a message to your brain that says, "Hey, this is new!" can help to pull you out of the doldrums and into a state of rewarding productivity.

Don't Overstructure

Some structure is good, but too much can undermine learning. Most of us learn more effectively when we pick up rules implicitly. Children provide a classic example of this principle. They don't learn to talk by studying grammar. Their brains unconsciously identify the patterns and rules that structure their native language. Most of them don't know the pluperfect from the indicative. They just know what sounds right.

Surprisingly, the work it takes to make sense out of something that is loosely structured, oddly structured, or even missing some key information can make it easier to remember than something that is carefully organized with everything in place.

In a presentation at the TEDx conference in Sitka, Alaska, Daniel Coyle, author of *The Talent Code*, showed the audience two columns of word pairs and gave them fifteen seconds to memorize as many items from the lists as they could.[30]

A	B
ocean / breeze	bread / b_tter
leaf / tree	music / l_rics
sweet / sour	sh_e / sock
movie / actress	phone / bo_k
gasoline / engine	ch_ps / salsa
high school / college	pen_il / paper

When he took away the lists, Coyle asked members of the audience to name as many pairs as they could recall. Their responses were lopsided. Combinations that they could remember from column B greatly outnumbered those from column A. In fact, when a similar study was conducted in a laboratory setting, subjects were 300 percent more likely to remember items from column B than from column A.[31]

What accounted for the dramatic difference in recall? Whereas the word pairs in Column A were easy to read—they were literally spelled out for them—the pairs in Column B were a bit of a challenge. That little bit of extra effort, that tiny gap in the structure, was enough to activate a burst of noradrenaline that provides just the right amount of extra oomph to make those word pairs memorable. A little bit of uncertainty helps things stick in one's mind.

Learn with a Friend

A revolution in what is known as social cognitive neuroscience is prompting scientists to completely revise or reexamine fundamental assumptions not only about the brain but also about society as a whole. As we'll see in chapter 8, many long-held beliefs about our basic needs have been totally turned on their head. The verdict seems clear and the data support it: First and foremost, we are social creatures.

This revelation has affected everything, including our understanding of learning. In many if not most cases, it pays to learn in groups instead of individually. The social interaction that comes from learning with someone else—a friend or a learning buddy—releases oxytocin, which, as we've already seen, enhances neuroplasticity and the possibility for change. This not only explains why falling in love can profoundly change your behavior and even your personality, but it's also why children learn so well when they interact with their parents. It also reinforces the importance of being a good role model for the people around you. After changing his diet and exercise routine, a successful CEO we know lost more than thirty pounds in less than six months. Although he's never discussed it at work, he's noticed that several of his formerly chubby direct reports have started looking fitter and healthier too. If you are the boss and everyone sees you are doing a great job, then they are more likely to pick it up from you! Social interaction makes us feel good. And when we feel good, we trigger chemicals that make it easier to learn.

Keep Things Manageable

One of the principal lessons learned from implementing kaizen (see chapter 4) is that goals are easiest to accomplish when they're taken in small steps. The same principle applies to learning. Undivided and uninterrupted, even valuable, interesting information can trigger a threat response. When it finds itself overloaded, your brain is likely to activate the amygdala, which is your body's equivalent of a burglar alarm. As UCLA psychologist and author Robert Maurer explains, the key is to find a way to "tiptoe right past your amygdala."[32] When you're learning, divide a big learning task into smaller manageable pieces and take frequent breaks to allow your memory to consolidate what you've learned so far. Likewise, the thousands of facts you may need to acquire will register as less threatening and more memorable if you place an emphasis on the meanings—the bigger picture that holds these facts together—instead of getting bogged down in a deluge of details that would also be likely to sound the alarm.

Use Multimodal Learning

The capacity of your working memory is surprisingly small, but it can handle words and pictures simultaneously. What's more, other senses, like our sense of smell, bypass the working memory entirely and yet can serve as an additional trigger for recall.

In fact, the more parts of the brain that are involved when you learn something new, the more likely you are to remember it. This is because memories of that information are stored in multiple regions in the brain, and neuronal connections are made between these far-flung locations. Then in the future, if you trigger one, the others will be activated as well.

And when more of the brain is involved, you are far more likely to remember more. Think of a conversation you might have on e-mail compared with one you have in person. Even the most emotionally involved e-mails are usually harder to remember than direct, in-person conversations, in which your brain, in addition to encoding what the other person says, also notes how it was said (the volume, intonation, etc.), the expression on the other person's face, his or her posture, as well as the location of the conversation, the time of day, and perhaps even the weather.[33] Each of these elements provides an additional handle that makes the memory easier to retrieve.

IMPROVE YOUR ODDS

There are certain steps you can take to increase the likelihood that what you learn will last. A healthy lifestyle of sleep and exercise can influence both learning and memory.

Sleep on It

Getting sufficient sleep not only aids in emotional regulation (see chapter 2), but it also improves your ability to learn. It reduces the levels of stress hormones such as cortisol in your bloodstream while encouraging the growth of new nerve cells that are necessary for learning and memory. And finally, it assists the hippocampus in determining which of the information you've recently learned will be stored in long-term memory for future use and which will be discarded.[34]

If you fail to get an adequate amount of sleep, the hippocampus is unable to do its job, and you fail to remember. You may *think* you remember, but you don't. Ironically, executives often refrain from sleep so they can spend more time learning. As counterintuitive as it sounds, it makes more sense to spend *less* time learning in order to make room for sleep.

Run with It

When it comes to learning, exercise can play a crucial role by promoting the growth of new neurons and increasing your cognitive performance. Things that require focused attention and a lot of coordination between body parts, such as dancing and tennis, trigger a burst of dopamine (released when you're having fun) and acetylcholine (when you're focusing your attention and are really present in the moment). Both of these neurotransmitters help your hippocampus to perform better. And, as we know, the hippocampus is the primary place where learning occurs.

FROM LEARNING TO TEACHING

The principles that support effective learning can also be used for more effective teaching. The paramount importance of emotional relevance in both learning and memory applies to teaching and training as well. The success of teaching often hinges on the mutual connection established between you and your audience. If you run a lecture more like a seminar and provide a series of leading questions that help participants to reach your desired conclusion, then they are more likely to adopt the ideas as their own.[35] And you're apt to benefit as well. When you have to teach someone who knows less than you, you often end up learning the material better yourself.[36]

Tell Me a Story

One of the most effective means of establishing an emotional connection is through stories. A carefully constructed argument full of facts and figures may seem like the best way to get your point across, but its impact pales in comparison to that of an engaging anecdote. As Nelson Mandela once advised, "Don't talk to their minds; talk to their hearts."

Using stories to support your ideas will stimulate the social brain. As you may recall from chapter 3, our default mental network is also known as the *narrative* network. That's because we contemplate our past and look ahead to our future by forging events into chains that make sense to our brains. In short, we create stories. This provides some insight into why stories may be so effective in engaging us: They echo the way that our minds already operate.[37]

One thing is clear: Storytelling is universal.[38] Some social cognitive neuroscientists have suggested that stories grew out of a group's need for social cohesion. The tales our ancestors told may have supplied a way of communicating the latest about each member of the group. If one group member ventured too far afield and narrowly escaped an encounter with a lion, the story of his adventure would not only raise his status, but it would also provide valuable, useful information for the other group members. After all, much of what we learn, we learn indirectly. If someone eats berries from a particular plant and gets violently ill, his cautionary tale saves everyone else in the group from making the same mistake. We don't all need to eat the same poisonous berries to learn that they are bad for us.[39]

Stories typically trigger either a reward or a threat response. They activate our emotions and increase our receptiveness to information. When we hear a story, we often feel a desire to connect it to our own life and experiences. Our insula (the part of the brain that detects body awareness) is activated, and we respond viscerally to the joy, pain, humor, and disgust of the narrative. All these reactions help us to become more receptive and engaged.[40]

In fact, when you truly have your audience rapt, the evidence from brain imaging indicates that they start to anticipate what you're going to say. This doesn't mean that your story is dull and predictable. On the contrary, it shows that your listeners are so fully engaged that they're excited to find out what's going to happen next![41]

Granted, not all stories are universally effective. A story that wins over one group may fall flat with another. Its effect can even vary within audiences that seem at first glance to be composed of like-minded people. Some level of connection is essential for a story to be successful. We need to be able to relate to it. A study by psychologist Melanie C. Green showed that prior knowledge and experience can influence the level on which you are immersed in a story. Thus, a story about a gay Boy Scout is more likely to resonate deeply with people who are gay or have been Boy Scouts. More likely, but not exclusively: Green also found that people who demonstrate a high level of empathy are more susceptible to being swept up by a story, regardless of their prior knowledge or experience.[42]

Recent neurocognitive research has revealed another fascinating aspect of storytelling. We are drawn to stories that we think will be emotionally relevant to others in our social group. So when we listen to a story, a part of our brain is deciding whether it's a story worth retelling. If we decide that it is, our attention intensifies and our learning and memory increase. If you convey information in a story that people want to share, whether that sharing takes place in person or via social media, then you have succeeded, not only as a storyteller, but also as a teacher.

From the standpoint of a leader and a teacher, the power of stories is not simply that they can be moving and entertaining. They can also be persuasive. Another study done by Dr. Green suggests that people are more receptive to ideas when their minds are in story mode as opposed to when they are in a more analytical mind-set.[43] If you can illustrate the points you want to stress by using stories, you are far more likely to get your message across—and have it remembered.

Using words and images in concert to tell a story will also improve the effectiveness of teaching. The more parts of the brain that are involved in acquiring new information, the better the chances are that it will be retained and remembered. That explains, in part, why the cartoons or memes we encounter in social media are often more vivid and memorable than the text-only articles we read or the detailed messages we receive.

USE AVERSIVE LEARNING WITH CARE

A training video for a major airline warns employees not to get too close to a jet engine when it's operating. Rather than providing rules or even text, it just shows a flight attendant who makes the mistake of walking too close and is sucked into the engine with a result that would make even seasoned viewers of Hollywood splatter movies feel nauseated. However, the video makes its point, and the airline has never had this type of deadly incident occur.

An elevator company wanted its mechanics to be well aware of the small space at the bottom of every elevator shaft that could conceivably save their lives if they were ever trapped beneath a free-falling elevator car. New mechanics were asked to crouch into a ball at the base of the shaft, and then the elevator was sent speeding down toward them. It was a harrowing and even sadistic experience, but it was a lesson that all of them survived and almost certainly will never forget.

Although teaching usually works best by appealing to our reward response, teaching that triggers the threat response can be highly effective—when used sparingly and responsibly.

Negative learning is good at inhibiting behavior, but it's terrible at teaching you to find creative solutions. That's because it activates a threat state, which means your PFC is temporarily shut down and with it your executive functions. Your reaction may be speedy and instinctive, but it isn't nuanced and thoughtful. In certain specialized contexts, that can be OK. In situations involving health and safety, such as the airline and elevator examples, fear conditioning can literally be a matter of life and death. The same applies to many military and law enforcement procedures, in which the moment you hesitate may prove to be your last. It's also valuable in cases of compliance, in which people need to know that if they break the rules or the law, then they will be punished.

THE mystery of Capgras delusion, the strange phenomenon that caused David to recognize his parents but fail to accept them as authentic, turned out to be a mystery of emotion. The connection in David's brain between his capacity for recognition and his ability to gauge emotional relevance had been badly damaged in his accident. When we see someone we love, our limbic system normally responds with emotion, sending a message to our autonomic nervous system. Our heart rate quickens and our perspiration subtly increases. In David's brain, the message was never sent.

Although it was the absence of emotion that created confusion for David as well as heartbreak and frustration for his parents, it was ultimately neuroplasticity that came to their rescue. As it turns out, Capgras doesn't have to be permanent. The condition appears to heal itself. Following his accident, David gradually regained the emotional response to his parents and no longer considers them to be impostors.

In short, he learned.

CHAPTER 6 IN A NUTSHELL

KEY POINTS FROM "FOSTER LEARNING"

Learning has no limits. Once believed to be hardwired by the time we reached our twenties, the brain has now been found to be far more malleable and plastic than even most neuroscientists imagined. You just need to know how to learn.

Learning is an emotional process. Learning will only happen when you are emotionally involved—either positively or negatively. Without emotional relevance, your long-term prospects for retaining new information are greatly diminished.

Passing the hippocampus test. The hippocampus weighs two factors in deciding whether information is worth remembering: emotional relevance and novelty.

It's all about survival. From the standpoint of your brain, only information or experiences that activate the reward or threat response are considered worth retaining.

While you were sleeping. Sleep is essential to learning because that's usually when the information deemed worth retaining is transferred from the hippocampus to long-term memory.

Get it right the first time. Good or bad, the strongest impressions are first impressions. That's why it's important to invest time and money to train people correctly at the outset.

Use aversive learning with care. By far the strongest form of learning comes from negative experiences. But aversive learning is ineffective for training positive behavior. Save it instead for those rare situations when you want to *inhibit* undesired behavior.

The company that learns together . . . As fundamentally social creatures, we learn better from others and in the company of others. This underscores the power of stories and the importance of being a good role model.

PART 3
BUILDING DREAM TEAMS

CHAPTER 7
THRIVE ON DIVERSITY

A Healthy Difference in Skills and Personalities
Can Make a Positive Difference in Your Business

IN 1961, writer-editor Stan Lee revolutionized comic books by combining a group of unwitting superheroes into a single team, the Fantastic Four. When their spaceship is bombarded by cosmic rays, Reed Richards; his girlfriend, Sue Storm; her kid brother, Johnny; and Ben Grimm, Reed's friend from college, find that radiation has mutated their bodies in peculiar and distinctive ways. Reed Richards now has the ability to stretch his arms and legs as though they are made of pliant rubber. Sue Storm is able to render herself completely invisible at will. Brother Johnny can turn himself into a human torch as readily as most of us switch on a floor lamp. Perhaps the most dramatic transformation occurs in Ben Grimm, whose body is now literally rock hard, making him hideous to look at but leaving him with incredible strength. Bitter about his transformation, Ben Grimm now calls himself the Thing. His colleagues follow suit by renaming themselves: Reed Richards becomes Mr. Fantastic, Sue Storm is the Invisible Woman, and Johnny is the Human Torch.

The genius of the Fantastic Four is that they echo the characteristics of the best teams in the business world. Each member has a unique and specific strength or skill that he or she excels at. Their approaches and personalities are different and occasionally at odds. Although they don't always get along outside work, when they pool their efforts they set their differences aside and team up to better humanity and to make the world a safer place.

WHAT IS DIVERSITY?

When most of us hear the word "diversity," we think of different nationalities, cultures, ethnic and economic backgrounds, genders, or sexual orientations. Although members of a team may look like the United Nations, they can still share a remarkably limited, homogeneous approach to problem solving. Another way to promote diversity is by forming teams in which each member has a specific strength or skill and there are a variety of personality traits. Working in a team of like-minded people can lull the brain into a state of complacency, diminishing performance and discouraging the chances of innovation and flow.

A team of like-minded people can lull the brain into a state of complacency.

SCIENCE AND PERSONALITY INTERSECT

Employers have been administering personality tests for more than a century. Unfortunately, most of these tests lack any real basis in neuroscience. Without a scientific basis, personality profiles can be susceptible to what is known as confirmation bias.

The Problem with Personality Profiles

In 1948, a psychologist named Bertram Forer administered a personality test to his students. When Forer received the completed tests, he promptly threw them all out and instead, unbeknownst to the students, returned one identical personality profile to every member of his class. Each student was then asked to read his or her own profile and rate its accuracy on a scale of 0 to 5, with 5 meaning "excellent" and 4 meaning "good."[1]

Incredibly, the profiles still received a cumulative average of 4.26 for accuracy. In other words, most of the students truly believed that the assessment had done a good job of describing their unique personality. What the students didn't realize—until he told them—is that Forer had clipped the profile out of a newspaper horoscope column. Like a typical horoscope, it was ambiguous but vaguely complimentary. The criticisms were mild. Thanks to what psychologists call "confirmation bias," most of the students who read the profile related to its positive elements, ignored those elements that were negative or didn't relate specifically to them, and then concluded that it was an accurate assessment of their particular personality traits.[2]

The risk of confirmation bias has been reduced and personality profiling has grown more precise as cognitive scientists have begun matching test scores with brain scans. For example, there have been studies comparing differences in the brains of introverts and extroverts.

Introvert or Extrovert? A Question of Energy

Introverts aren't necessarily shy. Nor are extroverts automatically empathetic. What typically distinguishes them is energy. Introverts tend to expend energy in social interactions, while extroverts look to the same scenarios as a *source* of energy.[3]

We find clues to these differences when we examine their brains. Introverts have larger and thicker gray matter in the prefrontal cortex. In people who are strongly extroverted, that gray matter is thinner, a trait that may suggest that rather than spending time in contemplation (that is, using the default network; see chapter 3), extroverts prefer to live in the moment, an approach that uses the direct experience network instead.[4]

Both introverts and extroverts seek rewards. It's in where they look for them that the difference lies. Conclusions from a Cornell University study of extroverts and introverts suggest that extroverts derive feelings of reward from their immediate environment, while introverts gain them from their inner thoughts.[5]

From a leadership standpoint, it's important to know that your introverts need solitude and downtime, while your extroverts will tend to get restless if they go too long without some sort of social interaction.

People in Glass Houses

This sensitivity to the diverse needs of your employees goes far beyond the way in which you conduct your performance reviews or choose your teams. It should also influence choices you make about the parameters that define their work environment.

One of the more conspicuous examples of extraordinary

tone deafness on the part of a company was a brand-new office design we once encountered. Instead of using traditional barriers to separate one work area from another, most of the walls were made from a durable, transparent glasslike material, which enabled everyone to peer into the offices of their coworkers whether their doors were open or not.

Although extroverts loved the new design, for the company's introverts the setup came very close to being a living nightmare. It took almost no time at all for the inward-focused coworkers to defensively adjust things to suit their own personalities. Much like the children who build "forts" in the middle of the living room by piling up pillows and couch cushions, the company's introverts barricaded themselves behind bookshelves, file cabinets, piles of boxes, or strategically hung-up parkas or suit jackets. In short order, this once gleaming, innovative design was transformed into a space that closely resembled the cluttered stockroom of a clothing store.

The well-meaning leader may have considered himself a visionary when it comes to office design, but he clearly overlooked the fact that between one-third and one-half of the population identifies as introverted.[6] (In fact, if you rely on the aggregate totals for the widely used Myers-Briggs Type Indicator, the Center for Applications of Psychological Type estimates the percentage of test respondents who had an *I* for introvert at the head of their four-letter MBTI score at somewhere between 47 and 55 percent.[7]) These people were suddenly expected to do their already challenging jobs over the insistent din of an instinctive threat response.

Teams operate best when they accurately reflect the varied strengths and styles of the company's employees and when the working environment accommodates as much as possible the diverse work styles of the team members. Of course, even in a company characterized by great diversity, it's still possible to form teams made up of members that seem almost like clones. These homogeneous teams may excel in comfort and collegiality, but they're more likely to falter when it comes to innovation and creativity.

Whether our innovative leader sought advice on the new office design by speaking to fellow extroverts or simply made the decision on his own, he seemed to have completely overlooked the fact that there might be people on his payroll with a radically different point of view. Had he addressed diversity at the outset, the design would've never left the drawing board.

MATCHMAKING IN THE MEETING ROOM

Although there are thousands of studies that add to our overall understanding of workplace diversity, the most useful, neuroscientifically based insights we've found thus far into differing personality traits come from an unlikely source, a Web site devoted to matching potential romantic partners.

The work of Rutgers University biological anthropologist Helen Fisher on the neuroscience of close relationships and underlying personality differences was initially designed to study the chemistry of romantic love. But the neurochemistry at the foundation of her analysis of potential romantic partners provides valuable insights into the interactions of team members in a corporate setting. And unlike commonly used personality assessment instruments, such as Myers-Briggs, Dr. Fisher's analysis is based on neuroscience.

Chemistry and Compatibility

"Why do we fall in love with one person rather than another?" That was the simple, basic question that originally drove Dr. Fisher's research. She set out to conduct a large-scale scientific study linking brain activity to mate choice. First, she studied brain systems and isolated four neurochemical systems, each linked with a specific constellation of biologically based personality traits. Next, she developed a questionnaire, the Fisher Temperament Inventory, to measure the degree to which individuals expressed the traits in all four brain systems. Then, by collaborating with a popular Internet dating platform, she was able to gain access to the profiles of more than 80,000 women and men who were seeking a partner, collect their data on each personality scale, and study whom they chose to meet in person. Fisher then used fMRI to analyze the brains of a group of individuals who had taken her personality test. By correlating the neuroscientific data of these participants with their behavior on the dating site, she discovered an astonishing pattern.

It is not by pure chance that we choose one partner over another. Certain people are drawn to each other, and the secret lies in their individual neurochemical balance. People differ to the extent to which they are modulated by certain substances in the brain. These neurochemicals modulate our behavior and, to a large extent, even our personality. Based on the activity of two neurotransmitters and two hormones (respectively, dopamine, serotonin, estrogen, and testosterone), Dr. Fisher identified four basic personality styles. She calls them the Explorer, the Builder, the Negotiator, and the Director.[8]

The Explorer

Explorers are sensation seekers. Remember the Inverted U model from chapter 1? Thanks to greater activity of the dopamine system in the brain and an extra burst of noradrenaline (the *D* and *N* in the DNA of Peak Performance), Explorers are usually the men and women whose performance curves are shifted to the right, that is, they require a higher level of arousal to achieve peak performance. This can lead them to search for new thrills, to take extraordinary risks, and to constantly shift gears, all in the pursuit of greater rewards.[9]

Explorers are sensation seekers.

But Explorers have a downside. Their constant need for new experiences means they don't handle boredom well. Unless they are truly interested in something or challenged by it, Explorers often find it difficult to sustain their attention. But when they are sufficiently challenged, Explorers are capable of remarkable, albeit short-lived, concentration. Explorers often feel an affinity with other Explorers, with whom they share a thirst for adventure.[10]

The Builder

Whereas an Explorer lives for dopamine, the personality of a Builder is largely defined by the stabilizing influence of serotonin.[11] In many respects, the serotonin that Builders express makes them the inverse of high-risk Explorers. In fact, psychologist Marvin Zuckerman calls people who express serotonin activity "low sensation seekers."[12] If you had to situate Builders on the Inverted U graph from chapter 1, it would almost certainly be to the left, where they would require less arousal to reach their performance peak.

This emphasis on caution and deliberation doesn't mean that Builders are wallflowers. On the contrary, they often thrive in social situations and can be excellent team players. Nor does it mean that Builders are fearful. They're merely deliberate and dependable, carefully taking the time to learn from past mistakes and to methodically prepare for the future.[13]

Of course, a Builder's dependability can lead to an obsession with sticking to the schedule no matter what as well as a general intolerance for deviating from the agreed-upon plan. But when you play to their strengths, they can provide the glue that holds a group together. Builders are usually drawn to other Builders.[14]

The Negotiator

Influence from the hormone estrogen is what differentiates the Negotiator from her colleagues. Or his. Although estrogen is generally thought of as a female hormone, men have it too. Male or female, Negotiators are normally very good at expressing themselves verbally.[15] In addition, they seem to possess almost a sixth sense of what others are thinking and feeling.[16] In fact, Negotiators who claim they "feel your pain" may not be exaggerating.

Negotiators who claim they "feel your pain" may not be exaggerating.

President Bill Clinton, who made that phrase famous, is a classic Negotiator.[17]

But this high degree of empathy can also push Negotiators toward losing themselves—they will go to great lengths in order to please others and to avoid conflict and disharmony. Moreover, their ability to see all sides of the picture will sometimes hinder their ability to focus on important details and make decisions.[18] It can take Negotiators forever to finally make up their minds regarding the direction to choose. Because their skill sets tend to complement each other, Negotiators often work well with Directors.

The Director

The Director is yin to the Negotiator's yang. Whereas the Negotiator's personality is influenced by estrogen, with the Director the defining hormone is testosterone. Once again, although testosterone is known as a predominantly male hormone, there are plenty of women Directors.[19] For example, while famously empathetic President Clinton exhibits the estrogen-linked characteristics of a Negotiator, his wife, former secretary of state and presidential candidate Hillary Clinton, fits the testosterone-influenced profile of a strong-willed, decisive Director.[20]

The Director is yin to the Negotiator's yang.

Male or female, Directors are defined by their competitiveness. They are tough, pragmatic, and extremely decisive, even when the choices seem complex and difficult. The skills we normally associate with the prefrontal cortex—such as logic and rational analysis—are among their key strengths. Yet, this doesn't mean that Directors lack creativity. On the contrary, the paths they take are often ingenious and bold but not always popular.[21]

In fact, if there's a key trait that Directors consistently lack, it's diplomacy. Their confidence, precision, and candor can sometimes make them seem boastful, stubborn, and rude. But Directors aren't usually loners. Their persistence, loyalty, and enthusiasm for ideas can make them great friends and colleagues, particularly with Negotiators, who can often help to smooth out some of the Director's harder edges.

What Does This Tell Us About Leadership?

According to the Center for Creative Leadership, unmanaged employee conflicts cause at least 65 percent of all performance issues at work.[22] Effectively identifying individual personality traits can be the first step in managing those conflicts. Focusing initially on romantic love, Helen Fisher developed a questionnaire based on her research that identified a person's neurochemical balance. Since then, Dr. Fisher has shifted her attention from the bedroom to the boardroom by designing a second personality test based on the same brain data, the NeuroColor Temperament Inventory, in order to provide a neuroscience perspective on work, communication, collaboration, and decision making in the business world. Depending on the activity of these different neurotransmitters and hormones, people prefer certain tasks and modalities of working to others.[23] Moreover, when forming a new team, you can increase productivity by balancing out the different personality styles.

Each of the personality styles can contribute certain skill sets that are complementary to each other. As an example, the fast-paced, curious Explorer will enhance the team with his creativity and drive and make working together fun. The Negotiator will be very sensitive to the "human" touch of collaboration and be particularly skilled at anything that has to do with verbal expression and communication. The Builder will add stability and the persistence to follow through with a task until the end. She's the one who will make sure that the timeline is respected and that commitments are taken seriously.

The Director, on the other hand, will reduce complexity and use his logical skills to cut through any seemingly confusing problems, keeping the team up to speed and on track.

Who You Gonna Call?

In most of us, a number of factors—genetic, experiential, and environmental—contribute to our overall personality and performance. That said, the fetal priming that results in the differing combinations of neurochemicals that underlie Dr. Fisher's four basic personality styles—Explorer, Builder, Negotiator, and Director—can make some team members better suited for particular roles or tasks than their colleagues.

Cooperation

Builders tend to be excellent team players. The serotonin that characterizes their personality trait has been shown in studies to produce employees who excel in "playing well with others." According to Dr. Fisher, "People who take serotonin boosters become more cooperative during group tasks."[24]

Builders tend to be excellent team players.

Decision Making

Decisiveness is often linked to testosterone. Perhaps it's no surprise, then, that Directors lead the way when it comes to making decisions. Although Explorers also make decisions quickly—primarily because they tend to be impulsive—Directors decide even faster because they are tough-minded.[25]

Negotiating

This one should be obvious. They aren't called Negotiators for nothing!

Writing
Verbal fluency has long been associated with estrogen, the dominant hormone in Negotiators.[26]

Big-Picture Thinking
According to Dr. Fisher, Negotiators excel in "web thinking," what many of us might also refer to as "seeing the Big Picture." She defines it as "the natural ability to collect many bits of data as you think, weigh the importance of these variables and envision the relationships between them. . . ."[27] Whatever you call it, Negotiators have it.

The Fine Print
Negotiators' sometimes-extraordinary ability to think in webs of factors instead of straight lines has a decided downside. It can make them susceptible to "system blindness," an inability to focus on important details while they're pondering the bigger picture.[28] If you want to make sure that every i is dotted and every t is crossed, look to your Directors. They tend to be nitpickers and hairsplitters.[29]

Administration
Builders make good managers and administrators.[30] In a meeting, although a Negotiator might be the best facilitator, the Builder is the one who'll make sure that you stick to the agenda.

Dealing with Chaos
Although true multitasking is extremely rare (see chapter 3), Explorers are generally better than average at responding to multiple inputs; they excel at dividing their attention.[31]

Clarity and Caution

A group dominated by Builders may be stodgy and risk averse. A group without them may be unfocused and reckless.

Meeting Deadlines

The downside of the dopamine motivation that drives Explorers is that it can sometimes lead to procrastination.[32] Look to your Builders if you're concerned with being on time.

Cheerleading

Explorers are the most optimistic and enthusiastic, traits typically associated with dopamine.[33]

High-Performing Teams

When creating high-performing teams it is particularly important to respect each other's needs. This is what you should pay attention to when having these people on your teams:

Explorers: Explorers tend to get bored easily. They reach their zone of peak performance at high levels of stress. Since they always need a new challenge, you shouldn't weigh them down with run-of-the-mill activities. They can be highly creative and quick thinkers, so give them a chance to engage in these kinds of activities.

Negotiators: Negotiators are very empathetic and see the big picture. They need to feel an affinity for and appreciation from their superiors and peers. Negotiators are highly sensitive to unresolved conflicts, and their performance will suffer if you don't create a trust-based, appreciative climate. Negotiators' strengths are their talent in handling people, their verbal fluency, and their ability to draw connections between seemingly unconnected topics.

Directors: Directors are tough-minded and highly analytical. They thrive in competitive environments where they can excel at their skills in problem solving and structuring. Due to their high testosterone levels, Directors can be pretty rough and undiplomatic in their communication. They work well only when the hierarchy is clearly defined; otherwise the risk for openly displayed conflict is high. Directors love to lead and to succeed. Don't deprive them of that pleasure!

Builders: As their name suggests, Builders are the pillars of society. You can always count on them to follow through with their tasks and responsibilities. Builders are very structured, loyal, and future-focused but can be thrown by unanticipated changes in schedule and agreements. A Builder needs the freedom to set up his own schedule and to work in a non-chaotic environment, such as the peace and quiet of his own home. Because the Builder often operates quietly behind the scenes, don't underestimate his work ethic, loyalty, and the value he adds to the team.

As with matchmaking in love, it is also important to find the right match at work and the appropriate means of communication in order to facilitate understanding and collaboration between the different personality types. And since it's a rare team that is perfectly matched, it is even more important to leverage the understanding of each other's biological preferences and the do's and don'ts of treating others. It will help you to play to your coworkers' strengths, even if they might be very different from your own.

WHY PERFORMANCE REVIEWS COULD USE A PERFORMANCE REVIEW

You wouldn't call an electrician to fix your sink. You'd call a plumber. And you certainly wouldn't tell the electrician, "Your electrical skills are great, but I think you really need to focus more attention on improving your plumbing skills."

We all have strengths and weaknesses. Many of us are proud of our strengths, and most of us are acutely aware of our weaknesses. Doing something we're good at focuses our attention, triggers a burst of dopamine, and often puts us into a rewarding state of flow. Working on something we're not so good at tends to lead to discouragement, frustration, and a dissipation of energy. The lessons from Yerkes-Dodson's Inverted U (see chapter 1) and Mihaly Csikszentmihalyi's model of flow (chapter 3) make it obvious that this is a losing proposition. As a leader, why in the world would you want to deliberately do something to rob your employees of motivation and energy?

You don't have to be a neuropsychologist to realize that the nearly universal dread surrounding the performance review process saps energy and deflates motivation. A 2012 study by the CEB Corporate Leadership Council found more than three-quarters of the managers, employees, and heads of human resources surveyed felt that performance review results were ineffective, inaccurate, or both,[34] while the title of an article in the *Washington Post* said it even more succinctly: "Study Finds That Basically Every Single Person Hates Performance Reviews."[35]

The performance review process saps energy and deflates motivation.

Although there are slight variations from one company to another, the annual performance review usually involves ranking each employee's strengths and weaknesses (often just with numbers but occasionally with comments as well) and, after briefly praising the high points, zeroing in on the low points and setting some measurable goals for improving them over the coming year.

Aside from the fact that it is typically tied to pay raises, very few managers and employees we know look forward to this process. On the contrary, they dread it. And it's no wonder. For the managers, it's often a lot of work. And for the employees, it can be stressful if not downright discouraging.

Why should an electrician feel like a failure because he doesn't know how to do plumbing as well? Why should an employee who excels at interacting with clients feel bad because she isn't a very good writer? Instead of building on the unique strengths of their employees, far too many companies are trying to iron out their weaknesses. The valleys may get shallower, but the peaks get lower in the process as well. Employees neglect the skills they're good at in order to improve the areas where they've never done well. Instead of aiming for excellence, far too many companies are moving toward mediocrity.

Occasionally the whole thing can get a little absurd. We know of a race car driver, one of the very best in the world. Yet he was awkward whenever he had to step in front of a microphone. Presumably, he didn't become a world-class race car driver in order to polish his public speaking. His performance behind the wheel spoke loud and clear. Yet if he had been an employee at a typical corporation, his manager might have helpfully suggested that although his ability to round corners at speeds that are faster than anyone else in the world is admirable, it would be a good idea to take some time off from racing to attend classes in public speaking and perhaps even debating. The world would've lost a great race car driver and gotten a mediocre public speaker instead.

Obviously, within limits, if an employee is failing to meet certain standards, then something definitely needs to be done about it. Rather than rating people on a 5- or even a 10-point scale, we limit things to just four areas:

1. Not acceptable
2. Acceptable standard
3. Professional standard
4. Best in class

Unlike with some of the scales used in companies today, in which it can be difficult to determine, for example, whether someone is a 4 or 5, it should be relatively easy to rate employees according to these straightforward rankings. Now, once we've assessed an employee's skills against the company's core standards, we can provide recommendations that will be best for that employee as well as for the company as a whole.

If we've ranked any of the skills as "not acceptable," we definitely need to do something to improve those specific areas. But here is where we deviate from the traditional performance review. Our goal is not to transform an area where the employee is clearly struggling into one of his greatest strengths. That's obviously not going to happen. Don't attempt to turn an employee into someone he or she is not. As the saying goes, "No matter how long the runway is, a pig won't fly."

"No matter how long the runway is, a pig won't fly."

Studies have found distinct differences in brain activity between subjects who exhibit a talent in a particular area and those who don't.[36] Moreover, tasks that employees find difficult or objectionable may trigger the brain's threat response, which can temporarily short-circuit rational thought, further undermining chances of success.

For whatever reason, this particular skill is against the employee's nature, his genetic disposition, or perhaps he simply doesn't like it. To some extent, the reason doesn't really matter. Our goal should simply be to lift that skill out of the hole of "not acceptable" and onto the firmer footing of "acceptable standard," but no further. That's it. Full stop.

Accentuate the Positive

Once we've raised any unacceptable skills up to an acceptable standard, we can focus the majority of the time on improving the employee's strengths. Instead of moving toward mediocrity, we're encouraging employees to develop their strengths with the goal of achieving world-class status. And unlike reviews that put weakness under a microscope, strength-based appraisals capitalize on the pride and motivation that most employees already feel for areas they are good at and inspire them to aim for the stars.

In the case of the world-class race car driver, his skills in front of a microphone regrettably fell into the "not acceptable" category, and it was clear that something needed to be done. But instead of taking time off from racing to enroll in classes for public speaking or debate, he learned just a handful of phrases in ten different languages. From then on, everywhere he went he was able to say a few well-rehearsed words to the general public in their native language. The crowds loved it. With a limited amount of time and effort, he had moved from "not acceptable" to "acceptable standard" and was able to focus the bulk of his attention where it belonged:

on his racing. As for any additional interactions with the local media, they could be delegated to a spokesperson who was "best in class" when it came to dealing with the press. That's how diversity works.

Although team assessments obviously differ from individual performance reviews, the underlying approach is the same. The emphasis should be on fielding a team of experts, encouraging them to make the most of their strengths, and devoting a minimum amount of time and energy to bringing any "not acceptable" skills up to "acceptable standard," but no further. In a nutshell, here are the steps we've successfully recommended with teams throughout the world.

1. List the KPIs (key performance indicators) that will determine the success of the team.
2. Evaluate each team member for each characteristic.
3. Identify the "not acceptables" and lift them up to the level of "acceptable standard," but no further.
4. Build on the strengths of each individual with the goal of ultimately achieving "best in class," and instill a sense of pride in the team.
5. In the event that the highest team ranking in a particular area is "acceptable standard," seek out and add someone to the team who is "best in class" in that area.

The lesson for teams and team building is simple: Not everyone needs to do everything. Strive to find a mix of people, with each excelling in a different area. Look for members who are professional class or higher in specific skills. If Reed Richards can't make himself invisible, that's OK. That's what

Sue Storm is there for. Likewise, nobody expects moody teenager Johnny Storm to be the team's leader. Older and wiser, phenomenally flexible Reed Richards has that covered. But when it comes to flying through the air in a self-generated fireball, Johnny is definitely "best in class." As for rock-hard Ben "The Thing" Grimm, his strength is literally his strength. The combined expertise of people with differing abilities and approaches will provide true team diversity.

Not everyone needs to do everything.

CHAPTER 7 IN A NUTSHELL

KEY POINTS FROM "THRIVE ON DIVERSITY"

People are different. There is a fundamental genetic predisposition to most personality differences. From these you can infer that people have different needs in the workplace, and if you respect the needs and try to accommodate them as flexibly as possible, people will perform much better and be happier at work.

The Fantastic Four. According to a scientifically sound psychometric tool devised by Dr. Helen Fisher at Rutgers University, four neurochemicals account for four key personality styles that she calls Explorer, Builder, Director, and Negotiator.

Explorers and Builders. Explorers are sensation seekers who inherit certain genes from the novelty-sensitive dopamine system. They exude optimism and excel in creativity. Builders, people valued for their loyalty, stability, and dependability, are characterized by the serotonin system, which is linked with a sense of calm and well-being.

Directors and Negotiators. Men (and women) with strong activity in the testosterone system are known as Directors. They tend to be consummate strategists, both decisive and logical. Women (and men) who demonstrate a dominance of estrogen are Negotiators. They are intuitive, sympathetic, and verbal and often exhibit superior executive social skills.

A team that looks like the UN may not be diverse. A group that looks different doesn't always think differently. Teams succeed not because of the variety of their appearances or backgrounds, but because of the diversity of skills and personality types they possess.

Best in class. Rather than trying to make everyone well-rounded, hire the people who have one or several top skills you need on your team and then develop them in the areas where they already excel, with the goal of helping them become "best in class."

Accentuate the positive. When dealing with a team member's weaknesses, move any behavior that qualifies as "not acceptable" to "acceptable standard" but no further. Then spend the rest of the time working on their existing strengths with the goal of helping them to become "best in class" in one or two areas.

Identify your experts. Make a list of the top skills that you need on your team and then rank everyone according to that list. Once you do this, everybody should be able to provide a clear and confident answer to the crucial question "Why am I on the team?"

Don't try to teach a pig to fly. Hire a bird. Rather than adopting the doomed strategy of attempting to develop weaknesses into strengths, hire new talent that already has a natural predisposition for the skill you require.

One size doesn't fit all. Don't expect everybody to be good at everything, but make sure that everybody is good at something. Develop people based on their specific strengths.

CHAPTER 8
CULTIVATE TRUST

....

More So Than Motivation or Money, Trust Is the Glue
That Holds Successful Groups Together

IT wouldn't be much of an exaggeration to suggest that a single raisin changed the world. In the early 1990s, scientists at the University of Parma in Italy were studying the neuronal activity of a macaque monkey's motor cortex while he was grabbing small food items, such as raisins and nuts. They had pinpointed a single neuron that was involved in the specific grasping motion. Every time the monkey reached for the food, the neuron fired and the scientists could hear the amplified sound of its neuronal activity through a speaker that had been set up in the lab.

But then one day, something surprising happened.

In between sessions, while everyone including the monkey was taking a break, one of the doctoral students decided to have a snack. The student grabbed the closest snack he could find, which just happened to be one of the monkey's raisins.

Suddenly, the amplifier connected to the monkey's brain

made the familiar sound of the firing neuron. The scientists were startled. Although the monkey wasn't doing anything at the time, his brain was sending the very same signals it would normally transmit if he were reaching for food. How could that be?

Thanks to this laboratory fluke, Dr. Giacomo Rizzolatti and his team of investigators made one of the most important discoveries in modern neuroscience. The monkey brain—and, as we now know, the human brain—has a function called a "mirror neuron system," a network of nerve cells that fire both when we engage in a particular action *and* when we observe someone else performing the very same action.

It is this second part that is truly extraordinary. Research has shown that the brain distinguishes very little between our own actions and the actions of others we witness. In fact, whenever we're in the company of other people, our brain continuously "mirrors" the behavior displayed by those around us.

Many neuroscientists assert that mirror neurons provide the basis not just for empathy but for all human communication. As Rizzolatti so eloquently explained to the *New York Times*: "Mirror neurons allow us to grasp the minds of others not through conceptual reasoning but through direct stimulation. By feeling, not by thinking."[1]

This discovery provided a paradigm shift in our understanding of human nature. Many well-established models will need to be reevaluated or completely dismissed. One of the first high-profile casualties of this momentous breakthrough is the well-known work of Abraham Maslow.

PYRAMID SCHEME

If you can remember only one thing from high school or college psychology, it's probably Maslow's "hierarchy of needs," the distinctive pyramid-shaped progression that starts with physiological needs, such as air to breathe, water to drink, and food to eat, moves steadily through safety, love and belonging, and esteem, then culminates in something that Maslow termed "self-actualization."

We have to hand it to Maslow. The pyramid design was a stroke of genius—both easy to remember and a little mystical and inspiring as well. That's no doubt why it has stuck with many of us for so long.

Unfortunately, Maslow's well-intentioned model lacked the evidence that cutting-edge neuroscience now provides. Although the hierarchy of needs was considered a foundational tenet of modern psychology, the truth is that it had very little scientific data to support it. As the acerbic journalist H. L. Mencken once said, "There is always a well-known solution to every human problem—neat, plausible, and wrong." Like the equally fallacious notion that we use only 10 percent of our brains, it captured the imagination of millions, not because it was backed up by any evidence, but because it just *sounded* right.

And yet, you only need to take a few minutes to consider the predicament of any infant to realize that without the support of a caregiver, none of us would've lasted for more than a few hours. That's why our social needs are absolutely essential to our survival. Rather than residing in the pyramid's midsection, they belong at its base. We have a basic craving for connection ingrained in us when we

We are fundamentally social creatures.

are born that persists throughout our lives. As humans, we are fundamentally social creatures.

As a leader, you overlook this core truth at your peril. Most of the behavior that constitutes what is sometimes called "group dynamics" hinges on our assessment of the people around us as either enemies or friends. Reward and threat, the two key circuits in our limbic system that we learned about in chapter 2, largely dictate our behavior around others. We make a snap judgment about each person we encounter and work with. Everyone is basically divided into two camps: "us" and "them."

For the sake of our survival, our default response is to treat the people around us as members of the "them" camp—in other words, as threats to our existence until we learn otherwise. As far as your brain is concerned, the general rule of thumb is "Better safe than sorry." This prompts what psychologists call "avoidance behavior," a tendency to fight, flee, or freeze, or at the very least, to watch our step. The flip side of avoidance behavior is "approach behavior," an equally primitive response that places people in the "us" camp and is based on a feeling of trust. It is approach behavior that prompts us to drop our weapons, lower our guard, and open up to the people around us.

No one is forever doomed to reside in the "them" column or guaranteed a lifetime membership in the "us" club. Although nearly everyone except our closest family members starts out in "them," there are ways in which we gain the trust of those around us that gradually diminishes their avoidance behavior while encouraging approach until we finally find ourselves considered a proud member of "us."

Of course, the distinction between "us" and "them" is largely dependent upon how the context is defined. Two rival departments in the same company may normally consider each other as residing in the "them" camp—until they're both faced with a challenge that affects them equally. Suddenly, the frame of reference shifts and they find themselves working together. Clever leaders sometimes use a trick to make their teams trust each other by conjuring up an outside enemy, whether it's the competition or even a threatening condition such as an economic downturn or an uncertain future. Politicians have been known to do the same thing in an attempt to unify the electorate. By the same token, it can also be helpful to encourage a "them" mind-set in certain situations. While "us" encourages cooperation and trust, "them" can increase motivation and focus.

Although it may seem a little more stable, that "us" status can also be precarious. Even loved ones or valued colleagues can sometimes fall from grace. By carefully examining brain scans, social cognitive neuroscientists have determined that social rejection, social neglect, or a violation of trust, whether real or merely perceived, can literally be as painful as a physical injury. In fact, most of the regions of the brain that light up when you are whacked with a tree branch or struck with a rock are the same as those that are activated when you are rejected or ridiculed by your peers. It's still true that sticks and stones may break your bones, but despite the school-yard saying, names will almost *always* hurt you.

If something or someone has caused you pain, avoidance behavior is not only natural but also prudent. If people you once trusted have hurt, betrayed, or in some cases simply disappointed you, then they may find themselves booted out of the "us" camp and stuck back in with "them." What's more, this change in status can even occur unconsciously. Your limbic system may have engineered a realignment without keeping your prefrontal cortex informed.

Obviously, as a leader, you can't let unconscious responses or even mere chance determine whether your team or your overall organization is harmonious or acrimonious, productive or paralyzed. You need the tools at your disposal to make your desired outcomes as predictable as possible.

THE FABRIC OF SCARF

Now that Maslow's pyramid has been largely debunked, where does that leave us? David Rock, author of *Your Brain at Work*, has devised a model for social interaction that reflects the latest findings in social cognitive neuroscience. It may not have a distinctive shape, but at least it comes with a memorable name: SCARF.[2]

The five letters that make up the acronym SCARF represent the five major factors—*s*tatus, *c*ertainty, *a*utonomy, *r*elatedness, and *f*airness—that determine whether groups are characterized by approach or avoidance behavior. Shifting each of these levers to the positive side can be instrumental in the success of a project, product, or company. Our understanding of mirror neurons makes it clear that as a leader you are in a unique position to model and encourage these changes. If you sense difficulties or friction in your group, you can employ the SCARF model as a diagnostic tool to pinpoint possible problem areas and then use what you find to help get everyone back on track.[3]

Status

Status might seem as though it refers to an expensive watch, a fancy car, or a bigger bonus. It can, but not always. From a leadership perspective, status refers to how people feel after they've interacted with you. Do they feel more important, more valued, or more appreciated? Or do they feel unimportant, inferior, or underappreciated?

From an evolutionary perspective, we all want to believe we are a key part of the group. In one study, 68 percent of sales reps sacrificed sizable commissions so they could literally earn a star (on their business cards), which indicated they were part of an elite Presidents Club. As strange as it may seem, the status of that star was more important than money.[4]

As a leader, you have a choice: You can treat the members of your team in such a way that they feel as though they are valued and make a genuine difference. Or you can treat them in a way that makes them feel inferior or insignificant.

Treat your colleagues with genuine respect, and make sure they know that you truly believe they are valued. It's not about pretending. In fact, like positive affirmations used by someone who doesn't have a positive self-image (see chapter 2), insincere attempts to ingratiate yourself with your colleagues can backfire. People want to feel important. Do you make them feel important, or do you devalue them?

Certainty

Our brain is constantly attempting to anticipate the future. According to philosopher and cognitive scientist Daniel Dennett, a human being is an "anticipation machine."[5] Based on the activities of our limbic system, it is continuously drawing conclusions and revising its predictions. Does this person make me feel comfortable or uncomfortable? Certainty is a lot about trying to predict the future.

Our brain is constantly attempting to anticipate the future.

Imagine that you left work early and have had to battle rush-hour traffic to get to the airport to pick up a relative who is flying in from overseas. But when you arrive at the terminal just in time, you discover that there's no listing for the flight on the arrival boards. No indication of whether the flight has been delayed. Or canceled. Nothing.

When you anxiously pump the nearest airline agent for more information, she calmly advises you to supply her with a contact number and informs you that the airline is "unable to provide any details at this time" but assures you that you will receive a recorded voice message as soon as definitive information is available. Unfortunately, this sort of response is likely to throw you into such a state of threat that your blood pressure will skyrocket and your body will quickly be coursing with so much cortisol that you'll practically be bouncing off the walls.

Luckily for all concerned, most airlines have long since learned that this is exactly the wrong approach to such a situation of uncertainty. Here's what they typically do instead: They advise you to remain inside the terminal, preferably within earshot, and then urge you to check back every ten minutes for a scheduled update on the status of your relative's flight. Even though the basic situation hasn't changed one bit, the airline has skillfully replaced "content safety" with "process safety" instead. The fate of the flight remains a mystery, but the process no longer is. That subtle shift is usually enough to neutralize the threat response and calm down all but the most high-strung among us.

You don't have to work for an airline to institute a similarly effective procedure for retaining a sense of certainty at your workplace, even in especially trying times. Although you may be unable to provide the sort of content safety that your employees may crave, you can often provide them with some process safety instead.

With layoffs looming, for example, most of the people

around you are likely to be in threat mode, wondering, "Am I on the list?" You can try to shed some reassuring light on the process by calmly mapping out the steps in detail so all your employees feel as though they have a clear sense of the procedure. This will often be enough to turn down the volume on the company's collective threat response.

Individual insecurity triggers instincts of self-preservation and drives people apart, while safety draws them together. The more transparent you are about the process, the safer people tend to feel. With process safety, even if the outcome is uncertain, they at least derive some solace from knowing the steps that are going to be taken. At the heart of this feeling of certainty is a sense of control, the same crucial factor that underlies another key element of the SCARF model, autonomy.

Autonomy

A colleague who grew up in a wealthy family had a curiously scarring experience as a child. Whenever he happened to mention a toy that interested him, whether it was a simple model train or a small LEGO set, his father would immediately rush out to buy the most elaborate and expensive version of whatever he had requested. Instead of feeling gratified, the boy felt utterly constrained. Moreover, whenever he showed even a casual interest in something, his father made it a mission to become an expert in whatever the boy had turned his attention toward. The father may have meant well, but he left the boy feeling embittered. "I quickly lost interest in those toys," he told us, "because I never really felt that they were *my* toys."

The irony of this story, which seldom fails to trigger a stunned silence of recognition and self-reflection whenever we tell it in our seminars, is that while the boy suffered throughout his childhood because of this experience, the father had almost certainly done what he did in order to demonstrate his love for his son.

These days it has become fashionable to refer to people like our colleague's father as "helicopter parents." In business, the phenomenon can be equally common, while the name for these people is even better known: We call them micromanagers. Although it may be borne of the best of intentions, micromanagement is a clear case of unintended consequences. It is a direct and potentially devastating assault on one of our most prized possessions: our autonomy.

Autonomy is the number one protector against stress.

Autonomy is the number one protector against stress. A remarkably varied array of inspiring and influential leaders (everyone from President Franklin Delano Roosevelt to anti-apartheid crusader Nelson Mandela) have used the final stanza of the Victorian poem "Invictus" as a philosophy of life:

> It matters not how strait the gate,
> How charged with punishments the scroll,
> I am the master of my fate:
> I am the captain of my soul.

Whether or not it's deserved, when people have a sense that they are masters of their fate (psychologists use the slightly less poetic term "locus of control"), their moods improve and their stress levels go down. The difference between working into the wee hours on a client pitch because it's due on your boss's desk tomorrow and doing so because you personally chose to is huge. Autonomy makes the difference.

As a leader, there are many ways that you can provide your team with a greater sense of autonomy without watching them go off and start their own company. One way is to grant them the freedom to work according to their own style as long as they are willing and able to meet the goals that you both agreed upon. As we learned in chapter 7, the strongest, most effective teams are often the most diverse, and that diversity will often include different standards and styles for getting the required work done. If, as a leader, you accommodate these differing styles, you will increase the sense of autonomy that each team member feels, and that will result in greater satisfaction, less stress, and, above all, a more productive and successful team.

Relatedness

Although pain may feel like a single sensation, it originates from two separate and distinct portions of the brain. The somatosensory cortex and the posterior insula, both of which reside in the back portion of the brain, track the sensory aspects of pain. At the same time, the dorsal anterior cingulate cortex (dACC) and the anterior insula handle the distressing aspects of pain. This is what makes us feel that pain is something we don't like.[6]

What is remarkable is that the brain's response to physical and social pain is virtually identical. In fact, some of the most painful life experiences are social pains, such as the death or loss of a loved one or the rejection by a favored person or group. Equally remarkable is the discovery that common painkillers, such as aspirin and acetaminophen, are as effective at easing social pain as they are at relieving physical pain![7]

In case you're wondering why a team member's pain should be any of your business as long as he or she works well, the fact is that a person in pain or feeling threatened is unlikely to be a peak performer. The threat response can undermine the ability to plan, to concentrate, and to create.

Researchers demonstrated the extent of social pain with a game they called Cyberball, in which each subject played electronic catch with two other players who were actually a clever computer program. As the subject became more adept at throwing and catching, there was a reward reaction that comes from playing any video game.[8] But when the other two players abruptly excluded the human player from their catch, the reaction of the subject's brain was almost the same as that of experiencing physical pain.[9]

What can we glean from this in a work context and from the standpoint of relatedness? Do the people in your group work well together? Is everyone included in important e-mails? Or are some people conspicuously missing? When you come into work one morning and hear everyone around you chatting animatedly about how much fun last night's barbecue was, the sudden realization that you weren't even invited can be every bit as painful as a punch to the solar plexus. In fact, it frequently feels worse. When people feel alienated or excluded, it hurts. Literally.

Our need for relatedness and our reaction to exclusion probably hark back to a prehistoric time when our ancestors survived in small groups. Back then, being cast out of the group was tantamount to receiving a death sentence. As a result, right up to the present day, situations in which we're excluded are perceived as threats—and not without good reason. The severing of a social bond is one of the greatest risk factors for depression and anxiety. The strength of our connections to others remains a key factor in determining how long we live.[10]

To foster stronger connections between you and the members of your group, devote some time to building good relations with them. Do you know, for example, about the family situations of the people you work with? Do you create an inclusive climate for new people joining the group, or is there an unspoken social barrier between the veterans and the newcomers?

> **Situations in which we're excluded are perceived as threats.**

One Friday, during one of our first visits to Google's campus in Mountain View, California, we noticed a lot of extra activity in one of the company's largest dining rooms. Our contact explained the reason for all the commotion. They were preparing for an all-company meeting with Google cofounders Larry Page and Sergey Brin, who would spend an hour updating the company's plans and taking questions from employees. The atmosphere is inclusive, and virtually no question is off-limits. Rather than being held once a year, once a quarter, or even once a month, the meeting, known internally as TGIF, is a once-a-week ritual. Although employee nondisclosure is obviously a key element of these get-togethers, they are an outstanding demonstration of the company's deep appreciation for the value of relatedness. In short, the *R* in SCARF is about building great relationships.

Fairness

If you found a five-dollar bill lying on the sidewalk along an empty street, would you take it? Most of us would. And yet, if a close relative who had just won the lottery offered us five dollars, most of us would turn it down. What's the differ-ence? The difference is fairness. Most people would rather get nothing at all than receive an unfair deal.

When it comes to fairness, perception is key. Whether or not a situation is actually fair is not as important as perceived fairness. The assessment of fairness is an emotional reaction.

When it comes to fairness, perception is key. It triggers a reward response when you sense that you, or those around you, are being treated fairly. In fact, the same part of the brain that responds to physical pleasures (such as eating choco-late) responds to fairness.[11] This response goes beyond simply a societal one for something like equal pay for equal work. It really appears to be hardwired.

On the other hand, any perception that you're being treated unfairly triggers a version of the fight, flight, or freeze response. Unfair offers are registered in the insula, the part of the brain that deals with body awareness. We feel it in "our gut" when we believe that we aren't being treated equitably. Moreover, people who are already under stress are more likely to view a situation as unfair, even if it isn't.

If your company's bonus situation or your team's setup is perceived as unfair, most people will respond with a very strong threat reaction. Fairness goes far beyond simply "doing the right thing." It has tangible consequences in a business context, affecting job performance, turnover, absenteeism, and organizational citizenship.[12]

One thing that has a surprising effect on the perception of fairness is oxytocin, the powerful "cuddle hormone" that is normally released when people fall in love, have a child, and even when they hug or just shake hands. Researchers found that people who were administered oxytocin in the form of a nasal spray were inclined to give far more money away.[13] Likewise, if the recipient of an unfair deal has had a snort of oxytocin first, he is less likely to be concerned about the inequity.

Why does oxytocin disrupt our traditional reaction to fairness? Like so many situations, this one has an evolutionary explanation. Oxytocin bonds couples and families together and tends to make them loyal and selfless. Although outsiders are often hired to provide childcare, it is a rare parent who would think to charge her baby for feeding and clothing her. That's because at its heart, a parent-child relationship is not an economic one. That's a truth that most of us understand and accept.

What's more difficult to accept but hard to ignore is that the fundamental dynamic between members of a team isn't economic either. If you have great relationships with your clients, negotiations will usually go more smoothly because they are less apt to count every penny. When people haggle over money, it's usually less about the money and more about status and fairness. They feel that their contribution should be valued. In these cases, the money they receive is not appreciated for its intrinsic value—that is, for its ability to place a down payment on a fancy car or to buy a lavish restaurant meal—but because it indicates that their contribution to the group is appreciated and that they are being treated equitably.

Rather than seeking a quick-fix way to introduce oxytocin into your workplace, it makes far more sense to trigger oxytocin the old-fashioned way, by doing the patient but rewarding work of building a cohesive, cooperative team. The SCARF model of status, certainty, autonomy, relatedness, and fairness doesn't come in a bottle or nasal spray. But together these five factors provide a clear, tangible, and potentially long-lasting remedy for common company ailments and a proven formula for cultivating trust.

CHAPTER 8 IN A NUTSHELL

KEY POINTS FROM "CULTIVATE TRUST"

Mirror, mirror. A network of neurons has been found to fire both when we engage in a particular action and when we observe someone else performing the very same action.

Lead by example. The implications of the mirror neuron discovery are clear. When you're a leader, the people around you may be mirroring what you do. This means you have a powerful, fundamental effect on the way that others act and feel.

Rewards drive performance. People perform better when they're in a reward state. The expectation of a reward, which can be anything perceived as pleasurable, triggers approach behavior, while anything viewed as onerous or unpleasant can lead to its polar opposite: avoidance behavior.

The fabric of SCARF. Responding to the realities of approach and avoidance behaviors, the SCARF model aims at minimizing threat and maximizing reward. The five letters in SCARF stand for *s*tatus, *c*ertainty, *a*utonomy, *r*elatedness, and *f*airness.

Status. Status refers to how people feel after they've interacted with you. As a leader, if you treat the members of your team in a way that they truly feel valued, it will lead them to believe they can make a genuine difference.

Certainty. Our brain is constantly attempting to anticipate the future. Uncertainty makes us uneasy and can lead to a threat response, while the perception of certainty is likely to trigger a sense of reward. As a leader, you can't always take the mystery out of certain situations, but what you can do is try to shed some reassuring light on the process.

Autonomy. When people have a sense that they are masters of their own fate, their moods improve and their stress levels go down. Leaders can provide their teams with a greater sense of autonomy by granting them the freedom to work according to their own style as long as they are willing and able to meet agreed-upon goals.

Relatedness. People perform better when they feel connected. To strengthen connections between you and the members of your group, devote some time to building good relations with them by fostering an environment of caring and inclusiveness.

Fairness. Instead of maximizing profit, we maximize relationships and fairness. In some instances, our brains even trigger a reward response when we see others being treated fairly. On the other hand, any perception that we're getting a raw deal can set off the threat alarm. As a leader, if you work to foster a climate of fairness, everyone and everything will likely benefit—including the company's bottom line.

Bringing a SCARF to work. You can use the five levers of the SCARF model to customize your workplace environment to meet the fundamental needs of your employees, to improve interactions between co-workers, to avoid or troubleshoot conflict situations, and to jump-start the change-management process.

CHAPTER 9
DEVELOP THE TEAM
OF THE FUTURE

....

How to Build One, How to Keep Everyone Happy, and
How to Create a Brain-Based Framework That
Encourages the Highest Performance

MOST high-performing teams look forward to those times when they can receive recognition for their efforts. In that respect, this group was no exception. Over the years, they had generated more than $8 billion in revenue and established a brand that was recognized around the world. The team's founding partners were past what would typically be considered retirement age. Yet when they came out on the stage in Melbourne, Australia, in November 2014, they had a youthful spring in their step. As the group stood before them, the crowd responded with a thunderous roar that is normally reserved for rock stars. And with good reason. By anyone's definition, the members of this particular high-performing team truly *were* rock stars.

Almost from the very beginning, with their formation in 1962, they were known as the bad boys of rock and roll. In

1963, while the Beatles were charming Princess Margaret and the Queen Mother at the London Palladium with their rendition of a popular Broadway show tune, the Rolling Stones were already gaining notoriety for their gritty, blues-inflected lyrics and their public acts of defiance. Everyone from parents to priests was issuing stern warnings to avoid them.

And yet just seven years later, following a rancorous rift between John Lennon and Paul McCartney, the Beatles had disbanded, while the Stones lived on. And on. And on. By the time they took the stage at Rod Laver Arena in Melbourne to play before a crowd of 10,000, comparatively modest for their concerts, the core team had been working together for more than fifty years. In fact, when they performed in Tel Aviv, Israel, earlier that year, all four members held the rare distinction of being older than the country they were playing in.

The Rolling Stones might seem like unlikely role models for a book designed to help business leaders use cutting-edge insights about the brain to achieve peak performance, but if you dig a little deeper, you'll find that they provide a remarkable example of how to face the changes and challenges of the "real world" and still manage to stay together and perform at your very best.

TO realize the team of the future, you need to build your team based on existing strengths, you need to keep them happy in times of both success and adversity, and you need to develop a framework that will encourage their highest performance and greatest satisfaction.

FIELDING A STRENGTH-BASED TEAM

When it comes to building top-performing teams, hiring always trumps training. Although training is important, it has its limitations. It makes far more sense to invest time and money into spotting talented people and hiring them than it does to spend it on training to cultivate talent that may not even exist. The ideal team is made up of talented people who are strong and getting stronger. Rather than setting a goal of a well-rounded worker, leaders should place an emphasis on turning a talented employee into a star. The best strategy is to hire those team members who have the strengths you require and then refine those strengths, instead of attempting to train someone to become an expert in an area where he or she doesn't already have talent.

That makes the ability to identify talent extremely important. While journalists may need a "nose for news," successful leaders must have a similar knack for recognizing talent.

LOOKING FOR TALENT

A colleague of ours was once a managing editor for a national newspaper. The entry-level employees he hired had to be proficient in using industry-standard layout software to create the newspaper's pages quickly and under the relentless pressure of deadlines. Not surprisingly, many of the candidates for the job had already taken an introductory course in using the software so that when the time came to apply, they could confidently list it along with their other skills.

Unfortunately, the contrast between using software in a controlled and comparatively comfortable classroom setting and using it in the fast-paced, deadline-driven environment of a newsroom was substantial. Our colleague would audition prospective employees and then assign them a single page to lay out. Many of these candidates with "experience" using the software failed miserably in their modest assignment.

Then one day, he interviewed a candidate with otherwise impressive credentials, but who had absolutely no experience using the required page-layout software. Normally, this conspicuous gap in her résumé would've been an automatic disqualification. But because she was already on-site and a workstation was available, he decided to give her a shot at laying out a page. It became clear to him almost immediately that she fully understood everything he was saying and had a firm grasp of her assignment, even though she had never seen the software before. The candidate completed her page quickly and accurately and was eager to try another.

That experience provided a memorable lesson in recognizing talent. Most of the candidates had the requisite skills, but very few of them had genuine talent. The knowledge and skills they had acquired from a minimum of practice gave them the thin veneer of competence but not the depth and flexibility that only talent can provide.

It also taught our colleague a valuable lesson in acting decisively. Although the woman with no experience in using the software was easily the most talented of the candidates he'd interviewed up to that point, he still had several more interviews scheduled for filling that particular post and decided to hold off making a final decision until he'd had a chance to interview everyone. His hesitation turned out to be costly. In the interim, the talented woman quickly landed a job with a rival newspaper, where she began an impressive career and a rapid rise through the ranks of the publishing industry. Our colleague, who still desperately needed to fill the open position, was forced to hire someone who had the requisite superficial skills but who lacked the same impressive level of talent.

The moral of this story is pretty straightforward: When you see talent, grab it. But be careful. Don't confuse genuine talent with well-practiced routines. Before you draw any lasting conclusions about a particular person's talents, it is important to assess those talents properly. Some talents can be shy and slow to surface, while other abilities that initially seem like talents are merely well-practiced—and often severely limited—routines.

When you see talent, grab it.

RECOGNIZING TRUE TALENT

A friend who is fond of Mexican food used to stop at a nearby taqueria for lunch several times a week and order the same beans-and-rice burrito. The food was delicious, the staff seemed friendly, and they soon grew to recognize him and his order. Nonetheless, although his order never changed, whenever he requested a beans-and-rice burrito, the pleasant woman behind the counter never failed to ask, "Super? Or regular?"—the burrito's two possible sizes—to which he would always reply, "Regular, please." From his perspective, although it may have seemed unnecessary and repetitive, it was their own little ritual, a bit like always asking, "How are you?" and always hearing, "Fine, thank you," in response— but with salsa on the side.

Then one day when he arrived at the restaurant and placed his usual order, he realized he didn't have enough change for an adequate tip. After fruitlessly digging through his pockets, he turned to the woman behind the counter and asked, "May I please get change for a dollar?"

When he asked, he was shocked by her response. Her

gaze was blank and her mouth was agape, almost as though she had suddenly been hypnotized. It was clear that the woman hadn't a clue what he'd just said. It was only then that our friend realized that she had carefully learned only a handful of questions and answers in English and was unable to respond to anything that strayed from the script. Rather than having a genuine talent for language, the cashier (like the race car driver from chapter 7) merely had an ability to memorize a few key phrases.

Although some people are truly talented, others have simply learned a set of skills that enables them to get the job done but that will fail them when the circumstances are changing and unpredictable. Of course, these are precisely the sorts of situations upon which the fate of a business so often rests.

TALENTS COME NATURALLY

Best known for its personal opinion polling, the Gallup organization has also devoted decades to studying talents. "Talents," according to Gallup, "are naturally recurring patterns of thought, feeling, or behavior that can be productively applied." Applying one's talents isn't merely admirable; it's essential. One person who has never even seen a piano may have more innate talent as a pianist than someone who has been practicing the piano for most of her life. A person with slow-twitch muscles who trains with the track team is bound to be a better sprinter than a person with fast-twitch muscles who has spent much of his time just sitting around. But should that couch potato ever decide to finally get up from his chair and start training, look out!

Debunking the "Blank Slate"

A significant body of evidence indicates that if your mother and father earned high grades on exams, then you are likely to as well. And it isn't simply a question of intelligence. Researchers at King's College London found that a number of other key traits that play a role in performance, such as personality, self-efficacy, and even behavior problems, are also genetically influenced.[1]

Genes can sometimes influence your temperament, and your temperament can in turn affect your talents. The so-called Big Five personality traits, sometimes known by the acronym OCEAN, are openness, conscientiousness, extraversion, agreeableness, and neuroticism. Researchers have begun establishing genetic links to these traits. Although not talents themselves, they often serve as the building blocks for particular talents.

Similarly, the reaction to stress or the appetite for sensation can both be genetically influenced. Recently, scientists identified gene variants that affect the expression of a molecule called neuropeptide Y (NPY), which activates a variety of functions, including your body weight and your emotional responses. Differing levels of NPY may help to explain why some people can withstand stress better than others.[2] Meanwhile, variants in the dopamine D4 receptor (DRD4) appear to influence novelty seeking and may even increase susceptibility to substance abuse, although the extent of these conclusions is still hotly debated.[3]

The key takeaway from this growing body of research is that the quaint notion of the "blank slate" (or tabula rasa), popularized back in the seventeenth century by British philosopher John Locke, is outdated. What these modern science-based studies tell us is that we are not all born the same and that it makes sense to treat people in line with their natural abilities. Although simply broaching the subject can trigger a threat response in many people, we feel we are doing everyone a favor by opening up an honest discussion about people's inherent differences. From our perspective, it will make the world a better place because it's much easier, more fun, and more likely to result in a success when you are working in an environment that makes your strengths shine and that takes your personal needs into account.

Make no mistake: Your genes aren't necessarily your destiny, but if you lack a "natural talent" in a particular area, it can make things more difficult. Your genetic makeup doesn't doom you to being terrible at math, for example. With patience and practice, you can still reach a minimum level of competency. But beyond that, any extra effort probably isn't worth it, especially when there are other areas of expertise that come more naturally to you and that you enjoy more.[4]

Epigenetics: What Turns On Your Genes?

A bomb isn't truly dangerous until somebody lights the fuse. By the same token, a birthday cake isn't truly festive until someone lights the candles. Like the inert bomb or the unlit birthday cake, not all of our genes are automatically activated when we're born. Some of them still need to be lit. A fascinating field called epigenetics provides evidence of how outside factors, such as diet, stress, and even parental affection, can influence your genetic code. The epigenome is the match that determines whether some genes are ignited while others remain unlit.

TALENTS DON'T CHANGE

Many people are familiar with theologian Reinhold Niebuhr's Serenity Prayer.

> *God, grant me the serenity to accept the things I*
> *cannot change,*
> *Courage to change the things I can,*
> *And wisdom to know the difference.*

Oddly enough, the basic message at the heart of this prayer is a crucial one for leaders: There are things about your employees that you can change, and there are things you cannot change. It is important to recognize the difference. At its heart, what distinguishes the things you can change from those you cannot is talent. Like muscles, skills may develop or atrophy over time, but talents remain constant. If the talent is there, some of the skills can be cultivated and developed. Unfortunately, if it isn't there, then they probably can't be.

There are things about your employees that you can change, and there are things you cannot change.

TALENTS VS. STRENGTHS

Even if you have the good fortune to come into this world equipped with all the right genes, the mere presence of a talent, no matter how impressive, is still no guarantee of success. A talent is an innate ability that can be cultivated or squandered. Strengths are talents put to productive use through the acquisition of skills and the accumulation of knowledge.

Skills are basic abilities that can be learned (through training and practice) and are specific to the situation. Learning to operate certain kinds of machinery, for example, is a skill. This can include everything from a cash register to a car. No one is born with the ability to drive an automobile. It's a skill that has to be acquired. Similarly, many readers may still remember the awkward experience of first learning to use a computer mouse, as well as its numerous variations on laptops. Some of these may be more intuitive than others and thus easier to acquire, but the fact is that they're all still skills.

If skills are your tools, then knowledge is the toolbox. It is your accumulated body of expertise. It's your storehouse of experience. It comes from the skills you remember and the information you retain and often depends on your ability to transfer information from one situation to another. If you first learned to drive in a Volkswagen, you don't usually have to start all over if you suddenly find yourself behind the wheel of a BMW. Learning to drive your first car was a skill. Operating all the cars you've ever driven since then depends primarily upon knowledge. And practice.

DOES PRACTICE MAKE PERFECT?

A 1993 study by Swedish psychologist K. Anders Ericsson, popularized by author Malcolm Gladwell in his 2008 book, *Outliers*, proposed what came to be known as the "10,000-hour rule." The basic idea was that you could succeed at almost anything if you put in 10,000 hours of practice.

It was an appealing idea. Appealing, but wrong. Unfortunately, although practice can often play an important role in achieving a level of mastery, its impact varies widely depending upon the field. A 2014 meta-analysis led by Princeton University psychologist Brooke Macnamara (now on the faculty of Case Western Reserve University) concluded that "deliberate practice is important, but not as important as has been argued."[5]

What does that mean in concrete terms? Macnamara and her colleagues found overall that practice accounted for only 12 percent of the variation in performance. The biggest bang for your practice buck appears to be in games like chess, in which the impact is 26 percent. It accounts for 21 percent of the difference in music and 18 percent in sports. Ironically, the area where practice seems to have the least effect is in the professions, at less than 1 percent.[6]

The Limits of Training

Practice can fix some things, but not everything. Only with talent can you be confident that all those hours of rehearsal will lead to mastery. That's why the best use of training is to help already talented people get even better.

In a corporate culture that predominantly focuses on identifying and improving substandard performance, training is often mistakenly viewed as an opportunity to help weaker employees to catch up. Unfortunately, you can only liberate and refine an employee's existing talents. You can't create them. You can't kiss a frog and expect that it will magically turn into a prince.

The best use of training is to help already talented people get even better.

From a practical standpoint, what this means is most attempts you make to cultivate talents in a person who doesn't already have them will be a waste of time and money and are almost certain to be a source of frustration for you both as well as a potential drag on everyone around you. In fact, if you're looking for a guaranteed method of robbing your

You can't kiss a frog and expect that it will magically turn into a prince.

team members of energy and motivation, then assign them tasks they aren't good at or don't enjoy. (By the way, you'll often find that one goes with the other. We tend to enjoy and become energized by the things we're good at and dread or loathe the things at which we don't excel. It's rarely the other way around.)

We are likely to learn and grow the most in our areas of greatest strength. Psychologists have known this for decades. More than sixty years ago, a Nebraska study that focused on improving reading speed yielded some startling, counterintuitive results. The most dramatic improvements came from students who were already fast readers. Students actually gained more by building on their existing talents than they did by trying to improve their areas of weakness.[7]

People with existing talents improve more with practice than people without them. You are likely to learn and to grow least in your areas of weakness. We do better improving strengths because this follows the path of least resistance. For most of us, that means it's more rewarding.

Of course, this doesn't mean the workday will be nonstop fun and games for talented people. From time to time, all of us are compelled to do things we don't enjoy. We know very few people, for example, who look forward to paying taxes, changing diapers, battling rush-hour traffic, or taking out the garbage. However, these onerous but comparatively brief tasks are usually more than outweighed by things we like doing and by the opportunities they often make possible. If they aren't, then you're probably in the wrong job, or at least in the wrong spot. As a leader, you can work to put employees in places and situations that make the most of their talents. Don't leave them where they're a bad fit. If you can't improve their existing conditions, move them to an environment where the fit is better.

RETAINING TOP TALENT

"Brains are like hearts," said Robert McNamara, former business executive and U.S. secretary of defense. "They go where they are appreciated." Once you've assembled a team of experts, it is essential to keep them happy, productive, motivated, and, above all, appreciated. You can do this by promoting a brain-friendly environment and by providing meaningful incentives.

CREATING A BRAIN-FRIENDLY ENVIRONMENT

The protection factors that ensure emotional resilience and regulation (see chapter 2) and the diversity that is key to a groundbreaking, innovative collaboration (see chapter 7) come together in a workplace environment that supports the members of your team as a team while accommodating the individual differences that make them unique and valuable contributors. And by "environment" we don't simply mean the walls, desks, and other amenities that make up a typical office. We're talking about the overall workplace atmosphere. Since exercise and nutrition are proven stress protectors (see chapter 2) and learning enhancers (see chapter 6), it is crucial to provide an atmosphere that makes these things feasible.

Organizations of the future will recognize that nutrition is as important to success as adequate ventilation or up-to-date equipment. They'll order in healthy food for meetings, install conveniently located kitchens so employees can address their nutritional needs at work, and hold off-site meetings where the catered meals are as rewarding and enriching as the conversation.

The same approaches can work with encouraging physical exercise. Sometimes the simple inclusion of a reliable shower and changing room will be all it takes to convince employees who live nearby to start bicycling to work instead of driving or taking the bus and instill a general philosophy of wellness throughout your company. At trivago, the world's largest online hotel search site, wellness and exercise are an integral part of the company's culture. "Golf, boxing, yoga, badminton. You name it, we've got it," says Malte Siewert, trivago's cofounder and managing director. "We have a big team in the HR department that just focuses on our employees' well-being inside and outside of work."

With a brain-friendly workplace, your employees will want to come to work. And with the right incentives, they will want to remain on the team.

PROVIDING MEANINGFUL REWARDS AND INCENTIVES

More than a hundred years ago, the discovery of quantum mechanics completely rewrote the rules of physics, yet most of us go through our lives as though the revolution never happened. And in many respects, that obsolete thinking still works. Except, of course, when it doesn't. Modern mainstays, such as CD players, laser surgery, grocery store scanners, and yes, even that indispensable tool of brain scientists, the fMRI machine, would be impossible without quantum physics.

Although it may not be quite as momentous, there's been

a similar revolution in business. Our basic assumption that we are motivated mainly by money has largely been debunked. And yet, many companies still cling to outdated notions of what drives their employees in order to determine the incentives they provide.

It's Money That Matters?

When a passerby stops you on the street and asks for directions, how much do you typically charge? When you bring in a plate of fresh-baked cookies to the office, do you accept both cash and credit as payment? Oh, and by the way, what's your going rate for taking out the garbage or doing the family dishes?

The concept of *Homo economicus* suggests that we, as humans, act primarily as self-interested agents. And if you selectively examine much of our behavior as a species, you'll find plenty of support for this notion even now. However, over the past twenty-five years, a wealth of data calls into question whether we're truly as self-interested as it once seemed.[8]

In instances of "impersonal exchange," such as investing in the stock market, for example, most people respond in a way that is consistent with the *Homo economicus* model.[9] But in what psychologists and economists call "personal exchange," transactions that involve people you know and interact with directly—such as your employees—the scenario is quite different. That's why you tip a restaurant server, for example, even though you may never see him or her again.[10]

The widespread, uncritical adoption of *Homo economicus* grew out of a misreading of evolutionary biology. Strictly speaking, *we* aren't selfish. Only our genes are.[11] Frequently, the most effective means of ensuring a future for our precious genes involves not selfishness and competition but altruism and cooperation. Fundamentally, we are a social species. This isn't simply homespun, feel-good philosophy. It's a brain-based assertion supported by mountains of scientific data.

A New Perspective on Incentives

How does this translate when it comes to providing incentives in the workplace? Don't worry. For the most part, money still rules as a universally acknowledged standard for measuring value and for triggering the reward response. But all those dollars and euros definitely have their limitations. They can be subject to the law of diminishing returns and in some instances may even have a negative effect. And in many cases they can be less effective than nonstandard, nonmonetary rewards.

Although you have numerous options for incentives, in general there are two key principles to keep in mind:

1. **Rewards are far more powerful when they're unexpected.** Most incentive systems are based on the idea of an expected reward: the quarterly dividend, the management-by-objectives bonus at the end of the year, or the prize for the successful completion of a project. Unfortunately, the expectations associated with these incentives can undermine the impact of the reward. What really stimulates our brains is novelty, which is why a predictable prize doesn't pack the same punch as one we weren't expecting. In fact, using a technique called deep brain stimulation, scientists have finally been able to prove in humans what they'd demonstrated in nonhumans for decades:

Unexpected rewards make us feel really good. They light up the reward center in our brain, causing clusters of dopamine neurons to increase their firing rate significantly.[12]

2. **Incentives for individuals have an impact on the entire team.** Don't make the mistake of believing that an individual incentive is just between you and the person who's receiving it. A prize or bonus (especially when it's unexpected) may produce a reward response in the recipient, but it can trigger a threat reaction from his colleagues. If the incentive is perceived as fair (see chapter 8) then it's likely that everyone will celebrate it or— at the very least—that few people will question it. But if your process of rewarding employees is considered unwarranted, unbalanced, or biased, the backlash you trigger from those who detect an inequity can cause the incentive to ultimately do more harm than good.

For the most part, these two principles can serve as your primary guidelines for arriving at rewards. In addition, cognitive neuroscience and behavioral economics have combined to reach a number of other counterintuitive conclusions about what works and what doesn't when it comes to determining incentives.

Paying Too Little Can Be Worse Than Paying Nothing at All

If you attach a trivial monetary bonus to something that is usually considered part of a job description (such as arriving on time to work), the incentive is apt to backfire. A chronically tardy person may conclude that forgoing the tiny bonus is worth the value of continuing to arrive late. He will likely see coming to work on time as something optional, a bit above and beyond what's expected.

Incidentally, the same approach can be just as ineffectual as a stick as it is as a carrot. A day-care center grew tired of having to stay open late to wait for tardy parents. So it instituted a fine for any pickups after official closing time in hopes that it would encourage increased punctuality. As it happens, the fine had the exact opposite effect. The number of late arrivals increased! Apparently, the moms and dads felt the extra cost was worth the convenience of arriving late. What should've been part of a social contract—being considerate of day-care employees who wanted to be able to go home to their own families—became a monetary one. Parents who showed up late believed that by paying the fine they were holding up their end of the transaction. In short, when the incentive or the punishment is too small, it can make matters worse.

A Rise in Pay Can Sometimes Lead to a Fall in Performance

You probably won't have a difficult time convincing whoever holds the purse strings in your company that you want to pay less for a job or a service. But in some instances, lower pay actually delivers better results. Attaching an inordinately high monetary value to a task may increase the perception that more is at stake and thus crank up the level of stress to a point where it interferes with productivity. The culprit in this case is noradrenaline, the fight-or-flight neurotransmitter that encourages alertness when released in moderate doses but can trigger panic when overdone. Although the threshold will vary from one employee to the next, if the stakes are perceived as being too high, a motivating challenge can sometimes morph into a debilitating threat. Granted, for some extreme sensation seekers, the stakes are almost never too high. Nonetheless, we all perform best when we are just slightly overchallenged, not completely overwhelmed.[13]

Intermittent Rewards Are More Effective Than Scheduled Ones

In a midsize, family-owned company we know, the managing partner and his team regularly go out for lunch. Although it would be relatively easy for him to pay for every lunch, he just foots the bill from time to time. Otherwise the team usually splits the check. Because his treating is unscheduled and unpredictable, it feels like a genuine reward, unlike the free food that many companies provide in the communal kitchen that quickly gets taken for granted. His staff enjoys the unexpected savings, as does the CEO, who saves money in the long run while also making everyone feel better. It's a win-win! This is a classic example of the power of an unexpected reward.

Personalized Incentives Can Cost Less and Mean More

Very few of us object to more money, but to trigger a reward response, it helps when the incentive is personalized. After all, money is a universal means of exchange. There's nothing inherent in a big fat bonus that says "this was designed especially for you." On the other hand, a weekend getaway for an employee and his or her spouse to their favorite destination or a pair of tickets to a popular play or a sold-out sporting event may cost less than a typical bonus and yet mean much more. In addition, researchers at Cornell University and the University of Colorado Boulder found that people get more retrospective enjoyment from experiences than they do from material purchases. In other words, well-chosen experiential incentives, such as the variety of sports opportunities that companies like trivago provide, may even be cheaper, but their positive motivating effects on performance will probably last longer.[14]

Even something as small as a bunch of flowers or a carefully chosen book can have a longer-lasting impact than a cash bonus. Providing an incentive that is custom fit to the employee's distinct personality sends a very strong signal: that you've been paying attention and you care. How much is that worth in dollars and cents? In many cases, the impact can be priceless.

Employees Are More Likely to Compare Than to Count

Often, the amount of money someone receives is not as important as how much he or she makes in relation to comparable colleagues or to counterparts in other companies. One study found that respondents would rather earn $50,000 a year while their coworkers made $25,000 than earn $100,000 a year while the others made $250,000.[15] This is fundamentally an issue of fairness. And as we learned in chapter 8, the perception of fairness triggers a reward response, while an employee who feels unfairly treated will react with an even more powerful threat response. It's also a matter of status. Money may not always be the most effective incentive, but it is definitely one important way we measure value. If an employee feels as though she is receiving less than her colleagues, then it's not unreasonable for her to conclude that her work isn't valued as much. Whether her conclusions are justified or not, this can inflict a level of social hurt that is every bit as painful as a physical blow. Sometimes, even more.

ACHIEVING COLLECTIVE PEAK PERFORMANCE

"It was almost as if we were playing in slow motion."[16]

That's how Hall of Fame basketball player Bill Russell described the "magical" feeling he experienced from time to time on the court when he was playing with his teammates, the Boston Celtics, and everything seemed to click. Hesitant to talk about it when he was still playing, Russell waited until he was retired to open up about those times when, in his own words, "all sorts of odd things happened."[17]

"During those spells," he wrote in his autobiography, *Second Wind*, "I could almost sense how the next play would develop and where the next shot would be taken."[18]

His premonitions were usually correct, and even though he was already one of the greatest to ever play the game, he could feel his play rising to an even higher level. And although in these instances he was often pushing his body to its physical limits, he rarely felt the pain.[19]

What made the whole experience so extraordinary was that Russell's feeling wasn't unique. In most of these cases, all his teammates felt exactly the same way. On one memorable occasion, when the buzzer finally sounded and the team walked off the court in victory, they looked at each other in amazement and said, "We have to figure out how to do that again!"[20]

FLOW FEELS BETTER WHEN YOU DO IT TOGETHER

As Bill Russell's story suggests, the flow that leads to individual peak performance can be extended to an entire team. Psychologist Mihaly Csikszentmihalyi, the man who originally coined the term "flow" to describe these peak experiences (see chapter 3), expanded his study from individuals to groups and was fascinated by some of his discoveries. The phenomenon was by no means limited to the basketball court. He found evidence for it in a remarkable number of settings.

Despite its strong association with sports and recreation, flow is actually three times more common in the workplace than it is during leisure time.[21] Teams of surgeons collaborating on a difficult operation have likened the sensation to performing in a ballet.[22] Other work groups have described the feeling as being part of a single organism. Perhaps not surprisingly, flow frequently plays a key role in start-ups, where the team is often collectively pursuing a clear goal while facing considerable time pressure.

Flow always feels good, but "social flow" feels even better. Research evidence suggests that when a team experiences flow collectively the experience is far more satisfying than it is when each member experiences it individually. According to St. Bonaventure University psychologist Charles Walker, the more social the activity, the higher the level of joy was for participants. It is precisely this social component that increases the feeling of satisfaction.[23]

Imagine if you and your team could achieve a collective state of peak performance whenever you needed it. In his book *Group Genius*, Dr. Keith Sawyer, an expert on creativity and a former student of Csikszentmihalyi's, arrives at ten conditions that encourage what he calls "group flow."[24] From our experience there are four major factors that encourage social flow: focus, flexibility, collaboration, and cost.

FOCUS: ZERO IN ON A CHALLENGING
TARGET IN ORDER TO GET IN THE ZONE

Social flow won't occur in an atmosphere of distraction. Focus is essential. A clear goal, complete concentration, and close listening will provide the focus a team needs to achieve the flow state. The expectation of getting closer to the goal or completing a specific step in the process triggers dopamine, the neurotransmitter that signals the anticipation of a reward and, more important, drives motivation. The right level of challenge provides the noradrenaline that ensures that everyone will remain alert. Finally, a clearly articulated goal encourages focus because it makes it easier to determine those stimuli that are relevant to the task at hand. The intensity of this focus is driven by another neurotransmitter, acetylcholine. Ultimately, skillfully given orientation toward an emotionally relevant goal will facilitate the DNA of Peak Performance (see chapters 1 and 3) and increase the likelihood of social flow.

With a clear goal in mind, concentration comes easier. To concentrate most effectively in a social flow situation, your focus should be on the task at hand, rather than on any external rewards or outside pressures that may be driving the group's activity in the first place. Challenges are essential to flow. Of course, the challenges that inspire the complete concentration that social flow requires should be intrinsic to the task rather than things that draw your attention outside the realm where your focus should be aimed. Social flow is also more likely when the group can draw a boundary between their group work and everything else.[25] Whether that boundary is physical, temporal, or merely symbolic, it is in this shelter of complete concentration that the most fruitful flow occurs.

The last component of the focus that is essential to social flow is close listening. In order to maintain a state of social flow for any prolonged period of time, team members must be acutely aware not only of their own actions but also of the contributions of their teammates. This hyperawareness is far more complex in a group context. The trajectory of everyone's actions and assertions must constantly be readjusted to reflect the contributions of his or her teammates. Jazz musicians understand this, as do actors in improvisational theater. Rather than planning ahead or thinking about what they're going to play or say next, they are responding in real time. Everyone is reacting to what he or she hears.[26] This not only encourages focus but also leads to flexibility, which, not surprisingly, is the second key condition for encouraging social flow.

FLEXIBILITY: WHEN IT COMES TO FLOW, "YES" BEATS "NO"

Focus is essential to social flow, but undue rigidity will discourage the flow state. It's one of many delicate balancing acts upon which social flow depends. It is important to build on the ideas of others, instead of rejecting them outright, and to surrender your normal tendency to assert your own ego in favor of group identity.

For stellar models of social flow and flexibility, we turn once again to improv. One of the cardinal rules of improvisational acting is known as "Yes, and . . ." Experienced improvisers almost never say no. They typically seek to extend and build on previous information instead of reversing or rejecting it. Saying no is almost guaranteed to activate the amygdala and trigger a threat response. In

With "no," there's no flow.

short, with "no," there's no flow. Saying yes is obviously preferable and can often prompt a reward reaction, but despite its affirmative nature, it usually brings any further progress to a grinding halt. If you want to keep things going, the "and" is essential. Actress, writer, and comedian Tina Fey, who began her career in improvisational theater, explains things memorably in her autobiography, *Bossypants*:

> If I start a scene with "I can't believe it's so hot in here," and you just say "Yeah . . ." we're kind of at a standstill. But if I say, "I can't believe it's so hot in here," and you say, "What did you expect? We're in hell." . . . Or if I say, "I can't believe it's so hot in here," and you say, "I told you we shouldn't have crawled into this dog's mouth," now we're getting somewhere.[27]

Flexibility also means learning to keep your ego in check. The temptation to take the wheel and steer the course of a group's efforts can be hard to resist. That's why both newcomers and superstars aren't always great team players. The former may be focused on establishing their reputations, while the latter are concerned with protecting theirs. With social flow, the participants are in sync and everyone seems to be thinking with one mind.[28] The key is to blend your ego with those of the rest of the team, to use deep listening to balance your voice with those of the others instead of trying to drown everyone else out.

Who is the leader of the Rolling Stones? Although many might say Mick Jagger, for those who follow the band closely, the picture is a bit more complex. Guitarist Keith Richards has been unsurpassed in writing some of rock and roll's greatest riffs. And yet fellow axman Ronnie Wood is thought by many to be the better overall musician. Meanwhile, the band members themselves have often pointed to drummer Charlie Watts as the key to holding the group together. As Richards wisely said, "I don't care who's leading, it's about whatever is best for the team."[29] You could hardly come up with a better example of people with the potential for king-size egos who are wise enough to know the benefits of keeping them under control.

COLLABORATION: WHY THERE'S NO "I" IN "TEAM"

The subordination of individual egos sets the stage for the third crucial component of social flow: collaboration. The idea is so obvious that it's often overlooked: Groups that work well together are more likely to experience social flow. The optimal level of collaboration is achieved when members have a basic familiarity with each other's processes and approaches but are not so comfortable as to become complacent, when everyone participates at equal levels, and when overall communication is effective.

Who wouldn't want to discover the recipe for surefire success? Northwestern University sociologist Brian Uzzi took a fascinating approach to this age-old challenge by closely examining the teams behind the most successful musicals in history as well as the biggest flops. What was it that made the difference between a Broadway blockbuster and a box-office bomb?

The answer was what many of us have long suspected: It depends on who you know. But that old adage may not mean quite what we thought it did. As it turns out, familiarity is a double-edged sword.

Uzzi established a five-point measurement he called Q to

gauge the number and the nature of the connections that Broadway collaborators had. If everyone on a particular team had worked together in the past, the group had a high Q. If the group was a team of total strangers, the Q was low.[30] What Uzzi and his partner Jarrett Spiro found is that the relationship between the creators was remarkably accurate in predicting a musical's failure or success. Shows that received a Q score of 1.7 or less were likely to fail.[31] But if the Q score was too high—greater than 3.2—the show was also apt to suffer, presumably because team members lacked the sort of diversity of thinking we stress in chapter 7, and innovation took a hit as a consequence.[32]

All these insights would be little more than curiosities if it weren't for one thing: What Uzzi and Spiro learned can be extended well beyond Broadway. With its stress-inducing deadlines, clashing egos, and relentless demand for the next new thing, Broadway provides a surprisingly good model for the general business climate.[33] On average, whether they work on the stage or at the stock exchange, the most successful creative collaborations are familiar but not too familiar. Without "new blood," teams who have worked together for a long time tend to fall into a rut. As Web anthropologist Stowe Boyd explains it, "There has to be a tension, a frisson, or outright disagreement—some working through of different perspectives and backgrounds—between those who have been in the clique for a long time, and one or more outsiders."[34] On the other hand, teams made up entirely of strangers may lose energy and momentum because they lack a tacit knowledge of how each member works. Creativity tends to dwindle when you have to clarify every idea or provide extensive context for every approach that you take.

Collaboration was the principal concern for a client who

hired us to help them improve the productivity of their meetings. Over time, their meetings had been taking longer and longer, yet their decision making was getting worse. Many in the group had been attending this meeting for years and were good friends both inside and outside the office. Everyone realized that something was fundamentally wrong. Most of them were bored, and yet not one employee was willing to speak up and point out what the others knew but didn't have the guts to publicly admit: Not only were the meetings sucking the energy out of everyone, but they were also eating up the better part of a morning. And for what?

In many respects, the format of the meetings would've been familiar to almost anyone. The group had a set of agenda items that they moved through systematically. Unfortunately, that's where the efficiency ended. When each item was brought up, absolutely everyone had an opportunity to contribute, regardless of whether he or she had any particular expertise in the area. And in many cases, everyone *did* contribute. Many team members spoke up, not because they had anything enlightening to say, but because adding to the conversation had become sort of a ritual, almost like a bad habit. Because most of the members were friends, the discussions were often congenial. But the thin foam of goodwill floated atop a deep ocean of boredom and discontent that nearly everyone felt but that nobody talked about—that is, until we arrived on the scene.

After suffering through our first meeting, we took the leader aside and recommended the following change: Each time a new agenda item was brought up, all meeting members not directly affected or who weren't experts on the subject would slide themselves and their chairs back a few feet. This left only the experts close to the table to discuss the current item. Everyone was still present in the room, of course, but the physical distance provided a powerful cue. Once the experts had reached a decision, the next agenda item was introduced and members of the team either pushed in or slid back their chairs depending on the topic. At all times the "outsiders" retained veto power, but except in extraordinary circumstances they let the experts discuss the details while they awaited their turn to step up and serve as the principal decision makers.

The group adopted the new procedure quickly and easily, and the results were almost instantly noticeable. The time spent in the meeting was cut back drastically, and everyone felt a renewed sense of enthusiasm. In a series of before-after measurements, we were able to reduce the time spent on topics by an average of 28 percent and raise the satisfaction with the meetings from 3.6 to 4.7 on a five-point scale—all by this simple intervention. In this case, our presence appeared to provide the "new blood" that the meeting sorely needed. Instead of dreading the meeting, all team members now looked forward to it.

Perhaps it's not surprising to learn that the Rolling Stones' Mick Jagger seems to have an intuitive sense of just what the equal participation aspect of social flow entails. "You have to realize," he told legendary rock journalist Jann Wenner in 1995, "that everyone in the band is all more or less together, and everyone has their own niche, and some people lead in some ways, and some people lead in others."[35]

Social flow is not only normally leaderless but it is most likely to occur when everyone is playing an equal role in the process. What this means is that all members, although they may come to the table with differing skills, should have comparable skill levels. No matter how good a professional athlete may be, he or she is unlikely to experience social flow when playing on a team of amateurs. They must also have equal authority. Managers can participate in social flow, but only as peers, not as bosses.[36]

The necessity for equal participation leads naturally to another key aspect of collaboration, *communication,* which comes from a Latin word for "sharing." To achieve social flow, a team requires constant communication. Some of it inevitably comes during regularly scheduled meetings, but much of it occurs spontaneously in more informal and less structured conversations that arise in office hallways or as asides in e-mails or telephone chats.[37] For the communication to be effective, it should be collaborative and candid.

One of the silent killers of effective communication—and with it, of social flow—is what psychiatrist Gianpiero Petriglieri, an associate professor of organizational behavior at INSEAD business school in Fontainebleau, France, calls "violent politeness." These are the situations in which people in groups would rather bite their tongues than openly express their disagreements or misgivings.[38] Problem solving and decision making suffer because the high cost of cognitive inhibition (see chapter 2) robs the brain of the resources that would normally be devoted to rational analysis. Meanwhile, the undercurrent of distrust triggers the threat response, which saps the energy from fruitful collaboration. In one fell swoop, we lose both our ability to speak our minds and our capacity to build meaningful relationships.[39]

Another problem with violent politeness is that it doesn't fade; it festers. Pulling your punches for now doesn't give you extra time to build up courage and resolve. Instead, it's more likely to make this damaging deference a permanent part of your corporate personality. The aversion to candor becomes a well-worn neuronal pathway. Hesitancy becomes a habit. Rather than consciously holding your tongue, you eventually do it without thinking. The higher you rise in the ranks, the more common violent politeness becomes. In fact, CEOs are often the unfortunate recipients of the bulk of this well-intentioned disingenuousness.[40] As one executive observed, "The neighborhood almost always seems to be free of crime when you view it through the windshield of a police car." Leaders who don't learn to tell the weather themselves may unwittingly wind up with a warm and sunny forecast for what in reality is a cold and stormy company climate.

The only way to break the cycle of violent politeness is with courage, the courage to say what you think and to respect those colleagues who are honest enough and conscientious enough to do the same. The result is more likely to build relationships than it is to endanger them. [41] And it will greatly improve the odds of achieving social flow. Of course, courage comes at a cost. But then, so does social flow.

COST: FLOW IS MORE LIKELY WHEN YOU'VE GOT SOMETHING TO LOSE

Have you ever used matchsticks instead of money to play poker? It can be fun for a while, but, ultimately, with nothing really at stake, it becomes far too easy to get distracted, to bet recklessly, and to gradually lose interest in the outcome of the game. It's not the money that matters; it's the fact that you're willing to risk something of value. In other contexts, that could be your job, your reputation, your self-respect, and yes, in some cases, even your life. (As eighteenth-century English author Samuel Johnson observed, "When a man knows he is to be hanged in a fortnight, it concentrates his mind wonderfully.")

Social flow seldom occurs when nothing is at stake. It requires a clear sense of control, which brings with it autonomy, as well as a genuine potential for failure. Everyone in the group should arrive at the same basic set of conclusions: It's our decision and it's a risky one, but we are willing to face the consequences in pursuit of our goal.

Although working together is essential to the success of the group, each group member should at the same time feel as though he or she is in control. The key is for everyone in the group to feel as though he or she has been granted autonomy by management.[42] A variety of studies have all reached the same conclusion: Team autonomy is a key predictor of team performance,[43] while an absence of autonomy can take the wind out of the sails of even the best teams. As Richard Ryan, a professor of psychology at the University of Rochester, explains, "Energy depletion effects are most apparent when people feel low autonomy."[44]

How can people in a group feel as though they have individual control? This is one of the fascinating paradoxes of social flow. The key is for all group members to feel as though they've been granted autonomy by management and that they are willingly surrendering their personal autonomy in favor of the collective autonomy of the group.[45]

For projects to have true potential and for meetings to really matter, everyone involved must have some skin in the game. We encountered a great example of what happens when there isn't enough at stake.

One of our clients, a CEO, wasn't simply annoyed; he was genuinely concerned. Once a weekly oasis of clarity and action, the Monday-morning meetings were gradually becoming a desert of indecisiveness and inefficiency. He noted with particular alarm how his trusted direct reports seemed to be demonstrating a dwindling lack of ownership.

By rights, the meetings should have been brief and efficient. After all, this was no standing-room-only convocation. There were only five direct reports. Ironically, it was a change that was originally intended as an improvement that caused the trouble. Each member was now able to bring along two staff experts to provide valuable details and data.

The idea was that everyone would benefit from the input of people who knew the topic better than anyone else. Rather than speculating about specifics, the team could turn to the experts in real time to confirm whether a proposal was actually feasible. It sounded wonderful in theory. But in practice, it was a disaster.

What happened is that the presence of two handpicked experts enabled each of the five direct reports to hang back and let his or her employees do all the talking. Even that seemed to make sense at first. After all, despite the love affair that many companies still seem to have with ideals of equal participation and consensus, decisions that require expertise are best made by the experts.

So what went wrong?

With the experts on hand, the attendance of the direct reports soon became superfluous. In fact, it was *worse* than superfluous. Not only did the experts do all the work (and most of the talking), but the reports also used this as an excuse to abandon any sort of personal accountability. If the advice from the experts didn't lead to a successful outcome, then they could blame the experts. Yet if things went well, most of the reports had no trouble taking the credit.

What to do? One possibility was to leave the direct reports in their offices on Monday mornings and let each handpicked pair of experts attend the meeting on their own. Of course, you don't have to have much experience in the business world to know how well that particular idea went over. Fearful of losing his job to a subordinate, each direct report activated his threat response and then under the pretext of rationality insisted that his presence at the meeting was absolutely essential.

The ultimate solution seemed counterintuitive: Get rid of the experts. The CEO limited the meeting to the original five direct reports. In the process, each report regained what he'd lost when the meeting had been expanded: accountability.

Not only did the meetings become more efficient, the change also strengthened the company as a whole by increasing the overall level of trust. The CEO signaled his trust in the conclusions of his direct reports by not turning to the advice of the expert guests for corroboration. The experts still played a key role, of course. But it happened behind the scenes. Instead of attending the weekly meeting, they met with their managers in advance and thoroughly briefed them so that they could discuss the topics with authority and make their cases clearly. This led to a two-way increase in trust. The experts had to trust that their managers would be able to relay their conclusions accurately and effectively, while the managers had to trust that their experts would provide them with reliable, well-supported advice.

What began as a problem was transformed into a breakthrough. Everyone emerged from the whole experience stronger and more confident. The increased levels of trust companywide weren't the only benefit. There was also an enhanced ability to communicate key ideas effectively as well as a greater sense of status and accountability.

What began as a problem was transformed into a breakthrough.

And with accountability

comes risk. After all, it's difficult to place the blame on others when you've already made it clear that you're in control. The sense that you are responsible for your own actions increases focus, and with focus comes flow. Daredevil climbers like Dean Potter understood this intimately (see chapter 3). It is the pursuit of the flow experience that leads them to tackle increasingly dangerous challenges.

Of course, corporate teams don't usually have to risk their lives to achieve social flow. But when the stakes are raised, the possibility of social flow increases. It's why experienced actors often learn to embrace the feeling of stage fright and use it as a way to jump-start the flow experience.[46] It's why many people rise to the occasion when the stakes are high but make regrettable mistakes when they let their guard down.

When the stakes are raised, the possibility of social flow increases.

The problem, of course, is that most businesses are designed to minimize risk. In fact, if you fail in business, you are often punished.[47] On one level, this is an understandable reaction to the threat response as well as to financial reality, but author Keith Sawyer reminds us of another reality: "Research shows us over and over again," he writes in his book *Group Genius*, "that the twin sibling of innovation is frequent failure."[48] Without the looming specter of failure, the chances of achieving precisely the sort of social flow you need to succeed are likely to vaporize. There's no question that social flow comes at a cost. But for those who have experienced its benefits in terms of both performance and profound satisfaction, the cost is definitely worth it.

As it happens, one of the Rolling Stones' greatest hits also turned out to be one of their biggest lies. Although the song, "(I Can't Get No) Satisfaction," may have once reflected the youthful angst of the era, time has shown that in more than fifty years together as one of the world's best-known, highest-performing teams, in addition to gaining great wealth and recognition, the band has achieved something we all seek, both individually and in teams: satisfaction.

CHAPTER 9 IN A NUTSHELL

KEY POINTS FROM "DEVELOP THE TEAM OF THE FUTURE"

T is for Team. *T* is for Talent. Creating a high-performing team is above all a question of recruiting and developing top talent. One of the most important roles of a leader is to recognize the presence of genuine talent. When you see it, grab it!

Target your development efforts. Don't dilute precious development time and money by devoting the same type of training to everyone. Training has a far greater impact on people who are already talented. Employees will gain more by building on their existing talents than they will by trying to improve their areas of weakness.

Create a brain-friendly workplace. Talented people still need an environment that makes them want to come to work and enables them to succeed. Since exercise, nutrition, and sleep make up the trio of stress protectors, it is essential to support and encourage an atmosphere that makes these things feasible.

Provide meaningful incentives. With a brain-friendly workplace, your employees will want to come to work. And with the right incentives, they will want to remain on the team. When providing meaningful incentives, keep two brain-based principles in mind: fairness and novelty.

Individual rewards are shared by the group. Like it or not, all compensation occurs in a social context. Money matters less than the perception that someone is being compensated fairly in relation to his or her colleagues. Fairness triggers oxytocin, and oxytocin promotes collaboration.

Everyone loves a pleasant surprise. Unexpected rewards are processed more strongly by the brain than incentives that a team member has been anticipating. The difference is dopamine, the novelty neurotransmitter, which can be a potent motivator. With this principle in mind, strive to set aside part of your budget for spot bonuses. You'll be impressed by how powerful these unscheduled rewards can be.

Social flow is flow on steroids. The flow that leads to individual peak performance can be extended to an entire team. Psychologists who have studied social flow closely have arrived at a set of conditions that can significantly increase the likelihood of its occurring. These four factors are focus, flexibility, collaboration, and cost.

Focus. Social flow won't occur in an atmosphere of distraction. A clear goal, complete concentration, and close listening will provide the focus a team needs to collectively achieve the flow state.

Flexibility. Undue rigidity will discourage the flow state. It is important to build on the ideas of others instead of rejecting them outright and to surrender your normal tendency to assert your own ego in favor of pursuing the cause of group identity.

Collaboration. Groups that work well together are more likely to experience social flow. The optimal level of collaboration is achieved when members have a basic familiarity with each other's processes and approaches but are not so comfortable as to become complacent, when everyone participates at equal levels, and when overall communication is effective.

Cost. Social flow seldom occurs unless something is at stake. A tangible, meaningful risk triggers noradrenaline, which sharpens everyone's focus. Both individually and in groups, a sharpened focus is a crucial precursor to the satisfying state of flow.

FINAL NOTE:
KEEPING THE BRAIN
IN MIND

GRANTED, we can't all be Mick Jagger (nor would some of us even want to be). And not every team can expect to achieve the stratospheric success of the Rolling Stones. But the latest developments in neuroscience provide us with an unprecedented means of fulfilling our dreams and aspirations in a way that wasn't possible even a decade ago. The goal of this book has been to make these groundbreaking developments meaningful, memorable, and, above all, useful. Supported by a mountain of data, what we now know about the neurochemistry of reaching our personal best, what we've learned about how neuronal pathways can be wired and rewired to our advantage throughout our lives, and, finally, the revolutionary insights we've gained into what really matters in building a happy and successful team have combined to provide us with an opportunity to thrive both in our businesses and in our personal lives and to truly become leading brains!

NOTES

PART 1: REACHING YOUR PEAK

CHAPTER 1: FIND YOUR SWEET SPOT

1   Cooper, Gordon, and Bruce B. Henderson. *Leap of Faith: An Astronaut's Journey into the Unknown.* New York: Harper Collins, 2000, p. 2.

2   Wolfe, Tom. *The Right Stuff.* New York: Farrar, Straus and Giroux, 1979, p. 402.

3   Ibid., pp. 334–42.

4   Ibid., p. 402.

5   Keim, Albert, and Louis Lumet. *Louis Pasteur.* Translated by Frederic Taber Cooper. New York: Frederick A. Stokes Co., 1914, p. 53.

6   Ibid., p. 65.

7   Ibid., p. 53.

8   Beilock, Sian. *Choke: What the Secrets of the Brain Reveal About Getting It Right When You Have To.* 1st ed. New York: Free Press, 2010, p. 40.

9   Bell, Vaughan. "The Unsexy Truth About Dopamine." *Observer*, February 2, 2013, http://www.theguardian.com/science/2013/feb/03/dopamine-the-unsexy-truth.

10   Beilock, *Choke*, pp. 81–82.

11   Doidge, Norman. *The Brain That Changes Itself.* New York: Viking, 2007, chap. 3.

12   Lusher, J. M., C. Chandler, and D. Ball. "Dopamine D4 Receptor Gene (DRD4) Is Associated with Novelty Seeking (NS)

and Substance Abuse: The Saga Continues . . ." *Molecular Psychiatry* 6 (2001): 497–99.

13 Rabl, Ulrich, et al. "Additive Gene-Environment Effects on Hippocampal Structure in Healthy Humans." *Journal of Neuroscience* 34, no. 30 (July 23, 2014): 9917–26.

14 Davidson, Richard J. *The Emotional Life of Your Brain.* New York: Hudson Street Press, 2012, p. 93.

15 Ibid., p. 101.

16 The Endocrine Society. "Older Age Does Not Cause Testosterone Levels to Decline in Healthy Men." *ScienceDaily*, June 7, 2011, https://www.sciencedaily.com/releases/2011/06/110607121129.htm.

17 Norton, Elizabeth. "Fatherhood Decreases Testosterone." *Science*, September 12, 2011, http://news.sciencemag.org/social-sciences/2011/09/fatherhood-decreases-testosterone. Barrett, E. S., et al. "Marriage and Motherhood Are Associated with Lower Testosterone Concentrations in Women." *Hormones and Behavior* 63 (2013): 72–79.

18 Author interview.

19 Zoefel, Benedikt, René J. Huster, and Christoph S. Herrmann. "Neurofeedback Training of the Upper Alpha Frequency Band in EEG Improves Cognitive Performance," *Neuroimage* 54, no. 2 (January 15, 2011): 1427–31.

20 Cohen, Sheldon, Tom Kamarck, and Robin Mermelstein. "A Global Measure of Perceived Stress." *Journal of Health and Social Behavior* 24 (1983): 385–96.

21 Keim and Lumet, *Louis Pasteur*, p. 70.

22 Wolfe, *Right Stuff*, p. 402.

23 Ibid., p. 408.

CHAPTER 2: REGULATE YOUR EMOTIONS

1 Pychyl, Timothy A. "Self-Regulation Failure (Part 4): 8 Tips to Strengthen Willpower." *Psychology Today*, March 3, 2009, http://www.psychologytoday.com/blog/dont-delay/200903/self-regulation-failure-part-4-8-tips-strengthen-willpower.

2 Derickson, Alan. "Real Men Go to Sleep." *Harvard Business Review*, November 11, 2013, http://blogs.hbr.org/2013/11/real-men-go-to-sleep/.

3 Anwar, Yasmin. "Sleep Loss Linked to Psychiatric Disorders." *UC Berkeley News* press release, October 22, 2007, http://berkeley.edu/news/media/releases/2007/10/22_sleeploss.shtml.

4   Ibid.
5   Breus, Michael J. "Insomnia Impairs Emotional Regulation." *Psychology Today*, July 5, 2013, http://www.psychologytoday .com/blog/sleep-newzzz/201307/insomnia-impairs-emotional -regulation.
6   Derickson, "Real Men Go to Sleep."
7   Anwar, "Sleep Loss Linked to Psychiatric Disorders."
8   Breus, "Insomnia Impairs Emotional Regulation."
9   Anwar, "Sleep Loss Linked to Psychiatric Disorders."
10 McNamara, Patrick. "REM Sleep, Emotional Regulation and Prefrontal Cortex." *Psychology Today*, December 28, 2011, http://www.psychologytoday.com/blog/dream-catcher/201112/ rem-sleep-emotional-regulation-and-prefrontal-cortex.
11 Ibid.
12 Sleep.org, "Sleeping at Work: Companies with Nap Rooms and Snooze-Friendly Policies," https://sleep.org/articles/ sleeping-work-companies-nap-rooms-snooze-friendly-policies/.
13 Derickson, "Real Men Go to Sleep."
14 Medina, John. *Brain Rules: 12 Principles for Surviving and Thriving at Work, Home, and School*. Seattle: Pear Press, 2008, p. 14.
15 Ibid., p. 16.
16 Ibid.
17 Ibid., pp. 16–17.
18 Ibid., p. 16.
19 Blumenthal, James A., et al. "Effects of Exercise Training on Older Patients with Major Depression." *Archives of Internal Medicine* (October 25, 1999).
20 Medina, *Brain Rules*, p. 22.
21 Schwarz, Joel. "Scenes of Nature Trump Technology in Reducing Low-Level Stress." University of Washington, June 10, 2008, http://www.washington.edu/news/2008/06/10/scenes-of -nature-trump-technology-in-reducing-low-level -stress/.
22 Wang, Shirley S. "Coffee Break? Walk in the Park? Why Unwinding Is Hard." *Wall Street Journal*, August 30, 2011.
23 Berman, Marc G., John Jonides, and Stephen Kaplan. "The Cognitive Benefits of Interacting with Nature." *Psychological Science* 19, no. 12 (December 2008): 1207–12.
24 Wang, "Coffee Break?"
25 Author interview.
26 Wurtman, Richard J., et al. "Effects of Normal Meals Rich in Carbohydrates or Proteins on Plasma Tryptophan and Tyrosine

Ratios." *American Journal of Clinical Nutrition* 77 (2003): 128–32.

27   Huang, Li., Adam D. Galinsky, Deborah H. Gruenfeld, and Lucia E. Guillory. "Powerful Postures Versus Powerful Roles: Which Is the Proximate Correlate of Thought and Behavior?" *Psychological Science* 22, no. 1 (2011): 95–102.

28   Cuddy, Amy J. C., Caroline A. Wilmuth, and Dana R. Carney. "The Benefit of Power Posing Before a High-Stakes Social Evaluation." *Harvard Business School Working Paper*, No. 13-027, September 2012.

29   Emmons, Robert A., and Michael E. McCullough. "Counting Blessings Versus Burdens: An Experimental Investigation of Gratitude and Subjective Well-Being in Daily Life." *Journal of Personality and Social Psychology* 84, no. 2 (2003): 377.

30   Korb, Alex. "The Grateful Brain." *Psychology Today*, November 20, 2010, http://www.psychologytoday.com/blog/ prefrontal-nudity/201211/the-grateful-brain.

31   Ibid.

32   Ibid.

33   Emmons and McCullough, "Counting Blessings Versus Burdens."

34   Bandura, Albert (1994). "Self-Efficacy." In *Encyclopedia of Human Behavior*, vol. 4, edited by V. S. Ramachaudran. New York: Academic Press, pp. 71–81. Reprinted in H. Friedman (ed.), *Encyclopedia of Mental Health*. San Diego: Academic Press, 1998.

35   Ibid.

36   Warrell, Margie. "Afraid of Being 'Found Out?' Overcome Impostor Syndrome." *Forbes*, April 3, 2014, http://www.forbes .com/sites/margiewarrell/2014/04/03/impostor-syndrome/.

37   Weir, Kirsten. "Feel Like a Fraud?" *gradPSYCH* (American Psychological Association), November 2013, http://www.apa .org/gradpsych/2013/11/fraud.aspx.

38   Warrell, "Afraid of Being 'Found Out?' "

39   Pinker, Susan. "Field Guide to the Self-Doubter: Extra Credit." *Psychology Today*, November 1, 2009, http://www.psychology today.com/articles/200911/field-guide-the-self-doubter-extra -credit.

40   Warrell, "Afraid of Being 'Found Out?' "

41   Weir, "Feel Like a Fraud?"

42   Pillay, Srinivasan S. *Your Brain and Business: The Neuroscience of Great Leaders*. Upper Saddle River, NJ: FT Press, 2011, p. 104.

43   Ibid.

44   Pinker, "Field Guide to the Self-Doubter."

45 Ibid.
46 Warrell, "Afraid of Being 'Found Out?'"
47 Weir, "Feel Like a Fraud?"
48 Ibid.
49 Ibid.
50 Pinker, "Field Guide to the Self-Doubter."
51 Carey, Benedict. "Feel Like a Fraud? At Times, Maybe You Should." *New York Times*, February 5, 2008.
52 Pinker, "Field Guide to the Self-Doubter"; Carey, "Feel Like a Fraud? At Times, Maybe You Should."
53 Ibid.
54 Pinker, "Field Guide to the Self-Doubter."
55 Ibid.
56 Weir, "Feel Like a Fraud?"
57 Pinker, "Field Guide to the Self-Doubter."
58 Ibid.
59 Carey, "Feel Like a Fraud? At Times, Maybe You Should."
60 Warrell, "Afraid of Being 'Found Out?'"
61 Pinker, "Field Guide to the Self-Doubter."
62 Ibid.
63 Weir, "Feel Like a Fraud?"
64 Warrell, "Afraid of Being 'Found Out?'"
65 Pinker, "Field Guide to the Self-Doubter."
66 Ibid.
67 Ibid.
68 Warrell, "Afraid of Being 'Found Out?'"
69 Ibid.
70 Pinker, "Field Guide to the Self-Doubter."
71 Weir, "Feel Like a Fraud?"
72 Pinker, "Field Guide to the Self-Doubter."
73 Weir, "Feel Like a Fraud?"
74 Pinker, "Field Guide to the Self-Doubter."
75 Ibid.
76 Dutton, D. G., and Aron, A. P. "Some Evidence for Heightened Sexual Attraction Under Conditions of High Anxiety." *Journal of Personality and Social Psychology* 30 (1974): 510–17.
77 Lieberman, M. D. *Social: Why Our Brains Are Wired to Connect.* New York: Crown, 2013, chap. 9.
78 University of California, Los Angeles. "Putting Feelings into Words Produces Therapeutic Effects in the Brain." *ScienceDaily*, June 22, 2007, www.sciencedaily.com/releases/2007/06/070622090727.htm.
79 Lieberman, *Social.*
80 Beilock, *Choke*, p. 161.

81   University of California–Los Angeles. "Putting Feelings into Words Produces Therapeutic Effects in the Brain."

CHAPTER 3: SHARPEN YOUR FOCUS

1   "U.S. Slackline Walker Dean Potter Crosses China Canyon." *BBC News* (Asia), April 23, 2012, http://www.bbc.com/news/world-asia-17811115.

2   Arnold, Katie. "The Man Who Thinks He Can Fly," *ESPN*, July 10, 2012, http://sports.espn.go.com/espn/magazine/archives/news/story?page=magazine-20071115-article43.

3   Chabris, Christopher, and Daniel Simons. *The Invisible Gorilla: And Other Ways Our Intuitions Deceive Us*. New York: Crown, 2010, pp. 5–6.

4   Ibid.

5   Ibid., p. 24.

6   Davidson, *The Emotional Life of Your Brain*, pp. 86–87.

7   Smaers J. B., et al. Primate Prefrontal Cortex Evolution: Human Brains Are the Extreme of a Lateralized Ape Trend. *Brain, Behavior and Evolution* 77, no. 2 (2011): 67–78, https://www.karger.com/Article/FullText/323671.

8   Kotler, Steven. *The Rise of Superman: Decoding the Science of Ultimate Human Performance*. Seattle: Amazon Publishing, 2014, chap. 3.

9   "Fuzzy Brain? Increase Your Attention Span." CNNhealth.com, December 9, 2008, http://www.cnn.com/2008/HEALTH/11/14/rs.increase.your.attention.span/.

10   Ibid.

11   Tierney, John. "When the Mind Wanders, Happiness Also Strays." *New York Times*, November 16, 2010, p. D1.

12   Medina, *Brain Rules*, pp. 86–87.

13   Ibid., p. 87.

14   Ibid.

15   Richtel, Matt. "Multitasking Takes Toll on Memory, Study Finds." *New York Times*, April 11, 2011, http://bits.blogs.nytimes.com/2011/04/11/multitasking-takes-toll-on-memory-study-finds/?_r=0.

16   Rock, David. *Your Brain at Work*. New York: Harper Business, 2009, p. 36.

17   Silverman, Rachel Emma. "Workplace Distractions: Here's Why You Won't Finish This Article." *Wall Street Journal*, December

11, 2012, http://online.wsj.com/news/articles/SB1000142412788
732433920457817325222302388.

18 Gold, Sunny Sea. "How to Be a Better Driver." *Scientific American Mind*, March/April 2013, http://www.scientific american.com/article/how-to-be-a-better-driver/.

19 Kotler, *Rise of Superman*, chap. 7.

20 Loh, Kep Kee, and Ryota Kanai. "Higher Media Multi-Tasking Activity Is Associated with Smaller Gray-Matter Density in the Anterior Cingulate Cortex." *PLOS ONE* 9, no. 9 (September 24, 2014), http://journals.plos.org/plosone/article?id=10.1371/journal.pone.0106698.

21 Poldrack, Russell. "Multitasking: The Brain Seeks Novelty." *Huffington Post*, October 28, 2009, http://www.huffingtonpost.com/russell-poldrack/multitasking-the-brain-se_b_334674.html.

22 Richtel, "Multitasking Takes Toll on Memory."

23 Poldrack, "Multitasking."

24 Richtel, "Multitasking Takes Toll on Memory."

25 University of Utah. "Frequent Multitaskers Are Bad at It: Can't Talk and Drive Well." *ScienceDaily*, January 23, 2013, http://www.sciencedaily.com /releases/2013/01/130123195101.htm.

26 Carr, Nicholas. *The Shallows: What the Internet Is Doing to Our Brains*. Boston: W. W. Norton & Co., 2011, p. 141.

27 Ibid., p. 142.

28 *Science Friday*. "The Myth of Multitasking," May 10, 2013 (radio show).

29 Mäntylä, Timo. "Gender Differences in Multitasking Reflect Spatial Ability." *Psychological Science* 24 (2013): 514–20.

30 Hassed, Craig. "Mindfulness, Well-being and Performance." *NeuroLeadership Journal* 1 (2008).

31 Lapowsky, Issie. "Don't Multitask: Your Brain Will Thank You." *Inc.*, April 2013, http://www.inc.com/magazine/201304/issie-lapowsky/get-more-done-dont-multitask.html.

32 Paul, Annie Murphy. "You'll Never Learn! Students Can't Resist Multitasking, and It's Impairing Their Memory." *Slate*, May 3, 2013, http://www.slate.com/articles/health_and_science/science/2013/05/multitasking_while_studying_divided_attention_and_technological_gadgets.html.

33 Hill, Audrey, et al. *Prefrontal Cortex Activity During Walking While Multitasking: An fNIR study*. Paper presented at the Proceedings of the Human Factors and Ergonomics Society Annual Meeting, 2013.

34 Cantor, Joanne. "Is Background Music a Boost or a Bummer?" *Psychology Today*, May 27, 2013.

35   Lapowsky, "Don't Multitask."
36   Poldrack, "Multitasking."
37   Blacksmith, Nikki, and Jim Harter. "Majority of American Workers Not Engaged in Their Jobs." *Gallup*, October 28, 2011, http://www.gallup.com/poll/150383/majority-american -workers-not-engaged-jobs.aspx.
38   Brewer, Judson A., et al. "Meditation Experience Is Associated with Differences in Default Mode Network Activity and Connectivity." *PNAS* 108, no. 50 (December 13, 2011): p. 20254.
39   Ibid., pp. 20254–59.
40   Tierney, "When the Mind Wanders."
41   Ibid.
42   Ibid.
43   Eisold, Ken. "Concentrating Makes You Happy." *Psychology Today*, February 8, 2011, http://www.psychologytoday.com/ blog/hidden-motives/201102/concentrating-makes-you-happy.
44   "Super Bowl XLVIII Most-Watched TV Program in U.S. History." NFL.com, February 3, 2014, http://www.nfl.com/ superbowl/story/0ap2000000323430/article/super-bowl-xlviii -mostwatched-tv-program-in-us-history.
45   Roenigk, Alyssa. "Lotus Pose on Two." *ESPN the Magazine*, August 21, 2013, http://espn.go.com/nfl/story/_/id/9581925/ seattle-seahawks-use-unusual-techniques-practice-espn -magazine.
46   Jha, Amishi P. "Being in the Now." *Scientific American Mind* 24 (March/April 2013): 28, http://www.nature.com/scientific americanmind/journal/v24/n1/full/scientificamericanmind 0313-26.html.
47   Davidson, *Emotional Life of Your Brain*, p. 235.
48   Brewer, "Meditation Experience."
49   Davidson, Richard J. "Transform Your Mind, Change Your Brain." YouTube video, 1:05:21, posted by Google TechTalks, September 23, 2009, https://www.youtube.com/ watch?v=7tRdDqXgsJ0.
50   Hölzel, Britta K., et al. "Mindfulness Practice Leads to Increases in Regional Brain Gray Matter Density." *Psychiatry Research: Neuroimaging* 191, no. 1 (January 2011): 36, doi: 10.1016/j.pscychresns.2010.08.006.
51   Murakami, Hiroki, et al. "The Structure of Mindful Brain." *PLOS ONE* 7, no. 9 (September 28, 2012), http://journals.plos .org/plosone/article?id=10.1371/journal.pone.0046377.
52   Konnikova, Maria. "The Power of Concentration." *New York Times*, December 15, 2012. Massachusetts General Hospital.

"Mindfulness Meditation Training Changes Brain Structure in Eight Weeks." *ScienceDaily*, January 21, 2011, www.science daily.com/releases/2011/01/110121144007.htm.

53 Murakami, "Structure of Mindful Brain."

54 Hölzel, "Mindfulness Practice."

55 Konnikova, "Power of Concentration."

56 Massachusetts General Hospital, "Mindfulness Meditation Training."

57 Brewer, "Meditation Experience," p. 20257.

58 Jha, "Being in the Now."

59 Davidson, *Emotional Life of Your Brain*, p. 238.

60 Ibid., p. 239.

61 Ibid., p. 243.

62 Stahl, Bob, and Elisha Goldstein. *A Mindfulness-Based Stress Reduction Workbook*. Oakland, CA: New Harbinger Publications, 2010, pp. 60–61.

63 Ibid.

64 Ibid.

65 Csikszentmihalyi, Mihaly, Sami Abuhamdeh, and Jeanne Nakamura. "Flow." Chap. 32 in *Handbook of Competence and Motivation*, edited by Andrew J. Elliot and Carol S. Dweck. New York: Guilford Press, 2005, p. 599.

66 Ibid., p. 600.

67 Ibid., p. 601.

68 Csikszentmihalyi, Mihaly. *Good Business*. New York: Viking, 2003, p. 75.

69 Kotler, *Rise of Superman*, chap. 1.

70 Pink, Daniel. "The Puzzle of Motivation." TED.com, July 2009, http://www.ted.com/talks/dan_pink_on_motivation?c=67552.

71 Herrero, J. L., et al. "Acetylcholine Contributes Through Muscarinic Receptors to Attentional Modulation in V1." *Nature* 454, no. 7208 (August 28, 2008): 1110–14.

72 Kotler, *Rise of Superman*, chap. 7.

73 Csikszentmihalyi, *Good Business*, p. 50.

74 Csikszentmihalyi, Abuhamdeh, and Nakamura, "Flow," p. 602.

75 Ibid., p. 603.

76 Ibid., p. 602.

77 Kotler, *Rise of Superman*, chap. 6.

78 "U.S. Slackline Walker Dean Potter."

79 Kotler, *Rise of Superman*, chap. 3.

80 Longman, Jeré. "900 Feet Up With Nowhere to Go but Down." *New York Times*, March 14, 2008.

81 Ibid.

82   Branch, John. "Dean Potter, Extreme Climber, Dies in BASE-Jumping Accident at Yosemite." *New York Times*, May 17, 2015.

PART 2: CHANGING YOUR BRAIN

CHAPTER 4: MANAGE HABITS

1   World Entertainment News Network. "Jennifer Aniston Beats the Habit, Quits Smoking." Contactmusic.com, October 27, 2011, http://www.contactmusic.com/news/jennifer-aniston -beats-the-habit-quits-smoking_1252963.

2   Ibid.

3   "Jennifer Aniston Kisses Justin Theroux, Smokes Cigarette at Birthday Party." PageSix.com, February 13, 2012, http://page six.com/2012/02/13/jennifer-aniston-kisses-justin-theroux -smokes-cigarette-at-birthday-party/.

4   "Barack Obama's Smoking Habit: Q&A." *Telegraph*, February 9, 2011, http://www.telegraph.co.uk/news/worldnews/barack obama/8313620/Barack-Obamas-smoking-habit-QandA.html.

5   Hurst, Steven R. "Obama Doctor: President Still Smoking Cigarettes, Needs to Lower Cholesterol." *Huffington Post*, February 28, 2010, http://www.huffingtonpost.com/2010/03/01/ obama-doctor-president-st_n_480450.html.

6   Ibid.

7   Diemer, Tom. "Has Obama Finally Licked His Smoking Habit?" *Huffington Post*, December 10, 2010.

8   "Barack Obama's Smoking Habit."

9   "Obama: I Quit Smoking 'Because I'm Scared of My Wife.'" *CBS Chicago*, September 24, 2013, http://chicago.cbslocal.com/2013/ 09/24/obama-quit-smoking-because-im-scared-of-my-wife/.

10   University of Southern California. "Habit Makes Bad Food Too Easy to Swallow." *ScienceDaily*, September 1, 2011, www .sciencedaily.com/releases/2011/09/110901135108.htm.

11   Duhigg, Charles. *The Power of Habit: Why We Do What We Do in Life and Business.* New York: Random House, 2012, pp. 13–14.

12   Ibid., p. 103.

13   Maurer, Robert. *One Small Step Can Change Your Life: The Kaizen Way.* New York: Workman Publishing Company, 2014 (Kindle edition), preface.

14   Ibid., chap. 2.

15   Ibid., chap. 3.

16 Ibid., chap. 4.

17 Ibid., chap. 5.

18 Ibid., chap. 6.

19 Ariely, Dan, Uri Gneezy, George Loewenstein, and Nina Mazar. "Large Stakes and Big Mistakes." *Review of Economic Studies* 76 (2009): 451–69.

20 Ibid., chap. 6.

21 "Making Money Fast." *Lewiston (Maine) Evening Journal*, July 7, 1893, p. 3.

22 Bonné, Jon. "How to Cure Airlines' Ills." NBCNews.com, February 18, 2003, http://www.nbcnews.com/id/3073562/ns/business-us_business/t/how-cure-airlines-ills/.

23 Gottman, John M., and Nan Silver. *The Seven Principles for Making Marriages Work*. New York: Three Rivers Press, 1999, p. 80.

24 Maurer, *One Small Step*, chap. 7.

25 Ibid., chap. 1.

26 Author interview with Dr. Schooler.

27 Schwartz, Jeffrey, and Sharon Begley. *The Mind and the Brain: Neuroplasticity and the Power of Mental Force*. New York: ReganBooks, 2002, pp. 79–91.

28 Ibid., p. 85.

29 Weil, Andrew. "Sure Cure for Nail-Biting." DrWeil.com, February 7, 2008, http://www.drweil.com/drw/u/QAA400350/Sure-Cure-for-Nail-Biting.html.

30 Schwartz and Begley, p. 83.

CHAPTER 5: UNLEASH YOUR UNCONSCIOUS

1 Klein, Gary A. *Sources of Power: How People Make Decisions*. Cambridge, MA: MIT Press, 1999, 32–33.

2 Tierney, John. "Do You Suffer from Decision Fatigue?" *New York Times*, August 17, 2011.

3 Snyder, Kristy M., et al. "What Skilled Typists Don't Know About the QWERTY Keyboard." *Attention, Perception, & Psychophysics* 76 (2014): 162–71.

4 Lehrer, Jonah. *How We Decide*. Boston: Houghton Mifflin, 2009, p. 159.

5 Couric, Katie. "Capt. Sully Worried About Airline Industry." *CBS Evening News*, February 10, 2009, http://www.cbsnews.com/news/capt-sully-worried-about-airline-industry/.

6   MacKay, Karen. "Intuition: How Leaders Use Their Bias to Evaluate Situations." *Phoenix Legal Inc.*, March 6, 2010, http://www.phoenix-legal.com/documents/articles/intuition_practice_bias.php.

7   "Wayne Gretzky." Wikipedia, http://en.wikipedia.org/w/index.php?title=Wayne_Gretzky&oldid=664984820 (accessed June 4, 2015).

8   Lehrer, *How We Decide*, pp. 37–38.

9   Beilock, *Choke*, pp. 194–95.

10   Sandbu, Martin. "Lunch with the FT: Magnus Carlsen." *Financial Times*, December 7, 2012, http://www.ft.com/cms/s/2/2164608e-3ed2-11e2-87bc-00144feabdc0.html#axzz2yo0k9wvd.

11   Fox, Justin. "Instinct Can Beat Analytical Thinking." *Harvard Business Review*, June 2014, https://hbr.org/2014/06/instinct-can-beat-analytical-thinking/.

12   Gigerenzer, Gerd. *Gut Feelings: The Intelligence of the Unconscious.* New York: Viking, 2007, p. 69.

13   Burton, Robert A. *A Skeptic's Guide to the Mind: What Neuroscience Can and Cannot Tell Us About Ourselves.* New York: St. Martin's Griffin, 2013, p. 51.

14   Eagleman, David. *Incognito: The Secret Lives of the Brain.* New York: Pantheon, 2011, pp. 107–9.

15   Thagard, Paul, and Allison Barnes. "Emotional Decisions." *Proceedings of the Eighteenth Annual Conference of the Cognitive Science Society.* Mahwah, NJ: Erlbaum, 1996, pp. 426–29.

16   Ibid.

17   Hayashi, Alden. "When to Trust Your Gut." *Harvard Business Review*, February 2001, p. 9.

18   Ibid., p. 7.

19   Ibid.

20   Christensen, Clayton M. *The Innovator's Dilemma: When New Technologies Cause Great Firms to Fail.* Boston: Harvard Business School Press, 1997.

21   Crovitz, Gordon L. "Who Really Invented the Internet?" *Wall Street Journal*, July 22, 2012, http://online.wsj.com/articles/SB10000872396390444464304577539063008406518.

22   Lazar, Sara W., et al. "Meditation Experience Is Associated with Increased Cortical Thickness." *Neuroreport* 16, no. 17 (November 28, 2005): 1893–97.

23   Stashower, Daniel. *The Boy Genius and the Mogul: The Untold Story of Television.* New York: Broadway Books, 2002, p. 23.

24   Lehrer, *How We Decide*, p. 118.

25   Lehrer, Jonah. "The Eureka Hunt." *New Yorker*, June 28, 2008, p. 43.

26   Norwegian University of Science and Technology (NTNU). "Brain Waves and Meditation." *ScienceDaily*, March 31, 2010, http://www.sciencedaily.com/releases/2010/03/100319210631 .htm (accessed January 1, 2014).

27   Jung-Beeman, Mark, et al. "Neural Activity When People Solve Verbal Problems with Insight." *PLOS Biology* 2, no. 4 (April 13, 2004): e97, doi: 10.1371/journal.pbio.0020097.

28   Ibid.

29   Lehrer, "Eureka Hunt," p. 43.

30   Bower, Bruce. "Road to Eureka." *Science News* 173 (March 22, 2008): p. 184.

31   Lehrer, "Eureka Hunt," p. 44.

32   Ibid., p. 45.

33   Winkielman, Piotr, and Jonathan W. Schooler. "Unconscious, Conscious, and Metaconscious in Social Cognition." Chap. 3 in *Social Cognition: The Basis of Human Interaction*, edited by Fritz Strack and Jens Förster. New York: Psychology Press, 2009, p. 62.

34   Andreasen, Nancy C. "A Journey into Chaos: Creativity and the Unconscious." *Mens Sana Monographs* 9, no. 1 (January– December 2011): 42–53. doi: 10.4103/0973-1229.77424.

35   Klein, Gary A. *Sources of Power: How People Make Decisions.* Cambridge, MA: MIT Press, 1999, p. 32.

36   Ibid.

37   Ibid.

CHAPTER 6: FOSTER LEARNING

1   Hirstein, William, and V. S. Ramachandran. "Capgras Syndrome: A Novel Probe for Understanding the Neural Representation of the Identity and Familiarity of Persons." *Proceedings of the Royal Society B: Biological Sciences* 264, no. 1380 (March 22, 1997): 437–44.

2   "Secrets of the Mind." *NOVA*, PBS.org. Public Broadcasting System, October 23, 2001. Web transcript.

3   Hirstein and Ramachandran. "Capgras Syndrome."

4   Barry, Dave. "Navigating London's Street Witness Protection Program." *McClatchyDC*, July 25, 2012, http://www .mcclatchydc.com/2012/07/25/157647/dave-barry-navigating -londons.html.

5   Maguire, Eleanor A., Katherine Woollett, and Hugo J. Spiers. "London Taxi Drivers and Bus Drivers: A Structural MRI and Neuropsychological Analysis." *Hippocampus* 16, no. 12 (2006): 1091–1101.

6   University of Oxford. "Juggling Enhances Connections in the Brain." *ScienceDaily*, October 17, 2009, http://www.science daily.com /releases /2009/10/091016114055.htm (accessed September 14, 2013).

7   Hamzelou, Jessica. "Learning to Juggle Grows Brain Networks for Good." *New Scientist*, October 11, 2009.

8   University of Oxford, "Juggling Enhances Connections."

9   Hamzelou, "Learning to Juggle."

10 Doidge, *Brain That Changes Itself*, chap. 3.

11 Ibid., chap. 8.

12 Carr, *Shallows*, p. 33.

13 Doidge, *Brain That Changes Itself.*

14 Ibid.

15 Lehrer, *How We Decide*, p. 50.

16 Doidge, *Brain That Changes Itself*, chap. 3.

17 Hendel-Giller, Ronni, et al. "The Neuroscience of Learning: A New Paradigm for Corporate Education." Maritz Institute, May 2010, http://www.maritz.com/~/media/Files/MaritzDotCom/ White%20Papers/Institute/Neuroscience-of-Learning.pdf (accessed May 23, 2014).

18 Doidge, *Brain That Changes Itself*, chap. 3.

19 Ibid.

20 Ibid.

21 Ibid.

22 Ibid., chap. 4.

23 Ibid.

24 Freeman, Walter J. *How Brains Make Up Their Minds.* New York: Columbia University Press, 2001.

25 Doidge, *Brain That Changes Itself*, chap. 3.

26 Carr, *Shallows*, p. 29.

27 Ibid.

28 Hofer, Sonja B., and Tobias Bonhoeffer. "Dendritic Spines: The Stuff That Memories Are Made Of?" *Current Biology* 20, no. 4 (February 23, 2010): R157–59.

29 Medina, *Brain Rules*, p. 116.

30 Coyle, Daniel. "Growing a Talent Hotbed: Dan Coyle at TEDx Sitka" (video file), http://www.youtube.com/watch?v=Aq0pH pNy6bs (accessed August 18, 2012).

31 Ibid.

32 Maurer, *One Small Step*, chap. 1.

33   Medina, *Brain Rules*, p. 111, with considerable extrapolations.
34   Wilhelm, I., et al. "Sleep Selectively Enhances Memory Expected to Be of Future Relevance." *Journal of Neuroscience* 31, no. 5 (February 2, 2011): 1563.
35   Ariely, Dan. *The Upside of Irrationality*. New York: Harper, 2010, p. 121.
36   Beilock, *Choke*, p. 18.
37   Hills, Jan. "How to Use Storytelling to Influence People." *HR Zone*, August 2, 2013, http://www.hrzone.com/feature/ld/how-use-storytelling-influence-people/140417.
38   Hsu, Jeremy. "The Secrets of Storytelling: Why We Love a Good Yarn." *Scientific American Mind*, August 1, 2008, http://www.scientificamerican.com/article/the-secrets-of-storytelling/.
39   Ibid.
40   Hills, "How to Use Storytelling."
41   Stephens, Greg J., Lauren J. Silbert, and Uri Hasson. "Speaker–Listener Neural Coupling Underlies Successful Communication," *PNAS* 107, no. 32 (August 10, 2010): 14428.
42   Hsu, "Secrets of Storytelling."
43   Ibid.

PART 3: BUILDING DREAM TEAMS

CHAPTER 7: THRIVE ON DIVERSITY

1   Carroll, Robert Todd. "Forer Effect." *The Skeptics Dictionary*, http://www.skepdic.com/forer.html.
2   Ibid.
3   Thomas, Ben. "Are the Brains of Introverts and Extroverts Actually Different?" *Discover*, August 27, 2013, http://blogs.discovermagazine.com/crux/2013/08/27/are-the-brains-of-introverts-and-extroverts-actually-different/.
4   Ibid.
5   Ibid.
6   Cain, Susan. "The Power of Introverts." *Huffington Post*, April 18, 2012, http://www.huffingtonpost.com/susan-cain/introverts-_b_1432650.html.
7   "Estimated Frequencies of the Types in the United States Population." *Center for Applications of Psychological Type*, http://www.capt.org/mbti-assessment/estimated-frequencies.htm.

8   Fisher, Helen E. *Why Him? Why Her?* New York: Henry Holt, 2009, pp. 7–8.

9   Fisher, Helen. "What's Your Love Type?" CNN.com, November 16, 2007, http://edition.cnn.com/2007/LIVING/personal/11/12/o.love.types/.

10   Ibid.

11   Ibid.

12   Fisher, *Why Him? Why Her?* p. 71.

13   Fisher, "What's Your Love Type?"

14   Ibid.

15   Fisher, *Why Him? Why Her?* p. 113.

16   Fisher, "What's Your Love Type?"

17   Fisher, *Why Him? Why Her?* p. 8.

18   Ibid., p. 121.

19   Fisher, "What's Your Love Type?"

20   Fisher, Helen. "Why the Clintons Are Married." *Big Think*, February 12, 2010, http://bigthink.com/videos/why-the-clintons -are-married.

21   Fisher, "What's Your Love Type?"

22   Malloy, Michelle. "Managerial Courage: Actively Managing Conflict." Center for Creative Leadership [PowerPoint presentation], 2011, http://www.ccl.org/leadership/pdf/community/ManagerialPresentation.pdf.

23   Wilde, Douglass J. *Teamology: The Construction and Organization of Effective Teams.* London: Springer, 2010.

24   Fisher, *Why Him? Why Her?* p. 72.

25   Ibid., p. 91.

26   Ibid., p. 118.

27   Ibid., p. 105.

28   Ibid., p. 121.

29   Ibid., p. 89.

30   Ibid., p. 72.

31   Ibid., p. 52.

32   Ibid., p. 53.

33   Ibid., p. 56.

34   Mueller-Hanson, Rose A., and Elaine D. Pulakos. "Putting the 'Performance' Back in Performance Management." Society for Human Resource Management and Society for Industrial and Organizational Psychology, SHRM-SIOP Science of HR White Paper Series, 2015.

35   McGregor, Jena. "Study Finds That Basically Every Single Person Hates Performance Reviews." *Washington Post*, January 27, 2014, https://www.washingtonpost.com/news/on-leadership/

wp/2014/01/27/study-finds-that-basically-every-single-person -hates-performance-reviews/.

36 Fox, Cynthia. "Brain Region for Musical Talent Found, Says New Study." *Bioscience Technology*, September 1, 2015, http:// www.biosciencetechnology.com/articles/2015/09/brain-region -musical-talent-found-says-new-study.

CHAPTER 8: CULTIVATE TRUST

1 Blakeslee, Sandra. "Cells That Read Minds." *New York Times*, January 10, 2006, http://www.nytimes.com/2006/01/10/ science/10mirr.html.

2 Rock, *Your Brain at Work*, pp. 195–97.

3 Ibid.

4 Lieberman, M. D. *Social: Why Our Brains Are Wired to Connect*. New York: Crown, 2013, chap. 11.

5 Gilbert, Daniel. *Stumbling on Happiness*. New York: Vintage, 2006, p. 5.

6 Lieberman, *Social*, chap. 3.

7 Ibid.

8 Eisenberger, Naomi I., Matthew D. Lieberman, and Kipling D. Williams. "Does Rejection Hurt? An fMRI Study of Social Exclusion." *Science* 302, no. 5643 (October 10, 2003): 290–92.

9 Ibid.

10 Lieberman, *Social*, chap. 4.

11 Ibid.

12 Ibid., chap. 11.

13 Zak, Paul J. "The Neurobiology of Trust." *Scientific American*, June 2008, p. 91.

CHAPTER 9: DEVELOP THE TEAM OF THE FUTURE

1 King's College London. "Why Is Educational Achievement Heritable?" *ScienceDaily*, October 6, 2014, www.sciencedaily .com/releases/2014/10/141006152151.htm.

2 NIH/National Institute on Alcohol Abuse and Alcoholism. "Genetic Factor in Stress Response Variability Discovered." *ScienceDaily*, April 5, 2008, www.sciencedaily.com/releases/ 2008/04/080402131150.htm.

3   Lusher, Chandler, and Ball, "Dopamine D4 Receptor Gene (DRD4)."

4   Rosen, Julia. "About Half of Kids' Learning Ability Is in Their DNA, Study Says." *Los Angeles Times*, July 11, 2014, http://www.latimes.com/science/sciencenow/la-sci-sn-math-reading-genes-20140711-story.

5   Macnamara, Brooke N., David Z. Hambrick, and Frederick L. Oswald. "Deliberate Practice and Performance in Music, Games, Sports, Education, and Professions: A Meta-Analysis." *Psychological Science Online*, July 1, 2014.

6   Ibid.

7   Clifton, Donald O., and Harter, James K. "Investing in Strengths." In *Positive Organizational Scholarship: Foundations of a New Discipline*, edited by K. S. Cameron, J. E. Dutton, and R. E. Quinn. San Francisco: Berrett-Koehler, pp. 111–21.

8   Aktipis, C. Athena, and Robert O. Kurzban. "Is Homo Economicus Extinct? Vernon Smith, Daniel Kahneman and the Evolutionary Perspective." *Advances in Austrian Economics* 7 (2004): 135–53.

9   Ibid.

10   Ibid.

11   Ibid.

12   Schnabel, Jim. "Scientists Measure 'Unexpected Reward' Response in Humans." Dana Foundation, June 4, 2009, http://www.dana.org/News/Details.aspx?id=42964.

13   Kamenica, Emir. "Behavioral Economics and Psychology of Incentives." *Annual Review of Economics* 4 (July 2012): 427–52.

14   Van Boven, Leaf, and Thomas Gilovich. "To Do or to Have? That Is the Question." *Journal of Personality and Social Psychology* 85, no. 6 (2003): 1193–1202.

15   Shermer, Michael. "It Doesn't Add Up: When It Comes to Money, People Are Irrational. Evolution Accounts for a Lot of It." *Los Angeles Times*, January 13, 2008, http://articles.latimes.com/2008/jan/13/opinion/op-schermer13.

16   Russell, Bill, and Taylor Branch. *Second Wind: The Memoirs of an Opinionated Man*. New York: Ballantine, 1979, p. 177.

17   Ibid.

18   Ibid.

19   Ibid.

20   Walker, Jeffrey. "Collective Flow State: From the Who to Your Team." *Huffington Post*, February 4, 2013, http://www

.huffingtonpost.com/jeffrey-walker/collective-flow-state
-fro_b_2614505.html.

21 Csikszentmihalyi, Mihaly, and Judith LeFevre. "Optimal
Experience in Work and Leisure." *Journal of Personality and
Social Psychology* 56, no. 5 (May 1989): 815–22.

22 Csikszentmihalyi, Mihaly. *Flow: The Psychology of Optimal
Experience.* New York: Harper Perennial Modern Classics,
2008, p. 65.

23 Walker, Charles J. "Experiencing Flow: Is Doing It Together
Better Than Doing It Alone?" *Journal of Positive Psychology* 5,
no. 1 (2010): 3–11, http://www.tandfonline.com/doi/abs/10
.1080/17439760903271116?journalCode=rpos20#preview.

24 Sawyer, Keith. *Group Genius: The Creative Power of
Collaboration.* New York: Basic Books, 2007, pp. 43–56.

25 Ibid., pp. 47–48.

26 Ibid., p. 46.

27 Fey, Tina. *Bossypants.* New York: Little, Brown and Co., 2011,
p. 84.

28 Sawyer, *Group Genius*, pp. 49–50.

29 Kerr, Michael. "Business, Teamwork and Creativity Advice
from Keith Richards?" *Humor at Work*, August 23, 2012,
http://www.mikekerr.com/humour-at-work-blog/teamwork
-business-and-creativity-advice-from-keith-richards/.

30 Lehrer, Jonah. "Groupthink: The Brainstorming Myth." *New
Yorker*, January 30, 2012, pp. 22–27.

31 Ibid.

32 Rosen, Rebecca J. "The Q Score: How Y Combinator's Startups
Are Like Broadway Musicals." Atlantic.com, March 2012,
http://www.theatlantic.com/technology/archive/2012/03/the
-q-score-how-y-combinators-startups-are-like-broadway
-musicals/254531/.

33 Burkus, David. "Why the Best Teams Might Be Temporary."
Harvard Business Review, September 17, 2013, https://hbr.org/
2013/09/why-the-best-teams-might-be-temporary/.

34 Boyd, Stowe. "What Makes the Most Creative Teams?"
Nexalogy Environics, February 17, 2012, http://nexalogy.com/
uncategorized/what-makes-the-most-creative-teams/.

35 Wenner, Jann S. "The Rolling Stone Interview: Jagger
Remembers." *Rolling Stone*, December 14, 1995, http://www
.jannswenner.com/archives/jagger_remembers.aspx.

36 Sawyer, *Group Genius*, p. 50.

37 Ibid., p. 53.

38 Petriglieri, Gianpiero. "Why Work Is Lonely." *Harvard Business*

Review, March 5, 2014, https://hbr.org/2014/03/why-work
-is-lonely/.

39   Ibid.
40   Ibid.
41   Ibid.
42   Sawyer, *Group Genius*, p. 49.
43   Ibid.
44   Villarica, Hans. "To Keep Willpower from Flagging, Remember
the F-Word: 'Fun.'" *Time*, October 21, 2010, http://healthland
.time.com/2010/10/21/to-keep-willpower-from-flagging
-remember-the-f-word-fun/.
45   Sawyer, *Group Genius*, p. 49.
46   Ibid., p. 55.
47   Ibid.
48   Ibid.

ACKNOWLEDGMENTS

FEW books are written in isolation. Like the best projects, *The Leading Brain* is the product of a "dream team" of experts, advisers, and inspirations.

Thanks to our agent, Jeffrey Herman, who recognized the promise of our book and used his considerable expertise to quickly find us a publisher we could be proud of. Thanks also to the team at TarcherPerigee, especially our editor, Marian Lizzi, who took a good book and made it that much better, and Brianna Yamashita, who has capably and enthusiastically handled the marketing.

The genesis for this book grew out of a presentation we initially gave to executives at thyssenkrupp. We are indebted to Dr. Janin Schwartau and Dr. Detlef Hunsdiek at thyssenkrupp for having the foresight to support what was then a relatively strange and new idea: applying insights from neuroscience to leadership training. Thanks for believing in us. It all started with you!

Thanks also to the participants in that original program: Dr. Kerstin Böcker, Dr. Jörg Breker, Martin Hurter, Ursula Kiel-Dixon, Dr. Uwe Kinski, Dr. Klaus Müller, Frank Rink, and Dr. Ulrike Weber. This was definitely a life-changing experience for us, and we know from your comments and enthusiasm that it was for many of you as well.

In addition to being coauthors, we are both a proud part of a much larger team, the Munich Leadership Group (MLG). Hans extends a special note of appreciation to Dr. Paul Schuermann, who cofounded MLG with him in 2008. Your advice and support in all stages of the book were invaluable; you are a true friend, a great business partner, and a role model for learning. Additional thanks to MLG experts Martin Spuetz, whose incredible wealth of talents and never-ending hunger for learning have served as the basis for some amazing work; Michael Knieling, for demonstrating extraordinary patience, stamina, and loyal support, especially when things are getting tough and schedules are growing tight; and Professor John Barr, whose unique wisdom and leadership knowledge have provided us with untold benefits for many, many years. We'd also like to extend special thanks to Stephanie Jagdhuber and Anja Wiendl, who've worked tirelessly to keep things in sync and on schedule throughout all the stages of putting this book together.

To all our MLG colleagues in the United States, in Europe, and in the Asia Pacific, who contributed so many examples for the practical application of the neuroscientific insights in this book—and who are working hard every day to make the business world a place full of respect, inspiring collaboration, creative innovation, and passionate performance, it is always a pleasure and a privilege to work with you: Margarita Aguilar, Simone Albrecht, Ulrich Albrecht-Früh, PhD, Monica Ambrosini, Deanna Banks, PhD, Matt Beadle, Martina Bohnenstiel, Klaus Dürrbeck, Roland Fichtel, Thomas Ganslmayr, Paige K. Graham, PhD, Mark Guo, Jürgen Hessenauer, Gabor Holch, David Hyatt, PhD, Glyn Jones, Kate Klawitter, Serdar Lale, Jane Millar, Vivianne Näslund, Susanne Rentel, Natalie Rosengart, Margaret A.

Sanchez, Georg Schuster, Laura Schwan, Heather L. Todd, Eric Vanetti, PhD, Christine Xue, Biran Yılancıoğlu, and Stephen Yong.

One thing that separates *The Leading Brain* from traditional leadership books is a fundamental reliance on valid neuroscientific research. Although we both have backgrounds in psychology and neuropsychology, we frequently turned to the wisdom of experts in the field to bolster our case. In that respect, we are indebted to Dr. Helen Fisher of Rutgers University, whose groundbreaking research provided the inspiration for chapter 7 and who was kind enough to read over that chapter and provide us with some helpful guidance. Likewise, Dr. Jonathan Schooler, professor of psychological and brain sciences at the University of California, Santa Barbara, provided deep scientific insights as well as inspiration during our many meetings with him.

Of course, *The Leading Brain* isn't solely about brain science. It's also a business book, and we were delighted to receive support and advice from some truly visionary business leaders. Liam Condon, board member of Bayer AG, has been dedicated to making the business world a better place. Not surprisingly, Uli Heitzlhofer, global people development program manager with Google, is a lightning-fast learner, who was always ready to share (and challenge!) with some unique and exciting insights. Peter Gerber, CEO of Lufthansa Cargo AG, used his impressive general knowledge and exhaustive practical experience to provide us with valuable feedback on an early draft of the book. Julie Teigland, a managing partner with EY, is a valued advocate of neuroscience-based leadership and has been steadfast in her pursuit of EY's goal to create a better working world. Alexander Wilke, head of communications at thyssenkrupp, has a passion for novelty and an unquenchable sense of curiosity that has set a wonderful example.

We are also indebted to numerous innovators in academia, whose patient and persistent work in laboratories and lecture halls has had an exciting ripple effect, generating waves that have turned the tide of the business world. Foremost among them is Ken Singer, managing director at the Sutardja Center for Entrepreneurship and Technology at the University of California, Berkeley. Ken is a true phenomenon, not simply because of his insatiable curiosity and his innovative theories and practices but also for his unique way of translating all this into stunning insights for start-up businesses. Ken's colleague at Berkeley, Professor Henry Chesbrough, has long emphasized innovation as one of the most relevant topics in leadership and responded enthusiastically to our efforts to add neuroscience to that leadership equation. Duke University's Dan Ariely, an author and authority on behavioral economics, was important both as a source of fascinating research and as a guide to navigating the sometimes confusing landscape of book publishing.

Each of us can point with great respect and gratitude to a mentor whose inspiring examples and invaluable support fundamentally altered the trajectory of our lives and careers. Hans wants to give special recognition to the late Lutz von Rosenstiel, from Ludwig Maximilian University of Munich, whose unrivaled understanding of psychology in both theory and practice made him a role model for his own passion for social life in organizations. Friederike is grateful to Dr. Wolf Singer, emeritus director of the Max Planck Institute for Brain Research, for sharing his considerable wisdom and knowledge, for providing many opportunities for her in the field of neuroscience, and ultimately for his support in creating this book.

ACKNOWLEDGMENTS

Each contribution to the writing of *The Leading Brain,* no matter how large or small, has played a vital role in the composition of the book you hold in your hands. That said, there are a handful of people who deserve special thanks: Matthias Hohensee, Silicon Valley bureau chief and columnist for the German national business weekly magazine *Wirtschaftswoche,* is a remarkable trend spotter, who recognized early on the tremendous potential of applying neuroscience to leadership. Dirk Kanngiesser, Silicon Valley networker extraordinaire, did an amazing job of linking us up with so many inspiring people from business and academia. Professor Dietmar Harhoff, PhD, director of the Max Planck Institute for Innovation and Competition, and one of the smartest people on earth, provided us with invaluable feedback and advice. Jeremy Clark, director of Innovation Services at the Palo Alto Research Center (PARC), always seemed to come up with an enlightening creative thought, precisely when it was needed the most. Navi Radjou, author of *Jugaad Innovation,* and a man who clearly practices what he preaches, was constantly inspiring us to think even faster, even leaner, and even more to the point. Angela Adams of the Saïd Business School at Oxford University generously shared her wisdom and experience in publishing, especially during the process of finalizing the manuscript as well as in the effort to find an agent and a publisher for this book. Laurence Williams, PhD, also at the Saïd Business School, is a true colleague and gifted coach, who accompanied us on our journey. Andy Goldstein, executive director of the Entrepreneurship Center at LMU, and executive director of Deloitte Digital, let us tap into his amazing personal network, enabling us to connect with so many interesting individuals. Koen Gonnissen, former coach of the Belgium Davis Cup Team, knows better than anyone else how to take the success rules for high performance in sports and apply them to the business world. We had the delight of working side by side with Koen on many executive leadership programs as well as the honor of sharing the stage with Marko Koers, Steffi Thomas, and other inspiring Olympic heroes. Finally, this list would not be complete without mentioning Viktoria Kraemmer, Andrew Wright, Peter Haugaard, Sebastian Kolberg, Lou Dobrev, Horst-Uwe Groh, Christoph Göbel, Wolfgang Zellerhoff, Marcus Krug, Arnie Wilson, Jutta Juliane Meier, Klaus Poggemann, Eric Strutz, PhD, Gwendolyn Owens, and Torsten Blaschke. Thank you all!

As for the actual and occasionally arduous process of writing, rewriting, and editing *The Leading Brain*, Ross J. Q. Owens was invaluable. He quickly seemed to grasp what we wanted to say and often made it better, ensuring that the book was not only scientifically valid but full of practical advice and a generous sprinkling of humor as well. We are immensely grateful.

Likewise, Friederike is grateful to Hans, who had the idea for this book and who has shared his wisdom from many years of leadership development. Thanks for always making me laugh when we work together. It is impossible to feel bored when you are around.

And Hans is grateful to Friederike: It is always such a pleasure to work with you. Writing the book together was a blast! You are the perfect combination of neuroscientific expert, stimulating thinker, and, above all, fun colleague.

From Friederike: I would like to thank Anna de la Roux, Elin Gustavsson, Sandra Harbert, Madelene Hjelm, and Baerbel Wayand for their friendship. In addition, I am profoundly grateful to my parents, Dr. Marianne von Siegfried and Dr.

Bernhard Wiedemann, as well as my siblings, Dr. Juliane Ebert and Konrad Wiedemann, for allowing me to grow up in an environment full of love and inspirational role models that gave me the strength and encouragement to pursue my passions wherever they might lead me. But above all, my deepest gratitude goes to my beloved husband, Jochen, not only for all your love and support but also for drawing on your personal leadership experience to make some remarkably astute comments on the manuscript. And finally, I want to thank our delightful children, Benita, Wolf, and Heinrich, who provide a boundless source of happiness. You mean the world to me.

From Hans: My love to my wife, Heinke, and my deepest thanks not only for sharing your life with me and for making my life so wonderful but also for your patience in reading and discussing all those details of the book that I am so enthusiastic about. Your wisdom in contemporary art was a surprising source of inspiration. Thanks also to our wonderful children, Oskar, Anton, and Tom, who represent a new generation that will hopefully find smart ways to make this world a better place.

ABOUT THE AUTHORS

Friederike Fabritius, MS, is the foremost neuroleadership expert at the global management consultancy Munich Leadership Group (MLG). As an executive coach and leadership specialist, she has extensive expertise working with top executives from multinational corporations such as Bayer, Audi, Montblanc, EY, and thyssenkrupp. Clients have raved about her seminars and coaching sessions, often describing them as "highly applicable" and even "life-changing." Friederike is also a sought-after keynote speaker and has addressed sizable audiences at corporate events hosted by large multinational corporations, such as EY and Audi.

A neuropsychologist by education, Friederike focuses on developing new methods and practices for leadership development based on solid scientific findings. She is also an expert in designing learning systems that draw on the brain's inherent capability to acquire and retain new information effectively. Friederike herself has used these methods to learn six languages that she now speaks fluently.

Friederike started her career at the Max Planck Institute for Brain Research and then continued as a management consultant at McKinsey before joining the Munich Leadership Group in 2010, where she has since supported many clients in reaching their full potential and delivering peak performance at critical moments.

Hans W. Hagemann, PhD, is managing partner and cofounder of the Munich Leadership Group, specializing in brain-based leadership. He is the leading expert for peak performance of individuals, teams, and organizations. Top executives and task forces from *Fortune* 500 companies in more than forty countries seek his advice. Hans counts Allianz Global Investors, Bayer, EY, Expedia, SAP, Siemens, and thyssenkrupp among his clients.

A psychologist and economist by education, Hans discovered the enormous potential of the neurosciences for leadership and innovation. When Friederike joined MLG, they started merging the latest research results with his wealth of experience. Hans and his team transform academic insights into pragmatic new tools and techniques that result in the strongest drivers for entrepreneurship and innovation in companies.

Hans is also active in the Silicon Valley, collaborating with leading companies and universities on groundbreaking new practices of entrepreneurship in the digital age. He is a cofounder of the German Silicon Valley Innovators (GSVI), an initiative based in Palo Alto, California, that makes firsthand Silicon Valley entrepreneurial practice accessible for innovative leaders from all businesses.

INDEX

Note: Page numbers in *italics* indicate tables and illustrations.